NEITHER

WAIF

NOR

STRAY

THE SEARCH FOR
A STOLEN IDENTITY

Perry Snow, B.A. (Hon), M.A.
Clinical Psychologist

For information address:
Perry Snow, B. A. (Hon), M. A.
Clinical Psychologist
#325 Market Mall Executive Professional Centre
4935 40th Avenue N. W., Calgary, Alberta, Canada, T3A 2N1
Phone: 403-288-4477
E-mail: psnow@cadvision.com

Universal Publishers/uPUBLISH.com
USA • 2000

ISBN: 1-58112-758-8

www.upublish.com/books/snow.htm

IN LOVING MEMORY OF
Frederick George Snow
(September 17, 1909 - September 17, 1994)

My Mother loved my Father for who he *was* -- not for *who* he was. My Wife Bonnie -- my truest friend for over 40 years -- had faith in all my projects, when sometimes I did not. My Daughters Charlotte and Elizabeth assisted as editors and supporters. My Nephew Alan Auld provided his computer expertise. My English friend Robin -- yet unmet -- devoted three years of his life to help me with my quest. He restored the Snow family faith in the "kindness of strangers." Gary, Karen, Sandy, Roger, and Wendy have made me proud to be their Brother.

To those who helped in the search, and those who did not, "What goes around comes around."

> Give, and it shall be given unto you; good measure, pressed down, and shaken together, and running over shall men give unto your bosom. For with the same measure that ye mete withal it shall be measured unto you (Luke 6:38).

Table of Contents

Introduction

My Father was a reserved and solitary man, who quietly stood at the fringe of conversations when others spoke of their past or families. His family was a mystery to him. He did not know who he was. He never had a Birth Certificate, and for the first 33 years of his life, had nothing to verify who he was. From the age of 33-48, he carried a tattered "To Whom it May Concern" letter for identification. It stated his name and identified him as "of British nationality." For the first half of his life, he had serious doubts if his surname was really "Snow." He wondered if someone had simply invented it and assigned it to him. When he was 48 years old, he obtained a Baptism Certificate that confirmed his name, and identified his Mother, but not his Father. From the age of 48-64, this was all he had for identification. When he was 64 years old, he received his Canadian Citizenship. All his life, he tried to identify his Parents and Family -- and find out who he was.

He became a ward of the Church of England Society for Providing Homes for Waifs and Strays when he was four years old in 1913. They placed him in a foster home in a small village in England from the age of 4-12. They then transferred him to a Home for Boys from the age of 12-15. When he was 15, they gave him the "choice" of emigrating to Australia or Canada. No one wanted him in England. They shipped him to Canada and sent him to work on farms in Ontario and Quebec. He was part of the little-known British Child Emigration Scheme. Fifty child-care organizations emigrated 100,000 children between 1880-1930 to Canada. These children ranged in age from 6-15 years old, and were known as "The Home Children." The organizations professed a dominant motive of providing children with better lives than what they might have had in England, but they had other ignoble motives.

Children worked as indentured farm labourers in harsh conditions until they were 18 years old. They were not allowed to go to school. They were not entitled to medical care. They had little protection under the law. They were not paid for their farm labour of 16 hours per day and six days per week. A third to a half of these children were neglected and abused, because the British organizations did not provide adequate inspections of their placements. They operated outside the control of the fledgling colony of Canada. The British Home Children were not voluntary "migrants" who "emigrated" to new lands. They were commodities that were deported because they were unwanted in Britain. The organizations expelled, banished, abandoned, and forgot them. A 'scheme' can be defined as a visionary plan, a foolish project, or a self-seeking, and underhanded plot. I prefer to call it the British Child Deportation Scheme.

7

From the age of 17-18, my Father was in a hospital for a year after he severely mangled his arm in a conveyor belt. He worked for a short time as a Timekeeper after they released him from hospital, but his work did not last long. From the age of 19-20, he enlisted in the Reserve Army Service Corps. He traveled to Western Canada to seek his fortune at the beginning of the Great Depression. From the age of 21-22, he was one of hundreds of thousands of single young men who rode freight trains in search of work. He met with "Help Wanted -- English Need Not Apply" signs when he sought work of any kind. From the age of 22-25, he lived in a highway construction Relief Camp in North-Western Ontario. He was an exile in a foreign and frequently inhospitable country. No one knew who he was. No one knew where he was. No one cared about a despised British Waif.

His life was irrevocably transformed on the Victoria Day Weekend of 1934 when he met and fell in love with my Mother. From that day on, he was never alone again. They married in the middle of the Great Depression in Port Arthur, Ontario. He began to live rather than subsist. For the first time in his life, he had someone who loved him, and someone for him to love. He had been deprived of so much love and human kindness in his life. In spite of this, he succeeded in becoming a loving Husband to his Wife and a devoted Father to his six children. Their early years of marriage were a struggle just to survive. They had two children during the Great Depression, three during World War II and one late in life in the 1950's. Their 59 years of marriage were a testimony of how their faith in God and their devotion to each other helped them overcome many challenges and adversities.

My Parents celebrated their Fiftieth Wedding Anniversary in 1985 in Thunder Bay, Ontario. The next year, my Mother wrote a book about their lives together. My Parents believed they had a love story to tell that might be of interest at least to their family. They had an everlasting faith in God. They firmly believed they were never alone, and a kind, loving God helped them along their way. In all things, they gave, "Thanks."

If I asked you to identify yourself, how would you answer? Invariably, you would volunteer your name. Although many others might have the same name, it is the first step in identifying yourself apart from others. Next, you might tell me your date of birth, because although many others might have an identical name, few others would have been born on the same day. Then you might tell me your Parents' names. Many others might have your name. A few might have been born on the same day, but no one -- apart from your siblings -- could have your Parents. You can only have one biological Father and Mother, and your moment of birth is unique to you alone. You might then specify where you were born. No one else on earth could have been born with your name, to your Parents, at a specific time, and in a specific place. You might produce a Birth Certificate to validate your claim to be who you say you are.

My Father was riddled with doubts every time he identified himself. All he could say was what his caretakers led him to believe was true. When he said, "My name is Fred G. Snow," he thought to himself, "I think." When he said, "I was born on Larch Road, Balham, London on September 17, 1909," he thought, "I have no birth certificate to prove this." When he said, "My Parents were John George Snow and Annie Gifford/Snow," he thought, "at least that is what they told me."

Your identity allows you to value yourself as a unique person of some worth. The absence of an identity contributes to your devaluing yourself as a useless thing. If you know who you are, you feel like a "somebody." If you do not know who you are, you feel like a "nobody." The majority of the British Home Children were labelled as worthless, and believed they were worthless. How can you feel like a person of worth when you have doubts that your name is really yours? How would you feel about yourself if you believed you were an orphaned, abandoned, unwanted, illegitimate, and inferior nobody? My Father was an intelligent and resourceful man who succeeded in overcoming his early childhood experiences, but many others did not. They were permanently marked by their traumatic experiences. Most lived their lives burdened with the disparaging identities that had been assigned to them. They were shamed throughout their childhood and lived with these feelings all their lives. Most died not knowing who they were.

Are any of your relatives of English, Irish, Scottish, or Welsh ancestry? Did any of them immigrate to Canada between 1880-1930? Are you certain they came with their families? Did they have Birth Certificates? Do you know your Aunts and Uncles on both sides of your family? Your ancestors may have been British Home Children. You may be one of their four million Canadian descendants.

My Father died on his unconfirmed 85th birthday in 1994. Shortly after his death, I told my Mother of my limited research of the Snow family the year before. I asked her for any information she had, and she gave me a file of their correspondence with England. Until then, I was completely unaware of their attempts to establish his identity over a period of 55 years. My Father's past was rarely a topic of family discussion. It was never a taboo subject, but rather one about which he could say so little. I read their file and concluded the Children's Society had given them the "run-around."

I combined information from my Parent's book and their correspondence file to write Part I: "A Life Without an Identity." It describes the life he had -- rather than could have had -- if he had known who he was. I had not intended to write a book about my search. At the start, I fully expected to find a few answers to his lifelong questions, and end the search by thanking his caretakers for their efforts on his behalf. It is the "Snow" way. Regrettably, my research led me to much different conclusions. The Children's Society never gave my Father the information that would have allowed him to know who he was, and to find his family. I could have written this book by simply presenting my discoveries as just another genealogical search. My Parents' lifelong search required more than just a summary of results. I wrote it as it unfolded, and how the secrets were revealed. The pieces of the puzzle did not come in an orderly or sequential fashion.

If one purpose of the British Child Deportation Scheme to Canada was to simply rid Britain of an unwanted element of their society, they only partially succeeded. They underestimated the strength of needing to know who you are. I hope the successful conclusion of my search will inspire others to persist until they re-establish their familial ties. No one should live their lives without knowing who they are and to whom they belong.

PART I: A LIFE WITHOUT AN INDENTITY (1913-1994)
Chapter 1: The Life of a Waif in England, 1913-1925

My Father had very few memories of the first four years of his life and could only retell this unvarying story.

I was born on Larch Road, Balham, London, England on September 17, 1909. My Mother was Annie Gifford and my Father was John George Snow. Something must have happened to my Mother. She may have died. That left my elderly Father to look after three young children by himself. Times were hard and there were no services available to help people in these situations.

I remember when I was about four years old being surrounded by 'Bobbies,' and taken away from my family. I might have been lost or perhaps I had run away. I never saw any of my family again. The Waifs and Strays Society placed me in a foster home in Rumburgh, Halesworth, Suffolk (Snow G. 3).

Imagine you are a four-year-old child living with your family in London, England in 1913. Your world is limited to your home and family. You are just beyond the toddler stage. All you really know is that your Parents love you. They would have told you this. You believe everything your parents and other adults tell you. One day there is a knock at your door. Some Policemen and strangers enter your home. All the adults argue and shout. They frighten you. You wonder why Policemen are in your home. You ask yourself what you did wrong. You try to understand what is going on, although all you can see is adult knees.

A Policeman picks you up and carries you away. You struggle and cry out, "Mommy!" The strangers shove your family out of the way. The Policeman carries you out of your home and away from your family. The last thing you see over his shoulder is your family crying and reaching out to you with outstretched arms. He tells you to stop crying. As they take you away, the image of your home and family gets smaller and smaller. When you look around, you realize that you have never been this far away from them before. You are terrified. You are afraid you will never see them again. You will wonder for the next 80 years of your life why this happened, and why you never saw your family again.

These people take you to strange surroundings. You wet your bed. They punish you. They are mean to you. They tell you that your Parents did not want you anymore. You do not believe them. You cry for your Mother. They tell you, "She is gone!" You do not know what that means. You know she is somewhere. They tell you that your Parents abandoned you, but you know the truth. They call you a "Waif," but you know you have Parents who love you.

You might be able to speculate a little how this experience might have felt. You can imagine being frightened and alone. You can imagine being taken forcibly away from your family at the tender age of four. At best, you can only imagine it as a temporary experience with a happy ending of a return to your family. Only orphaned, abandoned, and kidnapped children can truly appreciate the actual trauma of being permanently separated from their families at a tender age. This was the experience of thousands of British Home Children.

Dr. Thomas John Barnardo was one of the evangelical "Child-Savers." He believed he could save their souls by removing them from their families and emigrating them to Canada (Bean 42-43). He was never affiliated with any established Church, and was a self-proclaimed Doctor who forged his Physician's title (Wagner 1979 307-308). He notified Parents he deemed "respectable," before he emigrated their children. He notified those Parents he regarded as "not moral," after their children had sailed. He sent 30,000 children to Canada (Wagner 1982 147).

For the first 25 years of the scheme, he boasted that he had conducted "Philanthropic Abductions." He took almost half of the children into his care on "moral grounds," or because he decided, they were in the care of a "not respectable" guardian. In many cases, it was sufficient for them to label the families as "bad." He forcibly removed one quarter of the children in his care from their families. He proclaimed that children would be damaged if left in circumstances of which *he* disapproved. Such evangelical "Child-Savers" felt poor families reflected only an "unintelligent and almost animal affection" for their children. Barnardo argued that only emigration to Canada would save them from their families' evil influences (Parr 67). Parents took him to court over 80 times on charges of kidnapping. When he lost a case and the courts ordered him to return the children, he emigrated them anyway (Wagner 1982 147).

As a young child, my Father's options were very limited. He could have believed what strangers told him about himself and his family. Alternatively, he could have believed only what *he* knew to be true of his first four years of life. In retrospect, I can only assume that he opted not to believe what strangers told him. Throughout his life, he always tried to make the best of the situation at hand. As a child, he must have told himself constantly that he was not an orphan, his Parents did not abandon him, and that they loved him. All he would have to hold on to were his vague memories of his Parents. He knew he was not a "Bastard." He knew he was not inferior. He resisted others' efforts to convince him otherwise.

I can only speculate how he survived his childhood traumatic experiences. I imagine he observed families and recalled memories of how his Parents treated him. This painfully reminded him of his loss, but he focused on the future when he would be free of his caretakers. He vowed to himself that someday if he ever became a Father, he would love his children as he had observed Parents displaying their love for their children. He noted how Brothers and Sisters related to each other. He imagined that if he ever had children of his own, he would make sure they would treat each other as he had noted. He knew he was on the outside looking in, so he decided that he might as well learn what he could from this. He sought solace in the Church, where he learned that God loved him and would take care of him. There was no one else.

Organizations saw the children as only living *things* -- a little more intelligent than animals. They treated them accordingly, and the children learned to regard themselves as things. The "Waif and Stray" label reinforced these attitudes. It is not enough to simply provide for only the physical needs of children. The medical diagnosis, "Failure to Thrive," describes children whose physical, cognitive, and emotional development is drastically arrested. This is a result of caretakers who exclusively provide for the child's physical needs of food, clothing, and shelter, but completely ignore the child's emotional needs. The literature describing the scheme rarely acknowledges the injurious effects upon young children of separation from their Parents. Stroud offered the rationalization that the child-care organizations did not realize that children had emotional needs, and it would take three generations before parents became aware of this (106).

I cannot accept the despicable assertion that no one knew children had emotional needs. The most primitive tribe knows that a child's survival depends upon love and affection. Six centuries before the British Child Deportation Scheme, people knew that infants could die if caretakers only attended to their physical needs. In 13th Century England, a ruler conducted an experiment to assess the effects of rearing children under psychologically deprived conditions. He wanted to know what speech children would develop if no one ever spoke to them. He speculated that children might speak Hebrew, Greek, Latin, or their Parents' language. He allowed foster mothers and caretakers to only look after infants' physical needs. They were not allowed to talk to them. All the children died of emotional starvation (Mussen et al. 163).

Their bodies slowly shrivelled as if they died of food starvation. The twinkle of life in their eyes dulled and then extinguished. Their last breaths were sighs of longing for any sign of human affection or attention. Did those employed by the child-care organizations not have children of their own? Perhaps they regarded the children in their care -- not as someone's children -- but as pieces of ownerless property.

The medieval term "wayves and streyves" described abandoned things. These things became the property of the Lord of the Manor, if their owners did not reclaim them. Edward de Montjoie Rudolf adopted the phrase for his child-care organization in 1881. The selection of this name was touted as a stroke of genius, because it opened Victorian hearts and purses (Stroud 62). They generously made donations. Children in care were regarded as things that did not belong to anyone. It suited the organization's monetary motives to portray the children as foundlings. Who could not feel pity for the abandoned orphans? The organization did not change their name until 60 years later in 1945 to the Church of England Children's Society. In 1982, it changed its name to The Children's Society, but the children formerly in their care are still commonly known as Waifs and Strays.

Vital learning experiences occur in the first three years of a child's life. The most important lesson children learn in the first two years is love and trust. These experiences are transformed into long-lasting neurological patterns. They are etched upon the mind and become part of the personality of the child -- and the adult. Parents provide nurture, affection, protection, and love. The quality and consistency of parenting in the first few years is critical to normal child development. This determines whether a child learns he is deserving/undeserving of love, and the world is a safe/frightening place. I can only hope my Father's Parents loved him enough to give him a tiny sense of his being worthy and deserving of love from others before he came into care. He was an optimistic man, who trusted himself and others. I can only speculate that these lifelong attitudes were a result of his early positive experiences with his family. I do not believe he learned love and trust from his caretakers.

My Father's caretakers never provided him with an accurate explanation how he came under their care. When he was a young child, they may have simply told him he was abandoned, or his Parents were dead. His simple choice as a young child was to either believes what he knew to be true, or to believe what they told him. Fortunately, he chose not to believe his family abandoned him. As young as he was, he knew he had been taken from his family. He did not believe he was an unwanted Waif or Stray. I would like to believe that he sustained this belief in spite of how others treated him and what they told him of his Parents. His belief in his being worthy of love and his ability to love another must have remained dormant during his childhood, adolescence, and early adulthood. His faith and trust in himself and God were all that he ever had. These beliefs allowed him to subsist, endure, and persevere alone for the first 25 years of his life. Falling in love with my Mother allowed him to extend his faith and trust to another. It must have taken tremendous personal strength for my Father to overcome his early feelings of abandonment and rejection. As an adult, he had a long-acquired habit of looking through and beyond a situation. To others it may have appeared that he was simply staring off into space. I learned that it was his method of ensuring that the immediate situation would never overwhelm him. While doing this, he would also tilt his head back and raise his chin in a determined way. I believe he learned this as a young child, as a method he adopted to protect himself from the efforts of others to diminish him. He would not speak, but rather simply raised his chin. It was enough.

Fred G. Snow (4-11): Eight Years in a Foster Home, Rumburgh, Halesworth, Suffolk, England, 1913-1921

It was unusual that my Father had so little to say of his eight years in foster care. If there were anything positive to say about foster care, he would have said it. Out of painful necessity, he repressed or blocked out many negative memories of this time. I can only conclude that he was unable to find much to be grateful for in this situation.

The next thing I remember was having a nametag pinned to my shirt, being put on a train by myself, and going to Rumburgh, Halesworth, Suffolk, where I was met by a Social Worker. She drove the pony and cart to the home of Mr. and Mrs. Smith. They lived about ten miles (16 km) from the train station. I stayed there eight years until I was 12 years old. I attended public school at Rumburgh.

I recall having to wear ladies' boots for some time. The Smiths were both white-haired and had no young children of their own, as their children were married and away from home. I used to run to the store for tobacco for Mr. Smith who always seemed to be cranky. I attended St. John's Church and sang in the choir at the age of six or seven as a soprano (Snow G. 3).

Your caretakers pin a nametag on your coat. You are too young to read, so you do not know what the piece of paper says. You have never been on a train before. A man plunks you on a seat. He tells you not to talk to anyone, and not to leave your seat. He leaves you there alone. You have no idea where you are or where you are going. You have never felt so alone. You know the train is not taking you home.

You only catch glimpses of buildings rushing by when you peek over the windowsill. You are very tired and want to lie down on the hard seat but are afraid that someone will punish you for that. You know it is best not to look back where you have been, because something says you will not be going back. You sit upright on the seat but your feet do not reach the floor and you are jostled back and forth by the train. You lean against the window. You pull your feet underneath you. You are frightened and suck your thumb. You have not done that in a long time. You wet your pants, because you do not know if there is a bathroom on the train. You were told not to move. You find a rag tucked between the seat cushions. You use it to dry yourself as best you can. You are cold because all you wear is short pants and a thin shirt. The shoes they gave you are too small and pinch your feet.

You peek out the window and no longer see buildings rushing by, but only trees and wide-open spaces. It looks very, very empty to you. The train slows down and a man tells you to get off when it stops. You tentatively step onto the train platform. A stern woman approaches and says, "Come with me!" She looks at your wet pants and wrinkles her nose. She shouts, "Filthy Guttersnipe!" You have no idea what that means. She harshly takes your hand and leads you to a pony and a cart. She puts you in the back of the cart, instead of beside her. You feel like the bag of potatoes you sit upon. You watch the countryside with interest. Something tells you to remember every detail of this trip. You worry that you might never find your way back to your Mother. You ride in the cart for hours. Already, you have learned not to ask questions of these strangers. The woman stops the cart in a very small village. There are only a few houses. There is so much open space around you.

She takes you to a house and knocks on the door. An old man and woman answer the door. The woman says, "Here is the Waif!" Does she not know your name? The white-haired couple tell you they are your Parents now. You do not know why they say this, but you decide it is best for you not to say anything. You live with these old people for the next eight years of your life. They are poor. You quickly decide that you cannot afford to feel lonely. You decide just to feel alone instead, because it does not hurt as much. You wear shabby clothes. When your shoes wear out, they give you women's boots to wear that are too small for you. They cramp your feet. Your toes grow crookedly. There is not much food to eat. The old people are not cruel, but they treat you no differently than the family dog. They speak to you in the same tone. They do not really talk to you, but just order you around.

You learn to make yourself smaller when you are in their home. You learn to make yourself invisible so you will not attract undo attention from them. You know they do not really want you there, so you try to stay out of their way. Seven Christmas' come and go and you especially try your best to become part of the shadows on these occasions. You are not expected to participate. Their family visits them and they act as if you are not there. The old people surprise you when they give you a handkerchief on your eighth Christmas there. It is not wrapped, but you are grateful all the same. There is no one at school whom you can call a friend. All the children were born in the little village and live close to each other. Most are related to each other. You are the outsider who does not belong to anyone. They know you are not related to your foster parents. Everyone calls you a "Waif."

You wonder what you did wrong to deserve this. You know you belong to someone. You know you have a Mother and Father. Why do they not understand this? You go to Church and Sunday school and sing in the choir. The hymns are comforting. Outside Church, you hum these hymns very softly to yourself. You need to know that someone cares

17

about you. You wonder all the time, "Why doesn't someone take me back to my Family?" As the years pass slowly, you realize this will not happen. When you ask the old people where your Mother is, they tell you she is dead. You do not believe them. You vow to find your Family yourself when you grow up and are free. No one ever told you when you were born and you never had a birthday. Every other child you knew in the village knew when they were born and had a birthday every year. You did not attend anyone's birthday, but you heard of them.

The Waifs and Strays Society regarded village foster homes as ideal placements for their wards. They would not place children with their relatives. As early as the 1890's, it was obvious that children were neglected in the foster homes. They were unwashed and wore ragged, dirty underclothes for months. They wore boots that were too small and permanently deformed their feet. They were infected with vermin, and years passed between inspection visits by local clergy (Stroud 68-73). The organizations persisted in fostering children in small villages for the next 50 years. My Father's experience indicated that little had changed in the years he was in foster care. The organizations were adamant that *any* circumstances were better than a child living with his natural family -- his evil associations.

Fred G. Snow (12-16): Four Years at St. Augustine's Church Home for Boys, Sevenoaks, Kent, England, 1921-1925

You live in this foster home for eight years. You are surprised one day when the Social Worker knocks at the door. She is the same one from many years ago who took you to the Smith foster home. You remember seeing her only a few times before this. She says, "I'm here to pick up the Waif." Mrs. Smith invites her in. The Social Worker says she is sending you to a Home, where you will be "looked after." You could not possibly have known that your placement in the foster home would only last until you were 12 years old. You do not know that being taken to a Home is for the sole purpose of holding you until you are old enough to be "emigrated" to Canada. She tells you to pack your tin trunk. It has been under your bed for all these years. When you pack your meagre things, you notice there is nothing new to add. What you put in the trunk is exactly what you took out of the trunk eight years earlier. You put on Mrs. Smith's boots and grimace because you are older and have trouble fitting your misshapen toes into these boots you have worn for years. The Social Worker says you will have new shoes in "The Home."

You pass through the doorway and leave the only "home" you have known. Mrs. Smith says, "Good-bye." Her face is expressionless. Mr. Smith does not say anything. He does not even look at you. The Social Worker tells you to get in the cart. You rode the same one years before. She lets you sit on the seat beside her this time. When you arrive at the train station, you remember the terrifying train trip you had many years ago. She pins a nametag to your shirt. This time you can read and make sure your name is on it. She tells you someone will meet you at the next station. She leaves you there and walks away without saying anything. You get on the train and try not to think of where it is taking you. You wonder what "Home" you will be living in. As the train slowly pulls out of the station, you do not look back. You learned not to do that when you were four years old. You are a little boy who does not know where he is, and does not know where he is going. There is nowhere for you to run. There is no one for you to turn to. No one knows who you are. You do not know who you are either. As you watch the scenery pass by, you know you will not pass this way again.

As the train slows to a halt at a London station, a Porter looks at your nametag and tells you this is where you get off. He smiles and gives you a wink. You are not used to having someone smile at you, so you give him a shy smile back. You do not know how to wink. You get off the train. Another Social Worker hollers, "Here, Boy!" You assume that is yourself. He checks your nametag and tells you to follow him through the station, and not to say a word. He puts you on another train. As it

19

quickly passes through London, you wonder where your Family lives. You were too young to know where you lived when they apprehended you. All the same, you tell yourself your Family is somewhere out there. You have thoughts that now you are in London, somehow, they will find you, or you can find them. The train stops and you get off. You wait for someone to holler, "Here, Boy!" Someone does. He does not need to tell you to be quiet. You are a quick learner. You follow this man. He takes you to your new "Home."

It is a large and imposing stone building surrounded by high stone walls. They cut your hair off in clumps. They "delouse" you. You want to tell them this is unnecessary, but you know better than to speak. They give you clothes to wear that are more worn than your clothes. They give you old boots. To you they are new. At least they are too large instead of too small. You wonder if your bent toes might still straighten out in time. You notice that all the other boys in the Home have "empty eyes." You wonder if they are sick. They have scabs on their faces and arms. The adults take your nametag -- and your name away. One of the Sisters says, "You are now Boy Number 18264." You put your tin trunk under your bed in the dormitory, and notice the straw mattress reeks of urine. The older boys in the dormitory do not look at you.

An eight-year-old boy sneaks a look at you. He looks like a frightened puppy. At least the dormitory has a window, and you can see a little over the high walls. At night, you wonder which chimney pot belongs to your Family's home. You wonder why the Home is so silent. It absorbs the sounds of footsteps. It is a very strange place, full of very strange people.

The Home held 48 boys who were 6-16 years old in six dormitories. We slept on straw mattresses. Master Jago was quite sadistic and treated us as if we were criminals or slaves. I helped him fix some electrical wiring and he asked me if he knew anything about electricity. I said, 'Not very much.' I stood on a ladder and he told me to grab hold of a pipe. He handed an electrical wire to me. When I touched it, the shock nearly knocked me off. Mr. Jago laughed.

At the Local Council School they used a form of discipline called the 'cross' system.' A Head Monitor kept daily track of your mistakes or 'crosses.' The Headmaster of the Council School gave you one strap if you had eight 'crosses' for the day. He gave you another strap for every 'cross' more than eight. You got the same number of straps again when you got back to the Home! For serious misdemeanours, you leaned over and touched your toes while they caned you on your bare back. If they considered the offences very bad, you had to lie on a table with one guy holding your hands and head and another holding your feet. They beat you with birch twigs across your bare backside.

Every night after supper, they lined us 48 kids -- big and small -- in a horseshoe formation in a big room. They punished kids in front of the whole school. They regarded running away, smiling, getting out of line while marching to school, and speaking back to your Head Monitor as very bad offences.

I got the cane only once after my friend Leonard Knell and I cleaned up the big hall after a meeting of some kind. We had a game of floor hockey using brooms as hockey sticks. Sneaky Sister Megan caught us and we both 'got the birch!' Sister Pickett and Sister Megan wore blue habits with white starched cowls. They were particularly mean. They would do anything to get us in trouble. They enjoyed punishing us.

One boy ran away from a Barnardo Home. They captured him and placed him in solitary confinement. They gave him a nightshirt and locked him in a room for seven days. They fed him only dry bread and a glass of water three times a day. When the week of solitary confinement ended, four boys held him spread-eagled over the end of a table, and gave him six strokes of the cane over his bare buttocks (Harrison 203). How much money did they save by forcing children to eat mouldy food or bread and water?

We had soccer practice three times a week, no matter what the weather. They put us on bread and water for a couple of days when we lost a soccer game. Can you imagine playing soccer all day and coming home to that? If a kid ran away, they beat him and locked him in the 'tower.' They gave him only bread and water for days.

Breakfast invariably consisted of porridge and two slices of bread with butter. There was also jam and tea. Lunch was a bowl of soup and two slices of bread. There usually was no dessert. If you did not eat all of your porridge at breakfast, they kept it and made you eat it the next day. If you refused again, they would keep this up for days until the porridge had meld on it. Still they forced you to eat it.

One Home Child gave a piece of candy to another child. Someone told the Matron. She used large tongs to carry the young girl up a flight of stairs. She called the girl "unclean (sinful)," threw her into a broom closet, and locked her in the dark. The rest of the children ate their meal in silence while the girl screamed and kicked her feet on the floor of the closet (Stroud 117).

We did all the cleaning in the Home. We scoured the rough-wood gym floor with a scrub brush. We got many splinters in our hands and knees as we wore only short pants. We mopped and scrubbed the kitchen and scullery. We scrubbed, waxed, and polished the linoleum on the front steps and big staircase. We scrubbed the marble back steps down to the basement. We tended the gardens. The older boys polished all the other boys' shoes. Every Saturday night, three of us 14-year-old boys bathed 20 of the five-year-old boys. I was a server at Church. Twice a week I went to Communion at 6:00 a.m. On Sunday, I went four times a day for early masses, Matins, Sunday school, and evening services. I felt safe in the Church (Snow G. 5-6).

The Waifs and Strays Society operated on a food budget of 3s 6d per child per week (Stroud 45-46). My Father's account indicated that the diet established in the 1880's had not changed for 40 years. How would you subsist on this meagre diet? Your weekday Breakfast is porridge, milk, and "dripping." On alternate weekdays, it is porridge, water, and "dripping." On Sunday mornings, you have bread, butter, and cocoa. Monday Dinner is soup, bread, and milk pudding. Every other Monday you have boiled apple, or rhubarb pudding. Tuesday Dinner is Irish stew with rice and carrots, or a "dripping crust." Wednesday, you have boiled suet (fat) pudding with treacle. Thursday Dinner is meat, bread, and green vegetables. Friday Dinner is soup, bread, and milk pudding. Saturday, you have baked suet pudding with raisins, apples, or carrots. Sunday Dinner is meat, vegetables, rice pudding, or stewed rhubarb. You could have fruit in the summer. Your Tea (Supper) during the week is bread, dripping, treacle, and milk. On alternate days, you had bread, dripping, treacle, and water. The Punishment Circle follows every Supper.

The rules of the Home were rigid (Stroud 43-44). How would you adapt to this unvarying routine? You wake up every weekday at 6:30 a.m., in summer and 7:00 a.m., in winter. You strip your bed. You open the windows wide -- "a little at the top," unless it is raining, snowing or foggy. You kneel at your bed and say the Lord's Prayer. You wash your hands and face. You wash your shorn hair and "rub it perfectly dry." You bathe once a week. You help wash the younger children. You say Grace before and after every meal. You say Prayers and read Scripture before breakfast. All of this takes about an hour every morning. You have breakfast at 7:30 a.m., in summer and 8:00 a.m., in winter.

After breakfast, you make your bed. You wash your bed-sheets every second week. You wash your blankets and quilts once a year -- only in the summer. You work in the kitchen or laundry after breakfast.

You attend school in the morning and return to the Home for Dinner at 1:00 p.m. You say Grace before and after Dinner. You attend school in the afternoon. You have Tea at 6:00 p.m., in the summer and 5:30 p.m., in the winter. You say Grace before and after Tea. You read Scripture and say Prayers after Tea. You gather for the daily Punishment Circle after Supper every night. You watch other children being caned with birch twigs. It is hard to watch the younger children being punished, but if you close your eyes or look away, they cane you too. You unfocused your eyes so you do not see.

Once the caning is done, they send you all to bed. Children under eight go to bed before 7:00 p.m. Those under nine go to bed by 8:00 p.m., and those under twelve go to bed by 8:30 p.m. You go to bed before 9:00 p.m. You kneel at your bed and say the Lord's Prayer. On Saturday, you clean the Home -- "from top to bottom." You attend Church on Sunday morning and Sunday school in the afternoon. You can attend evening Church -- but only in the summer. You spend as much time in Church as you can. It allows you some respite from this place, if only for a while.

Every Friday night, they "dosed" the children with a mixture of castor oil and liquorice powder. A single spoon was licked by one and passed to the next. Ringworm, vermin, and chilblains were rampant in the Homes. They allowed the children a one-day outing per year. They did not allow them to go outside the gates of the Home except briefly during school holidays. Children could go out on the large paved areas that were surrounded by high walls, but there were no toys with which they could play (Stroud 113-115). They had to refer to themselves by their number at all times. Perhaps there was another motive to their numbering of children. In 1911, a Canadian eugenicist suggested all of humanity should be numbered. He contended that if numbers replaced names, over time everyone would develop pride in their assigned digit (McLaren 25). I do not think many British Home Children developed pride in their digits. I am surprised the organizations did not tattoo the children's arms with, "Waif Number 18264." This might have made it easier for them to locate children, since they lost track of so many in Canada.

The Homes strictly enforced the Rule of Silence, especially when children were outside the Home. They could talk quietly amongst themselves for an hour between tea and bedtime (Stroud 112-113). The Punishment Circle was held every night after Tea, so there could not have been much time left for communication. What could they talk about after they were forced to watch other children being caned? The organizations justified the Rule of Silence by saying that the prevailing attitude of the time was, "Children should be seen and not heard." If they were seen and heard at the wrong time and place, the organizations feared the loss of the gentry's goodwill -- and their financial contributions (Stroud 106-107).

The dominant motive of the Waifs and Strays Society was to permanently isolate children from their families and deport them overseas. Their 1893 constitution stated their primary mission as one of doing "all things expedient" to assist the emigration of children (Stroud 229). They wanted to rescue children from their bad surroundings and permanently place them in Canada to prevent them from drifting back when they were no longer under their care. The entire emphasis was upon breaking "old evil associations." The Waifs and Strays Society regarded their efforts as wasted if children re-established their associations. Admission was made contingent upon the nearest relative handing over the child "unreservedly" into their care (Stroud 80). The child-care organizations conducted a Holy Crusade against poor families.

They appeared to have modified their objectives in 1952 when they professed their first priority as one of providing financial assistance to families so that children could remain with them. The provision was whether they judged the homes as "reasonably satisfactory." Their second apparent priority was adoption, if they decided it was "inadvisable" for children to stay in their homes. Their third priority was to board children with foster parents, and their final option was to send children to the Homes until they were of employable age (Stroud 230). There was no mention of child emigration in their policies, even though they were very much involved in the British Child Deportation Scheme to Australia until 1967.

When I imagine St. Augustine's Home for Boys, I see only grey. I see the sun shining overhead -- but not on this building. Inside, I see spirits frozen in the still air. They are images of children with hurt but tearless eyes. They all wear numbers. I see cold stone walls saturated with their muffled cries. I do not hear echoes of children's laughter, because this is a silent place. Instead, I feel the vibrations of their unspoken pleas. I feel a silent, "Please help me." I see my Father's dormitory, and imagine him sitting by the window, leaning on the sill, and praying to the night sky for deliverance. I see a children's prison.

Chapter 2: A British Home Child Deported to Canada, 1925

The child-care organizations regarded the children as simply commodities for export. It cost them 10-15£ each year to keep a child in their care. It cost them only 2£ to emigrate each child. They saved a great deal of money by exporting children at the earliest possible age -- many as young as six years old. Not only did they save money, but also they profited. Canada's need for cheap farm labour was insatiable. For every child sent, there were requests for ten more.

The Canadian government paid the organizations $2.00 for each child (Wagner 1982 154). The British Parish Guardians paid them $75.00 for each child they emigrated. The Canadian government paid them a cash bonus of $5,000.00 for every 1,000 they sent (Bagnell 1980b 69). The organizations sold the children as slave labour. The Canadian government bought them. The scheme was always about money and never about the best interests of children. There are many similarities between the British Child Deportation Scheme and Black Slavery in the US in the 19th Century.

The Waifs and Strays Society saw Canada as a void to fill with their "surplus" children. By 1919, the scheme had been in operation for 50 years. Fifty British child-care organizations sent 73,000 to Canada unaccompanied by parents or guardians (Stroud 78-79). Between 1882-1908, Barnardo shipped 14% (4,500) of his children to Canada illegally -- without parental consent. A further 9% (3,000) were sent because of court orders and the Home Secretary's authorization, but not parental consent. One quarter (7,500) of all Barnardo children were sent to Canada illegally (Parr 67).

Few of those in the organizations had ever traveled more than a few kilometres from their place of birth. They had no appreciation for what was involved in traveling across the ocean and could not comprehend the vastness of Canada.

Boys were shipped in the spring and girls in the fall. Each child had a metal suitcase that contained what the naïve English considered necessary for survival in Canada. The suitcase contained a cap, a suit, belt, ball of wool, boot brush, one pair of rubber boots, one pair of slippers, one pair of overalls, one pair of underwear, two long nightshirts, two pairs of woollen socks, two shirts, two handkerchiefs, some needles, and thread. Each case also contained four books: The Travelers Guide, Holy Bible, New Testament, and Pilgrim's Progress (Corbett 123).

The clothing was quite inadequate. Many farmers did not replace children's clothes when they wore or outgrew them, and many wore the same clothes for years.

Fred G. Snow (16-18): Two Years of Indentured Farm Labour, Sherbrooke, Quebec, 1925-1927

In 1925, Master Ernest Jago of St. Augustine's Church Home for Boys called my Father and 40 other boys over 14 years old to his office. He gave them the choice of "emigration" to either Australia or Canada. He did not give them the choice of staying in England. No one wanted them there. He gave them two days to get ready to leave the Home. No one saw them off on their journey. No one waved, "Good-bye." They led my Father to believe he would have a better life in a land of prosperity and opportunity. He could only hope that his life would be better than what it had been to date.

He was a young boy who had only known eight years of life in a foster home in a small village and 3½ years in a sequestered institution. All he had seen beside the inside of the Home and school, was the sidewalk he walked on from the Home to the school and back. The boys silently walked single-file, with downcast eyes. They were punished if they looked around while they walked. He must have been a little apprehensive about what lay ahead. When they deported him from England, he faced the prospect of not being able to find his Family.

You are 15 years old when you are told to choose between "emigration" to either Canada and Australia. What would you choose? How would you feel to know that staying in England was not an option for you? They say you will have a better life in Canada. Given what you had experienced to date, you think, "Anything would be better!" You choose Canada, only because one of your friends chose Canada before you. Two days later, they gather you up and march you down to the train station. You feel a little strange, because they let you look around while you walk. Some people look at you, and you see a little sadness in their eyes.

You march up the gangplank, and Master Jago gives you a photograph of the ship. "SS Andania" is written in ink on the back of the photograph. You look at the photograph and then look up at the ship. The ship in the photograph has only one smokestack. The ship you board has two smokestacks. Do they simply pass out pictures of any ship, and think you do not know the difference? You keep this picture all your life. You seem to know how important it is to keep a record of your travels.

You go down many ladders into steerage class. The three-tiered bunk beds have metal frames with chains to support the mattresses. The space between the bunks is very narrow. As the ship leaves the port and the shores of England, you go to the stern with the rest of the boys to have a last look.

SS Andania: London, England to Halifax, Nova Scotia, 1925

You silently say, "Good-bye" to your unknown Family, and tell yourself you will be back someday. You go to the bow of the ship to stare out over the grey sea and try to imagine what Canada will be like. You know you will have to work hard, but you are used to that. You wonder about Cowboys and Indians, because you once saw these things in a picture of Canada. It is an awful trip. Everyone is seasick. The crew treat you as if you were livestock in the hold of the ship. They open the door and leave food on the floor. At least it is better than what you usually ate in the Home. Master Jago stays in his quarters nearly all the time. You see him only twice in the two weeks it takes to sail to Canada. He is drunk both times and seasick the rest of the time.

When the ship arrives in Halifax, you march down the gangplank into a large shed. A man in a uniform asks you how old you are. You say, "Fifteen, Sir." You watch him write, "Boy -- 15 years old," on a piece of paper. He has a gold patch on his arm that reads, "Department of Agriculture." You wonder why he did not ask you for your name. You were looking forward to using it again as you had not spoken your name aloud very often in the past 3½ years. You consider telling him you are, "Boy Number 18264," but change your mind. You hope you might not have to identify yourself again this way once you are in Canada. Another man who looks like a Doctor goes down the line. He pulls your eyelids back and looks inside. He tells you to open your mouth and he looks down your throat. It is dark in the shed and you do not think he can see anything, but you know enough not to talk to your "betters." You were told everyone is your "better." They told you never to forget you are a "Waif," and that your Parents were "vicious." The Doctor moves quickly down the line and only looks in a few boys' eyes. He announces, "Forty-five medically fit!" The man in the uniform makes a note of this.

My Father arrived in Canada on April 17, 1925, in Halifax, Nova Scotia. They placed him on a train alone with his nametag to Montreal. I do not know if his nametag read, "Boy -- 15, Boy #18264, or Fred Snow." Someone met him at the station and put him on another train to the Gibbs' Home at Sherbrooke, Quebec. It was a Distributing Centre where they sent boys to work on farms.

The vastness of the country must have been imposing to a young boy from London. When he rode the train for hours in the middle of winter, he must have wondered just how inhospitable the country might be. He could not have anticipated the prejudice that would make the country all the colder for him. There are lies behind the public portrayal of the British Child Deportation Scheme to Canada.

> . . . more than 80,000 children, many just out of infancy, were gathered from the poor neighbourhoods of Britain's cities - London, Birmingham, Liverpool, Manchester - and sent to Canada to live on farms, some in the Maritimes and Quebec, but most in Ontario and Manitoba. During the peak period of the movement, the early 1900's, scores of organizations and individuals were busily shipping children to Canada.
>
> Some of these children, those too young to work, were adopted into families, often informally, but most were expected to spend the years of their childhood working in fields or tending the cattle in an indenture that was stern and lonely. It was a practice that in some cases revealed the dark side of early Canada. . . . From 1882 to the early 1930's there was scarcely a farming district in Ontario or Manitoba that did not have a number of Barnardo boys and girls, with their cockney accents, their plain clothes, and often, too often, their lonely and frightened faces.[1]

Sir Francis Galton used the term eugenics in 1883 to describe a movement dedicated to the improvement of the human race by selective breeding. He automatically classified the upper and middle classes as fit, and the criminal, alcoholic, feeble-minded, and poor as unfit (McLaren 14-15). The upper classes feared the growth of the poor working class. They believed paupers bred paupers, and the working class were mentally deficient, irresponsible, and negligent because of their biological destiny (Kevles 114). The British Home Children suffered the imposed eugenic curse of "tainted blood." Canadians were contemptuous of their "uncertain parentage," and treated them abominably. Their attitudes towards these children persisted long after the scheme ended. These children were victims of very mixed messages. The British organizations regarded them as a valuable, exportable, breeding stock that could improve the quality of the Canadian gene pool. At the same time, they did not want them in England because they believed they were tainted by their family origins. Canadians welcomed them only as cheap labour, but believed these children carried inherited physical and moral deficiencies.

They saw them as a potential plague that threatened to contaminate the healthy Canadian gene pool (Bagnell[b] 77-78).

Medicine, Psychology, and Social Work exploited Canadian fears of the threat posed by British child immigrants. Their onslaughts were clearly self-serving, and they ensured their careers and professions by appointing themselves as defenders of the race (McLaren 66-67). Dr. C.K. Clarke was a Professor of Psychiatry who attacked the inferiority of the British Waifs. He announced that proof of their degeneracy could be found in their symmetrically shaped heads and their stunted bodies (Bagnell 1980b 206). Canadians labelled the British Home Children as criminals, imbeciles, paupers, Cockney sneak thieves, pickpockets, Street Arabs, and carriers of syphilis.

A Master and Servant Act bound children until they were 18 years old. Those who ran away could be found guilty of desertion. They could be fined and jailed (Parr 92). Ontario Police were convinced these children had criminal natures because depraved parents had raised them. This made them physically weak and unable to resist temptation. The Ontario Prison Reform Commission in 1891 attributed an increase in drunkenness and prostitution to the presence of the British Home Children (Parr 53). These attitudes contributed to the extreme physical and social alienation of the Home Children. It was common practice for farmers to make sure their children were segregated from the British Home Children. Ontario Physicians cautioned Canadian families about contact with British Home Children. They believed them to be carriers of syphilis that could be transmitted to Canadian children through simple play (Bagnell 1980a 80).

Many British Home Children did not see the inside of the farmer's homes. They ate and slept in the barn with the animals. The organizations were to provide Inspectors to frequently visit the children. Some children worked for years without ever seeing an Inspector. The rare meetings with Inspectors were usually at the farmer's kitchen table -- with the farmer included. What were the children free to say? At least in Canada, my Father was free to use his name again. The Canadians did not call him "Boy Number 18264." They had many more derisive names for him.

The agencies promoted the myth that children would benefit from the more egalitarian Canadian education system. Barnardo's indenture of 1913 recommended that boys under 14 years old should be allowed to attend to attend school for five months per year. While 66% of his nine-year-old boys went to school regularly, 33% did not. While 25% of the boys 10-12 years old attended on a regular basis, 75% did not, or did on an irregular basis. Almost 75% of boys 13-14 years old never attended a

Canadian school. Their Masters suffered no penalties for denying these children their right to attend school. Those attended school were publicly ridiculed because of their speech and clothing (Parr 109-110). In late 1924, the Bondfield Commission from Britain investigated the scheme and concluded the children suffered from loss of education, overwork, and non-payment of their labour. They recommended -- 40 years after the beginning of child deportation -- that children should be given long winter pants to replace their short pants. The British government finally decided that children under the British statutory school-leaving age of 14 years old should not be emigrated to Canada. The Canadian government complied, and the child-care organizations decided to keep children in their Homes until they were over 14 years old (Bagnell 1980a 23-24).

The scheme still had enthusiastic supporters in 1925. Some proposed that Britain should ship 200,000 children between the ages of 14-18 to Canada. They hoped to reduce their unemployment rate at save "dole (welfare)" money. Over a twenty-year period, they wanted to send four million children to Canada. They regarded the English child as "magnificent material" who would ensure the racial unity of the Empire (Wagner 1982 232). How did they plan to recruit four million children? Where would they find so many "Orphans?" The Great Depression put a halt to this eugenic scheme.

Barnardo deported a group of 89 children in 1888. Twenty-two children (25%) were between 6-12 years old. Sixty-seven (75%) were more than 12 years old. Sixty children (67%) had lived in the Homes for less than 1-3 years. Twenty-nine children (33%) had lived in the Homes for over 3 years (Corbett Appendix). Any trauma these young children experienced by being separated from their families and raised in institutions would have been compounded by their deportation. They were sent to a cold and inhospitable country. Children are more likely to reflect their traumatic experiences in their behaviour rather than their words. Bed-wetting was a prevalent indicator of their responses to traumatic experiences. An Ontario Immigration official noted that two-thirds of the British Home Children suffered from enuresis. He referred to this as their "dirty habits" that were proof of their immoral parents' lives. Many children who did not overcome their enuresis were deported back to England (Parr 103-107).

My first farm job was at East Angus, Quebec where they treated me as if I were a dumb farm animal. When the farm owner had visitors, he brought us English boys into the house. He ridiculed us because of our accents. I was there for about a year. They took me by horse and wagon to Sherbrooke, where I saw Mr. Keeley to get another job.

My next position was with a young couple that were Agricultural College graduates. They kept bees and had an orchard. I stayed farming for a few months but did not like it very much, as I had to eat in the kitchen apart from the others (Snow G. 10).

The organizations placed young children on isolated farms in Quebec, even though none of the children spoke French. Some children spent their entire indentures on these Quebec farms. As adults, they would have conspicuous English names, but were fully Quebecois. A Chief Medical Officer of the Canadian Department of Immigration in 1916 wrote that the rate of feeble-mindedness of British Home Children was twice as high as that of Canadian school children (McLaren 25, 59). This report strengthened Canadian beliefs that the British Home Children were not only genetically tainted but also intellectually slow. The 1924 Social Service Congress of Canada concluded that the importation of child immigrants had added to the incidence of pauperism, vice, crime, and insanity" (McLaren 46).

What many children would remember all their lives was the work, long, hard, and unrewarding. . . . Ellen Keatley was sent by train from Halifax to a farm in the Nova Scotia settlement of Pictou country. Within a few days of arriving there, she was, though only 11, carrying sacks of potatoes to the cellar, picking boulders from the fields, carrying all the water to the house and barn, and wielding a buck-saw in a vain attempt to cut the wood.

For eight years, during which she was never visited by the organization that sent her there, she rose before anyone else and retired after them. Finally, when she was reaching 18 and facing another winter without even warm clothes, she wrote the Home and asked to be removed. She was.

Some, like Amy Norris, who came to Canada when she was 12, were not kept in one place very long but were shunted from farm to farm all through childhood. . . . Whatever the reason, the frequent moving from place to place left many of them bewildered and hurt and, they believe, unsettled for the rest of their lives. Amy Norris was moved 14 times in four years.[2]

31

Fred G. Snow (18-19): A Lonely Year in Hospital, Sherbrooke, Quebec, 1927-1928

My next work was for a sawmill operator. I was responsible for making sure the belts on the saw did not slip. I applied a dressing of resin and oil to the belts. It was dangerous work. I got my arm caught between the belt and the pulley. My elbow suffered a compound fracture.

The nearest doctor was five miles (8 km) away and came the next day. He looked at my elbow and said I had badly bruised and sprained it. He gave me a few painkillers, put my arm in a sling and left. After a week of unbearable pain, I insisted my employer take me to a hospital in Sherbrooke. It took another week for the swelling to go down.

I had to have two more operations. They broke and reset the bone and put a metal plate in my arm. I was in the hospital for a year, as I had nowhere to go where someone could look after me while I mended. I had no money. While I was in the hospital, I met the General Manager of Ingersoll-Rand Company. He asked where I was going to work when I left the hospital and offered me a position as a Timekeeper. I had to write and type with my left hand (Snow G. 11).

You are 17 years old and you work in a sawmill. You lubricate the belts on the saw. You carry a heavy bucket full of a sticky mixture of resin and oil. You dip a short, rag-covered stick into the bucket and carefully lubricate the rapidly moving belts. They do not shut the machine off while you do this. You are not very tall, so you have to stand on an upturned bucket to reach one of the upper belts. You are hungry and tired. The sawmill is hot, dusty, and noisy. You step on the upturned bucket, and lose your balance. You fall. Your arm is caught on the lower belt. It quickly carries you along to the pulley at the end of its loop. Your elbow is crushed as it is carried completely around the pulley. The belt releases you from its grip. You are fortunate that the pulley has a smooth, flat surface. A slotted pulley would have severed your arm.

You howl with pain. A few men rush over to look at you. One says, "You are lucky to still have your arm!" Another is concerned enough to telephone the nearest Doctor 8 km away. It is late afternoon, and he decides to wait until the next day to come. You tell him what happened and he raises his eyebrow when he hears your English accent. He gives you a disparaging look. You are now used to people looking at you with disdain when you speak. He briefly looks at your arm and tells you it is only badly bruised and sprained. You already know that. You are worried the bones are crushed or broken. He gives you a few painkillers and puts your arm in a sling. He sees no reason to see you again. The

Foreman tells you to take a few days off -- without pay. You stay in your rented room alone and suffer unbearable pain for a week. No one calls to see how you are doing. Your arm swells up and turns ugly colours of yellow, green, and brown. You cannot move your fingers. They swell to the size of sausages. You hope somehow your arm might heal itself, but you worry that you might lose the use of it. You are right-handed and it is awkward to use your left hand for shaving. You learn to write with your left hand.

It has been a week since the accident. You run out of food and painkillers. You have no money. Your weekly rent is due. You were last paid the day before the accident. You will not be paid for the week you have been off work. You cannot stand the pain any longer. You walk 8 km down the long, dusty road to the sawmill. You carry your tin trunk in your left hand. Every step sends spears of pain through your right arm. You set your sights on the road ahead, and plant one foot in front of the other. You are determined. Tomorrow, you have nowhere to live, and no way of providing for yourself.

You insist your employer take you to the hospital to have someone attend to your arm. He gives you, "The Look" when he hears your accent. You hold your breath, and pray he does not say, "No." If he does, you do not know what you will do. He notices your swollen hand and fingers. He sighs, and calls someone to drive you to the hospital. They admit you the minute you take your arm out of the sling. They do not need to examine it. You are indigent, so they put you in a large hospital ward. There are only old men in the other beds. The swelling in your arm gradually dissipates after the first week. The first operation on your arm is not successful. They perform another to break, and reset the long bones in your arm. They put a metal plate in your elbow to hold the shattered, smaller bones together. You are in this hospital for a year.

You spend most of your time learning how to talk like a Canadian. The staff are kind and treat you like a person. This is a new experience for you. They seem to care. For the first time in your life, people call you by your name. You are very happy about that. You observe how everyone acts. You are amazed the staff treat patients with the same respect they treat each other. The food in the hospital is monotonous but the meals are balanced. You grow an inch and a half (3.7 cm) taller in a year and you become muscular. You walk the hospital grounds every day, partly to get out of the confining ward, and partly to explore the environment, and observe people. All you saw since you came to Canada two years ago were isolated farms. The only people you met were farmers and labourers. You spend Christmas in the hospital alone. They discharge the other patients to their homes for the holiday

A Nurse gives you a little wrapped present on Christmas Eve. It is a tin of Player's Cigarettes. You had always rolled your own cigarettes. The Nurse has a confused look on her face when she sees your face light up like a young child. She does not know this is the first wrapped Christmas present you have ever received. You are too ashamed to tell her, so you just say, "Thank you very much." You hold back the tears that well up in your eyes. There are no churches nearby. Even if there was one, you are not sure if they would allow you to attend. You wonder what these Canadians have against you. Why is it so bad for you to be English? You find a little chapel in the hospital. You read every book you find, regardless of the subject matter. You find hope and comfort in the chapel and the books.

No one visits you. You have no money. You have nowhere to live. You worry about how you will be able to work with your mangled arm. The only work you have ever done is labouring. How will you provide for yourself if you cannot do this kind of work? You have no one -- other than someone at the Gibb's Home -- to notify where you are. You are almost 18 years old. You will no longer be in their care. They did not care much about you when you were in their care. Why would they care about you afterwards?

A man regularly visits someone in your ward. One day, he happens to notice you, and asks what happened to you. When you tell him, he notices your accent but does not give you, "The Look." He asks you about your family, and you say, "I don't have a family." He changes the subject and asks where you will go when you get out of the hospital. You tell him you do not know where you will go, but you will try to find a job anywhere. He offers you a job as a Timekeeper. You explain that your right arm might not work very well once the cast is removed. He tells you not to worry about that. After he leaves, you look out the window and up above the dense bush. You say a silent, "Thank you!" When they discharge you from the hospital, you pack your tin trunk. You had grown so much that your shirts barely fit. There is little original material left in your socks as they had been darned so often.

My Father was fortunate to get medical treatment. In 1924, a Manitoba farmer was accused of abuse and mistreatment of a British Home Child. The boy died of double pneumonia. The judge criticized the farmer for his "harsh" and "cowardly" treatment of the boy, but acquitted him of the manslaughter charge. He ruled the farmer had no legal responsibility to provide medical care for the boy (Humphreys 126). John R. Seeley was a British Home Child deported to Canada in 1929. He endured considerable physical abuse at a farmer's primitive log cabin in the bush. The organization that deported him to Canada abandoned him after his indenture. He sold donuts on Toronto streets he could afford a bed at the YMCA. Someone recognized his potential and arranged an intelligence test for him. He obtained an extremely high score. He quickly finished High School and obtained a Sociology degree in three years. He became Head of Sociology at York University, Toronto and later Assistant Dean at a private college in Los Angeles. He never forgot the loneliness and hardship of his life as a British Home Child, nor those who befriended him and gave him hope. When he addressed the American Academy of Psychoanalysis, he said, "I know that for brief times, on small scales, as far as an arm will reach, good people still do good things" (Bagnell 1980b 6).

One man's kindness allowed my Father to work as a Timekeeper for a little over a year. I imagined how he spent his first pay cheque. He would have first bought a suit, shirts, and tie. Then he would have found the best fitting shoes he could. He would have gathered all the clothes he brought from England and burned them. It would not be enough to just discard them. He would have watched the smoke curl up into the air and hope his past followed the same path. He would have felt extremely proud of his work. He would have worn his suit, tie, and polished shoes. He would have replaced his British Home Child cap with a Fedora. He would have walked tall, with his chin held high. The only remnant of his past would be his accent. He knew he would have to lose it if he was to survive in Canada. Others he met had English accents, but they were not branded "Waifs." His job ended in late 1929 as the Great Depression descended upon the world. He enlisted in the Reserve Army Service Corps at Sherbrooke, Quebec. With the threat of the Great Depression, he was assured of a place to live and food to eat for a year.

Fred G. Snow (19)   Right: Leonard Knell (19)

Fred G. Snow (20-22): A Single Homeless Man in the Great Depression, Western Canada, 1930-1931

He was finally free to do whatever he wanted and go wherever he wanted. His emancipation coincided with the onset of the Great Depression. He was 21-30 years old through the Great Depression years of 1929-1939. He traveled Western Canada by boxcar for a year and worked in a Highway Relief Camp for three years. He prospected for gold, married, and had two children during the Depression years.

Leonard Knell (20), Fred G. Snow (20), Sherbrooke, Quebec, 1930

The two million young, unemployed men who struggled to survive the "Dirty Thirties" had the weather as an adversary. In 1930, there were blizzards and winters with record low temperatures of -34° to -40°C. Spring droughts and dust storms caused crop failures on the prairies in 1931. In 1932, the worst grasshopper plague in 50 years devastated Manitoba's crops. A cycle of droughts and severe winters ensued from 1933-1935. Normal weather patterns did not return until 1939. Travel by foot or boxcar through bitterly cold winters, broiling hot summers, dust storms, and grasshopper plagues, was daunting (Mennill 14).

Unemployment Rates in Canada: 1921-1940

1921	6 %	1926	4 %	1931	10 %	1936	12 %
1922	5 %	1927	2 %	1932	12 %	1937	10 %
1923	2 %	1928	2 %	1933	18 %	1938	12 %
1924	5 %	1929	2 %	1934	20 %	1939	12 %
1925	6 %	1930	8 %	1935	15 %	1940	10 %

Although many would say he was not alone during these times -- he was very much alone. Unemployed single men had families from whom they could derive a measure of support. The British Home Children were on their own through the Great Depression, as they had been on their own all of their lives before these times. My Father found work with a rubber company, seed supply store, and shoe store, until each of these companies went out of business. He got behind in his rent at a boarding house and his landlady took his suitcase that contained all of his worldly possessions. He never saw it again.

He sold most of his clothes to get money to buy food. He bought a pair of overalls to wear over his suit while he rode the freights. He looked his best regardless of his circumstances. Approximately 100,000 men rode the freights during the Great Depression. They traveled everywhere to look for work of any kind. They chased moving freight trains and hopped on them. They either found a place inside to curl up, or clung to the outside of a crowded boxcar. It was very dangerous. If a man did not tie himself to the roof of the boxcar, he could fall asleep, and fall off to his death. His dangling feet could be amputated at a bridge crossing. A slip or fall under the wheels could be fatal. Men who crossed between the boxcars had to be careful that their feet would not be caught in the couplings. The -34° to -40°C temperatures of winter contributed to many deaths by freezing. Finding enough food was a constant problem. Men found companionship and a chance to wash clothes in the hobo camps (Berton 153).

Leonard Knell and I stoked and hauled grain from daylight to dark in Saskatchewan. When the sun set, we lit straw stacks on fire so we could see to work. We worked steadily seven days a week. The only way we got a break from work was to drop a pitchfork down into the beaters. It would take them a while to repair the machinery. We finished threshing in the fall and moved on to Hatzic Island, BC to pick raspberries. Secretaries and Schoolteachers did this work during the summer. At the end of the fruit-picking season, we drove to the Okanogan Valley in an old car to pick peaches, apricots, and apples. We stayed there about a month and then headed to Vancouver.

We were only there a few days, as we could not find work or somewhere to sleep. We hopped a freight train in Vancouver to get to Winnipeg. It took days to cross the Rocky Mountains. We rode the freight through the long Connaught Tunnel that spiralled right through the middle of the mountains. If you needed a rest or somewhere to sleep, you looked for a hobo 'jungle.' You cooked up a meal of sorts on an open fire and slept in your overcoats.

The RCMP pulled us off the train in Calgary. They lined fifty of us up in a row and made us put all of our belongings, identification, and wallets on the ground. I did not have any identification. They inspected our things, returned them to us, and let us go. The group included educated people such as Doctors and Lawyers. We would have appreciated being locked up, as that would have provided us with a meal and a bed. The Mounties told us to, 'Get out of town!' We walked along the track for many miles to reach the outskirts of town to catch a freight train to the next town. 'Get out of town -- don't stop here!' This was the welcome wherever we went for the next few years. Some train engineers soaked us with water when we pulled up to a station. We were wet and cold the rest of the ride.

Once, I wore a long overcoat when I ran to jump into a boxcar. I slipped on the gravel and nearly went under the wheels. One of the guys in the boxcar reached out, grabbed my coat, and pulled me up. He saved my life. By the time we reached Winnipeg, it had turned cold enough to make it very dangerous to run along the tops of the boxcars and jump from one to the other. The best place to ride was in the 'icebox' (the refrigerator car). It was insulated and one could stand upright but the danger was that some 'car knockers' (trainmen) would lock down the lid. We found ways to keep the lid from being locked. Even so, some men were locked in and froze to death. Deadly fumes could accumulate in the cars as well (Snow G. 18).

He might have been killed while hopping a freight train. Who would have found his corpse? How would they identify his body? Whom would they notify of his death? He likely would have been buried as a "John Doe" in some "Potters Field." Men often were not paid actual wages. The farmers determined what to pay men in excess of their room and board, or what they could afford to pay them. My Father's farm work provided him with only a place to sleep and food to eat. Married men worked on the farms so their families far away could qualify for relief. Any man who refused farm work was ineligible for relief. They were supposed to work 10 hours a day, 7 days per week, with every second Sunday off (Mennill 11).

Have you ever slept, "rough?" You are on your own in a foreign country. Everyone speaks English, but your accented English prevents you from getting work. You travel with one change of clothes you carry on your back. You no longer have your British Home Child tin trunk. You have no identification. You are 21 years old and utterly alone. You sleep on the cold ground in your clothes every night, with only a thin blanket to keep you warm. If it rains, you are soaked. If it snows, you shiver to keep warm. If it is hot, flying insects torment your sleep. At night, unknown animals howl in the bush and scurry around you in the dark while you sleep. You have only the stars to keep you company. You worry about being injured or sick, because no one would know where you were. In the morning, you wake up hungry. You eat whatever you carry with you. You trap small animals.

You continue to tell yourself, "Things will get better." You live in hope -- for that is all you have. To avoid crushing despair, you hum your favourite hymns to yourself. If traveling alone, you sing these hymns at the top of your lungs. You hope God hears you. You hope another train comes along or you will have many kilometres to walk along the endless track. You study the weather, and become an expert at reading the sky for inclement weather. You learn how to cook out of a tin can over a fire of twigs. You hop a freight train and hope for some companionship in the boxcar. When the train slows at the next town, you jump off and try to find work wherever you can. You are confused when you read posted signs saying, "English Need Not Apply." You wonder why. They now call you a vagabond and a hobo. You have been called a Waif, Stray, and Orphan before. Others you travel with talk of their families. You keep silent while they talk. If asked, you tell them your Parents are dead, and you have no family. They give you strange looks and continue the conversation without you.

We arrived in Winnipeg and received a warm reception from the 'CPR Bulls' -- the dirtiest of all cops. They chased us out of the train yards. We bummed money and food and slept at the Salvation Army, or in the 'jungles' where all the 'boxcar travelers' hung out. We had to walk many miles to reach the city limits. Some train engineers were kind enough to slow the train down when they saw 25 guys waiting to get on. We got off the freight at the outskirts of Fort William to avoid being picked up by the cops.

I found room and board for $10.00 a month in Port Arthur and tried to sell Life Insurance. It was a hard way to make a living so I quit that. The landlady had a relative who owned a farm near Murillo. I worked there as a farm hand where I cleared land by digging and hauling rocks. I also worked at haying, threshing, harvesting, ploughing, and milking. The work was much the same as the farm work I had done when I first came to Canada six years earlier. They treated me as if I was just another farm animal. I enjoyed going to Church and singing in the choir. I stayed at this job until the highway construction work began. I met some nice people on the farms.

My Father jumped off a boxcar outside Fort William and walked through the town to Port Arthur, where he rented a room in a boarding house. He must have been impressed with his first look at the grain elevators, Lake Superior, and the Sleeping Giant. He could not have known, as he sat in his room overlooking the imposing lake, that he was destined to spend his life in this area. My Mother was 18 years old and had just finished High School. He may have passed her home while he walked to Murillo. She was used to seeing young men tramp the streets of Port Arthur looking for work, as her five Brothers were part of this army of the unemployed. Had she been looking out her window this day, she might have noticed one young man in particular. He would have been a clean-shaven, 22 year-old man who wore coveralls over his suit. She might have noticed that he seemed determined as he walked with his eyes locked on the road ahead. While others walked with their eyes downcast, he walked with his head held a little higher. They were destined not to meet for another three years.

He had no proof of his identity, and officially did not exist as a person. There was no one in all of Canada how could 'vouch' for him. How many lonely days did he walk the streets of Canadian towns and villages looking for work? How many lonely nights did he spend sleeping in a ditch alongside railroad tracks, or in fields in the middle of nowhere? How many times did he envy a family sitting at a supper table, or having a picnic in a park? He felt different and inferior as a child in England. How did he feel as an unemployed, homeless, and unwanted foreigner in Canada? All he had for comfort was his belief that God knew where he was, and was looking out for him.

Only married men with families qualified for Relief. In 1931, a man had to prove he was unable to support himself and that no relative was able to help him. He had to turn in his liquor permit, license plates, driver's license, and telephone. He had to register for work on Relief projects (Mennill 10). In 1926, a British biologist proposed compulsory sterilization as a punishment for parents who had to resort to public assistance to support their children (Kevles 114). In Canada during the Great Depression, one out of five Canadians subsisted on Relief and could have become the focus of attention for such eugenic ideas. I am surprised that the British Home Children were not considered as candidates for compulsory sterilization. Canadians could have met their labour needs *and* eliminated the threat of contamination of their gene pool. The Home Children had no one to protect them from such prejudice.

Involuntary sterilization was not simply a hypothetical idea proposed by eugenic enthusiasts. Thirty US states passed compulsory sterilization laws by 1940. From 1907-1941, 60,000 people underwent involuntary sterilization in the US. In Nazi Germany from 1933-1937, 400,000 institutionalized people were involuntarily sterilized. Most US sterilization laws were in effect until the 1960s (Allen 1999). In some Canadian provinces, these laws existed until the early 1970's.

Fred G. Snow (22-25): Great Depression Relief Camp, North-Western Ontario, 1931-1934

My Parents lived their lives in the vast area of 777,000 square km known as North-Western Ontario. Residents affectionately refer to the thousands of lakes and dense forest as "The Bush." One predominant feature of the area is Lake Superior -- the largest freshwater lake in the world. It is formidable in its fury and almost all of England would fit into it. The region is sparsely populated, and 60% of the current population (200,000) live in the City of Thunder Bay. Port Arthur and Fort William amalgamated in 1970. Long distances from the nearest large cities contribute to the unique nature of its people. Thunder Bay is almost 1,609 km from Toronto, 321 km from Duluth, Minnesota, USA and 804 km from Winnipeg, Manitoba. The region enjoys an annual 2,000 hours of sunshine, 50 cm of rain, 180 cm of snow, and temperatures that range from -40°C to +40°C. It requires a special resilience to adapt to both the land and the climate. They command respect from those who choose to live in this unique part of Canada. The phrase "people need people to survive" takes on a literal meaning. A graceful solitude cannot be found elsewhere.

North-Western Ontario was very much undeveloped during the Great Depression. There were very few roads and only a single rail line connection to Eastern Ontario and Western Canada. It was an ideal location for the highway construction projects of the Great Depression. These projects contributed to the development of the Trans-Canada Highway. The work was hard and monotonous. The living conditions were primitive. The summers were hot and plagued with flies while the winters were bitterly cold with heavy snowfalls.

The government created Relief Camps to isolate the huge single jobless population because they feared a potential revolution. They considered interning men who refused to work in Relief Camps in special Discipline Camps. These camps were to be located in isolated areas, and surrounded by barbed-wire fences. Men were to be confined in isolation cells and not allowed to speak for two weeks at a time. Fortunately, the government abandoned this scheme (Berton 275). The camps would have been similar to the WWII Prisoner of War camps, and would have held young, single, men, who would have been guilty of no crime other than being unemployed.

Relief work was called the "moving of dirt. The Relief Camps were designed to house 2,000 men but swelled to 11,000 in the first year and 170,000 men after five years. If a man left, he would not again qualify for relief. He stayed or starved. Single, healthy, unemployed men over 18 years old were paid 20 cents per day. In 1931, 88 men lived in one tarpaper shack. The air was foul, the outdoor toilets were unsanitary, and the food was bad. Two men shared one double-decker bunk (Mennill 11, 26). When others complained of the living conditions in the Relief Camps, my Father kept quiet. He had lived under worse conditions.

Fred G. Snow (23)

Front Right: Fred G. Snow (24) Relief Camp, Niblock, Ontario

I became very ill in the Relief Camp. The Boss thought I was simply sick because of the poor food and only gave me some aspirins. Some of the boys thought I needed real medical attention. They hitched up a team of horses and a sleigh and took me to the nearest whistle-stop.

There was a lot of snow so it was tough going. They put me on a train and I was admitted to hospital in very bad shape. They removed my appendix.

I developed pneumonia and was in the hospital for two weeks. I recuperated with friends at Murillo for two weeks before I returned to the Relief Camp. They put me to work in the commissary and I helped the illiterate fellows to read and write. Most had been signing their paycheques with just an "X." I enrolled in an International Correspondence School course to upgrade my education and improve myself (Snow G. 20).

Fifteen hundred Relief Camp workers went on strike in BC in 1935 to protest the living conditions. They intended to ride the freights for 4828 km to Ottawa to present their simple demands of a minimum pay of 50 cents an hour for unskilled labour and union rates for skilled labour. They wanted adequate medical supplies, work to be insured by Workman's Compensation, and control of the camps to be taken out of the hands of the Department of National Defence. They wanted the right to vote. The RCMP halted the strikers in Regina, Saskatchewan. This led to a two-hour riot. One RCMP and one striker were killed. After the riot, wages were increased to 40 cents an hour, and most camps were controlled by the Forestry Department (Mennill 26-31).

Chapter 3: Love at First Sight, Port Arthur, Ontario, 1934

My maternal Great Grandfather George Perry was a 33-year-old printer in London, England when he died in 1881. His Wife was widowed with two young children -- my Grandfather (4) and my Grandaunt (1). Given the times, she was fortunate not to have *her* children taken and swallowed up by the British Child Deportation Scheme. My Grandparents immigrated to Canada and settled in Port Arthur in 1905. My Mother was born in 1913 -- when my Father (4) was sent to the foster home. She is the sixth youngest of seven children.

My Father planned to rent a room at a boarding house in Port Arthur on the Victoria Day Weekend. My Uncle worked at the same Relief Camp and invited him home for a visit. He introduced my Parents to each other. My Mother knew the minute she saw my Father that he was "the one" for her. He said of their first meeting, "From that time on, I have never had to worry about having a place to hang my hat. We have always had a home with lots of love in it -- even if there was not always a lot of monetary value" (Snow G. 12). He was inclined to understate.

From the age of 4-25 years old, he never experienced the security of being loved by his Family. No one comforted him, paid attention to him, took an interest in him, kissed him, or hugged him. No one told him he was special, celebrated his birthday, or encouraged him to dream. His lifelong and solitary anguish of being plagued by unanswered questions about his unknown family began when he "came into care." Who are my Parents? Do I have any Brothers and Sisters? Do I have any Uncles and Aunts? Why am I named, "Frederick George Snow?" Is this really my name? Why did I never see my family again? Do I have "tainted" blood? Why did those people take me away from my family? Is there something about my family I should not know?

Twenty-one of his 25 years of life to date had been dominated by subsistence and survival. He had lived a life devoid of love and affection. He had very little -- if any -- experience with women in his life before he met my Mother.

1- 4 years old	1909-1913	Lived with his parents	England
4-12 years old	1913-1921	Lived in a foster home	England
12-15 years old	1921-1925	Lived Boys Home	England
15-18 years old	1925-1927	Indentured Labourer	Quebec
18-19 years old	1927-1928	Hospitalized	Quebec
19-20 years old	1928-1929	Timekeeper	Quebec
20-21 years old	1929-1930	Reserve Army	Quebec
21-22 years old	1930-1931	Riding Freights	Canada
22-25 years old	1931-1934	Highway Relief Camp	Ontario

It was a momentous meeting and truly love-at-first-sight. Perhaps my Mother saw a man who had not experienced love. Perhaps my Father saw a woman capable of infinite love. Each had found their soul mate. For the first time in his life, he heard and said the words, "I love you." From the day they met, their separate lives merged into one, and they spent the rest of their lives devoted to each other and their children.

When they first met, my Father spoke of returning to England to find his Family. Fortunately, he reconsidered this plan. The Victoria Day Weekend became for them, and our Family, a time as important as their Wedding Anniversary. He must have been very apprehensive when he asked my Grandfather for her "hand" in marriage. My Grandmother was sympathetic to the plight of the British Home Children and regularly chastised a dairy farmer for how he treated these boys. They accepted my Father for who he was -- someone who dearly loved their Daughter.

He was not content to stay in town and idly subsist on welfare. He heard of possible prospecting work, so he loaded his packsack, and hopped a freight train to Jellicoe -- 209 km from Port Arthur. He was lucky this time, because the Ontario Provincial Police did not stop the train at a rock-cut outside town. Had they done so, he would have had to walk all the way back to town.

Gertrude Perry (21): Engaged, Port Arthur, Ontario, 1934

The winter in North-Western Ontario can be brutally cold. As temperatures drop and the snow piles up, life in the bush can be miserable. The prospecting camps were separated by many kilometres of very thick bush. Prospectors wrote notes to each other on birch-bark and tacked them to trees. He lived in a tent and slept on a bed of fir boughs covered with a blanket. It was a lonely time for him in the barren and desolate wilderness. Prospecting for gold was not just a "pipe dream." Gold had been discovered in the area. Many years later, the largest gold deposit in Canada was found at Marathon. The present-day Hemlo Gold Mine has one of the richest sources of gold outside of South Africa.

My Parents had been together a few weeks when they were apart for four months while my Father prospected for gold. He kept a diary on 25 small scraps of paper. He wrote in pencil and fountain pen on both sides of the pages. There was very little money for envelopes and stamps. Mail deliveries to the prospecting sites were sporadic. My Mother knew how important her mail was to him. She knew she was all he had.

Fred G. Snow (25): Diary of a Gold Prospector, 1934

October: Left Jellicoe for Corrigan Lake -- a 2½-hour hike. Made camp for the night. Four-hour-hike to Taylor's camp and then a 4-mile (6.4 km) hike to Maloney's. Had a mishap at the Chute and had to make camp at the side of the river to dry out my clothes. Finished the walls of the shack. Put in the floor and tent on the roof. Received a letter from my Sweetie. Wish I could see her. Slept in the bunk, felt like a sardine in the morning. The plane landed 20 miles (32 km) off their course. Put them up for the night. Had another little accident today. Slid down the rock slide of a mountain for a ways and got scratched up some but no bones were cracked. Laid up in camp all day and recuperated. Should have Skeets up here so she could doctor me up a little.

Jellicoe, Ontario, 1934

Had partridge for supper. Knocked it off with a rock. Primitive hunting, but it tasted good. The pilot and I went fishing and caught a pike. We cooked him -- the pike -- for supper. I'm living in hopes of getting mail pretty soon. Cold, and no pan gold as yet. Made a pie, some tarts, and two cakes today. Gee, I miss you. Sent $40 to my Sweetie to bank for us. I'll have to start writing on the backs of these sheets, as this is all the paper I have. Your letters Darling are what are going to keep me from going mad. Every time I get lonesome for you, I'll read the words you underlined on that song sheet you sent me. I'll imagine you are saying the words to me. Sweetie, I've got to write down my feelings. It's so hard to get mail out to you and I feel by doing this that I am keeping in touch with you. After receiving your loving letters, all I can say is that I love you and I always will. It's hard for us to be apart this way, but then, it's all for our own good, someday. Darling, I've got to turn in. I dream of you. I still wear your initial, and have your picture on my watch, so every time I look at it, I see you.

November: We found a vein just at quitting time. Not feeling so good tonight. Have a pretty bad toothache. Was up most of the night, but I guess I can stand it for a while anyhow. I had to go into Jellicoe to get a tooth pulled. I only got back last night. The lake was partly frozen over and we had quite a time to get out. I paddled across the lake and hiked to Nezah. Is it ever a tough road! I made Jellicoe by 6:20 p.m. Got my tooth all fixed up. I left Jellicoe this morning at 9:30 a.m., and arrived at camp at 8:30 p.m. Only about 35-40 miles (56-64 km). Was it dark! I thought for sure I was lost. I was never more glad to see camp than I was that night. Well, Sweetie, back on the job - rather sore and stiff from the double hike - but I'm OK. We caught a rabbit in a snare made out of my wire armbands. The lake is frozen over. I miss you more every day. It seems a long way off until Dec. 15, but I'll make it. I'll have to. Boy, we found some swell mineralized quartz. If only we could find just one speck or two of that stuff called GOLD! It would mean so much to us. Imagine my name in the paper! Worked all day and panned for the 'bug' but was very disappointed. I just snared a bunny. Andy cut my hair tonight with a razor. That is the first one I've had for about three months! We just caught a weasel outside our door and Andy is skinning him right in the tent. We went to Springer's camp to take over our mail and see if there was any for us. I guess mine must still be in Jellicoe. I might get it in a couple of weeks, if I'm lucky. We walked over three lakes on the ice, and it was shaky in spots. You could just feel it bend underneath. Today we left for Twin Falls. We sure had a tough time of it, too. We walked about 16 miles (19.6 km) and crossed the rapids on logs. They sure were shaky. We are going to board at Rene's. Am writing this with pencil, as I have no ink. There was a knifing party on before we got here. Three guys got into the lemon extract. No one was injured and of course, they got fired.

Hardrock, Ontario, 1934

Hello Skeets, I'm not so hot myself on account of having the blues tonight. Today we trenched all day and didn't find anything. It's monotonous. After receiving your letter, I feel like quitting and leaving for Port Arthur -- but can't do that. Guess I'll have to hang on for a while yet. Well, I'm not feeling too bad tonight as I have just received a couple of letters from you. If only it was nearer Christmas. Oh well, another 30 days and I'll be seeing you - if I can just stick it out that long. I guess I can for our sake and what it means to us. Well, here's the news from Sturgeon River coming over station L.O.V.E. Your announcer is F.G.S. (Fred G. Snow) and we hope the only listener is G.M.E.P. (Gertrude Mabel Emily Perry). About a foot of snow fell last night. Every day is like a nightmare. Now all I look for is seeing my Sweetheart. Found some viable gold today - not much though. I guess we'll be coming back here after Christmas.

December: It snowed about two feet (60 cm), so we washed our clothes instead of working. Gee! I want to get out so bad. Some of the other boys are in a bad way, today. I miss you so much Dear, don't know if I'll make it yet or not. I sure am getting restless. Hope the plane will come in and take us out.

If not, it will be a long hike -- about 25 miles -- (40.2 km) and a rough trail. Two more days to work and then I'll be seeing you. What fun we will have! I want to make this the best Christmas yet for both of us. Mail came in by dog-team but none for me though. One of the gang got 'bushed.' He quit at noon and got his time. He was sure fed up proper. It gets to a guy. He hiked 25 miles (40.2 km) to Jellicoe and left at noon. Well, tomorrow we blow out of here, and am I glad! Guess I'll pack my 'Glad-Rags' and be all set to leave. I'll finish off these pages tonight and whenever you read them, I'd like to you to think of me. I hope these pages will give you a little idea of what I have been doing out here, and the thoughts I have been thinking of while longing to see you. So, Darling, I hope you'll keep these and remember that First, Last, and Always - I Love You. Fred.

My Father was very much 'Love-Struck.' My Parents were always at their best, as long as they were together. His constant search for work in the bush separated them far too often in the early years of their marriage. He referred to "having another little accident," where he "slid down the side of a mountain and was scratched up some." What likely happened was that he fell a considerable distance and got severely bruised, scraped, and cut. He always minimized incidents such as this. He struck partridges down with rocks, and trapped rabbits with metal armbands. He suffered a toothache for six days under primitive living conditions. He had a high tolerance for pain. He paddled a canoe across a lake, and then hiked 11 hours through 64 km of bush to the nearest town. He repeated the trip the day after he had his tooth pulled. He crossed rapids by walking over slippery logs, and crossed frozen lakes with the rubbery ice undulating beneath his feet. A man on a prospecting crew had a mental breakdown. It was called, "Getting bushed." He lost his job and made his way back to civilization alone. Bush pilots often lost their way and landed planes on any available lake. Many have never been found. Men often resolved their interpersonal difficulties with a "knifing party." These were hard times in a hard country. This is an intimidating part of Canada. Wind, rain, snow, and cold can easily take the life of the uninitiated.

These months were particularly difficult for my Father, because he had fallen in love. Before this, he had no one to miss. Now he had to bear a new loneliness -- missing someone he loved. It was a new experience for him. They spent Christmas together, and he returned to the bush. He hopped a freight train and had a long, cold, and miserable trip in the dead of winter. There were no open doors on the boxcars, so he rode on the roof, or hung on to the ladder for the five hours it took the freight to cover the 209 km to Jellicoe.

Fred G. Snow (25): Diary of Cutting Lake Ice and Prospecting for Gold

His diary described his six months of cutting ice and prospecting for gold, and three months of labouring in a gravel pit in 1935. He slept on a pool table when he arrived in Jellicoe. When that was not available, he slept on the ground in the bush -- regardless of the weather. It took him four hours to hike 48 km through the bush with a 75-pound (165 kg) pack to get to a prospecting site, where he thought there might be work. There was not, so he turned around and made the same trip back! It was a hike through deep snow, rough bush, and frozen lakes. He got a job to build a log shack in Jellicoe. When it was half finished, the tent roof caught fire and the shack burned to the ground. He started over and cut 47 trees down with an axe. He trimmed the branches, dragged the logs to the site, cut them to size, and fitted them together. He chinked the spaces between the logs with moss and worked in snowstorms when the temperature reached -45°C. A strong wind could add a chill factor to lower the temperature to -56°C. He found odd jobs loading and hauling freight by horse and wagon. He hopped a freight train to Port Arthur to see my Mother in February. They went to a show and a dance.

Fred G. Snow (25)   Jellicoe, Ontario, 1934

He rode the freight train to Jellicoe and found work, cutting trees. He was paid $3.00 a cord for wood cut, split, and piled. The employer charged him $1.25 a day for room and board. In March, he had a contract to cut lake ice. He built an icehouse and cut the ice with a long saw that he pushed and pulled vertically through the ice. The cakes of ice were awkward to move with only ice tongs. He single-handedly cut 491 blocks of ice from the lake over eight days. They paid him four cents for each block, so he earned less than $20.00.

He returned to Port Arthur for a few days and again rode the five-hour freight train to Jellicoe. He slept in the pool hall and got work, cutting trees. This work lasted a few weeks, and he was paid $9.00 for cutting six cords of wood. At the end of April, he hopped a freight train to Geraldton and arrived at 3:00 a.m. He slept in the bush in the snow. He could not find work, so he returned to Port Arthur but was unable to find work there, either. During May, he hauled ice and freight until he found work prospecting again from June - July. It was an 8½-hour hike through the bush from Jellicoe to the prospecting site.

June-July: A Black Bear visited me and came within 20 feet (6 m) of the camp! These bears are a damn nuisance! One woke me up at 5:00 a.m. this morning. They are eating sugar out of my bag no more than 10 feet (3 m) from me! Too damn close for me! Millroy came in last night from Nezah. The bear came again. Either he gets out or he gets us! Moved out of camp as the bear was in this morning. Going to Jellicoe for a rifle and ammunition. Back at Corrigan Lake again with rifles. Went to work with a rifle. No sign of bear as yet at 7:00 p.m. A bear at Boylen's camp sure raised hell. Smashed the log camp all to pieces and broke open all the supplies. Did some trenching close to camp. We eat our meals and go to bed with the rifles beside us. Stayed on guard all night. Slept most of the day. Saw a bear close to the camp about 2:00 a.m. Well, we were in luck today. At 5:30 a.m., Mr. Bear woke us up by coming into our tent and getting a box of crackers for himself. We jumped up and grabbed our rifles, and Millroy 'bumped him off.' We buried him and I cut off one of his paws for a souvenir. Saw a bear swimming across the lake. I took off after him in the canoe but was too late to get a shot at him. Left Nezah for Corrigan Lake. 2½ hard hours walking in the rain. Still at the trenching. A skunk paid us a visit and swiped some pork and ham. Packing up and leaving for Twin Falls. Leaving for Jellicoe in the morning. All through. Sent Skeets a telegram to meet me in Port Arthur.

After nine months in the bush, through a bitter winter and a scorching summer, he found work in the Ozone gravel pit just before they were to be married. He worked all day with a pick and shovel, and spent every other available hour building a log shack that was to be the matrimonial home. They charged him $1.25 a day for board whether he worked the day or not. They paid him only 35 cents per hour or $2.80 per day. The net pay for an entire day's work in the gravel pit was $1.55. He used the money he made from cutting ice to buy their first piece of furniture -- a kitchenette set of a table, four chairs, and a buffet.

August: Hopped a freight train to Ozone. Helped unload freight. Tired tonight. Miss Skeets. Really hot here. Nice gang to work with -- all English-speaking. Worked shovelling gravel and loading wagons. Darn hot all day. Worked in the pit.

Sunday -- bummed around all day. Picked some blueberries for supper. Time drags on. Eight men laid off. I'm not working. Board has to be paid at $1.25 a day anyway. Our engagement was announced! Moved to the clay pit. Really hot. Went to Port Arthur to see my Sweets. Left for Ozone at 11:30 p.m., arrived at 2:00 a.m. Worked in the clay pit all day. Hot as Hell! Received the tent roof from Skeets. Start on the shack tomorrow. Put up the walls and put the tent on for a roof. Chinked one wall. Worked on the hill and in the pit. Finished the floor and will put in bunks tomorrow. Put up bunks in our shack. It's going to be OK, too. Shack is almost finished. Arrived in Port Arthur 8 p.m.

September: Skeets and I went to the church tonight and saw the Minister. Got my check. Skeets and I went shopping. Bought a stove.

September 05, 1935 -- MARRIED TODAY! Skeets is now Mrs. Gertrude Snow.

I do not know if my Father had any difficulty when he saw the Minister before being married. He was the same one who visited him after his emergency appendix operation a few years earlier. My Father did not have a Birth or Baptism Certificate as identification. The Wedding Announcement stated he was the youngest Son of John Snow and the late Mrs. Snow, Dean Cottage, Dean Road, Croydon, Surrey England. He believed his Mother was deceased. His own wedding may have been the first one he ever attended. Their friends picked flowers from their gardens to make bouquets for the wedding party. My Parents had only had enough money for one night in a hotel.

They married at the height of the Great Depression when the unemployment rate peaked at 20%. The marriage rate across the country had declined as the unemployment rate rose. My Parents had hope.

Fred (26), Gertrude (22): Engaged, Port Arthur, Ontario, 1935

Gravel Pit, Ozone, Ontario, 1935.

Chapter 4: Honeymoon in a Tent, Ozone, Ontario, 1935

Fred (26) & Gert (22) Snow, Ozone, Ontario, 1935

They took the train to Ozone in the middle of the night. If they did not have money for tickets, my Mother readily would have hopped the freight train with him. The train stopped just long enough for them to throw their things onto the ground. Her plain cedar "Hope Chest" survived the trip. A man appeared out of the darkness and took them to his tent for coffee. They visited until sunrise and walked through the bush to their new home. My Father carried my Mother across the threshold of their new home. It had a small, hinged table that folded up against the wall and a camp stove with a small stovepipe that went out a hole in the tent roof. My Mother did laundry by hand in a tub with a washboard and hung clothes on a line strung between the trees. They hauled water from the Ozone Creek for washing and laundry.

The Matrimonial Home, Ozone, Ontario, 1935

My Mother had not spent a night in the bush before, but readily adapted to the primitive conditions. They stayed at Ozone for about three months until it was too cold to live in the tent. They returned to Port Arthur and found rooms to rent. They were very happy with the attic suite they rented because they were able to use their kitchenette set. He had worked so hard at cutting ice at Jellicoe to save up the money to buy this one. They had some bedroom furniture so they were quite comfortable. They heated the place with short lengths of railroad ties they carried up three flights of stairs. They carried their laundry to my Grandmother's home. They were always cold in this place and often the water in the kitchen pail would freeze overnight. They carried cooking and drinking water from the bathroom on the second floor. They did not complain, as the owners were so kind to them. This was one step up from the tent in which they had lived. They said, "When you start out in a tent, you could only go up from there!"

Work was scarce, and he sold wringer washers and vacuum cleaners' door-to-door. He tramped around in the bitter winter without sufficient warm clothes. He was still forced to apply for Welfare Assistance. They were cruel to him because he was not a "local." I imagine they noticed his English accent. They told him he "should not have married if he was unable to look after a wife." He found a job washing dishes for $1.00 a day in a bush camp at Mobert -- 281 km East of Port Arthur. The food was awful and the working conditions were deplorable. He did not stay long there as he felt they had been apart too much already. In the winter of 1935, my Mother was pregnant when they rented a two-room, single-story 'shack' across the street from my Grandmother for $10.00 a month.

Pit Gang, Ozone, Ontario, 1935

Port Arthur, Ontario, 1936

He found work for a few days a week shovelling snow on city streets. They paid him partly in groceries and cash. It was not much, but they were grateful. Their rented home had neither an indoor toilet nor running water. They carried water for cooking and washing from my Grandmother's home.

My Brother Gary Frederic Snow was born on June 01, 1936. He may have been the first newborn my Father ever held in his arms. After years of being told that his blood was "tainted," he must have worried more than most about the health of his firstborn. There were no Snow's anywhere in the world for him to notify about his Son's birth. My Father had his first true Christmas for the first time in his life that year. In eight years in the foster home in England, he received an unwrapped handkerchief one Christmas. I doubt Christmas was much of an event for him in his 3½ years at St. Augustine's Home for Boys. From the ages of 15-25, he worked on farms, spent a year in hospital, rode boxcars, and lived in a Relief Camp. I imagine that Christmas was a bleak affair for these nine years. This Christmas was special, because he had been married for a year, had a loving Wife, and a six-month old Son. He was a Husband and a Father and had his *own* family, even if he had never had a family of *his* own.

Fred G. Snow (27): Fighting Forest Fires, Big Santoy Lake, North-Western Ontario, 1937

In June 1937, he found work with a construction company in Beardmore, 184 km North of Port Arthur. The working conditions were terrible and the flies were awful. Men slept in tents without screens. Fly repellent -- commonly called "gravy" -- was ineffective. The flies regarded it as a condiment. Northern Ontario flies are famous for their ability to drive animals out of the bush and sometimes people out of their minds. Some people are immune to their torment whereas others -- like me -- seem to attract every fly within sight. The smallest "No-See-Ums" are the size of a grain of pepper. The largest are Horse Flies the size of a thumbnail. Mosquitoes rule the bush. Their Black-Fly cousins swarm around in clouds to attack any exposed flesh. They are adept at burrowing through clothing. Men worked eight-hour days for six days a week in the camp. They had very little money to send home after they had paid room and board from their small wages. My Father tolerated these conditions longer than most, but finally quit.

Every summer in North-Western Ontario is fire-fighting time in the bush. Lightning strikes start many forest fires but humans cause as many or more. Perennial rumours circulate that desperate people start fires simply to create work for themselves. These fires destroy thousands of hectares of forest each year as they rage across the country driven by high winds. There is little to stop them when they became airborne and cross open lakes and highways. This part of the country is sparsely populated and there are few roads through the bush. Inaccessible fires are left to burn themselves out. This work was often the only work available for men during the Great Depression. It was hot, dirty, and dangerous work.

My Father described fighting one forest fire at Big Santoy Lake -- 248 km North of Port Arthur.

A crew of 50 men cut pulpwood at a camp on the Big Steele River. A lightning strike may have caused a fire in the bark piles. When the fire came close to the camp, the pulp-cutters ran away. They packed up as much food and supplies as they could carry, but soon found out these slowed their escape. They dumped bread, bacon, and beans, as they fled along the Big Steele River.

Firefighters could 'commandeer' anyone to fight forest fires in an emergency. The pulp-cutters refused to help and argued it was not their job to fight forest fires. Two fire-fighting bosses flew to Port Arthur to see our employer, because we needed everyone's help. He told his employees that any of them who refused to fight the fire would be fired.

The fire-fighting crew -- that now included some pulp cutters -- had to cross the lake to get to the fire. They tied four canoes of four men each together in a line. They attached a 'kicker' (an outboard motor) to the lead canoe. No one ever did such a dangerous thing as this! One canoe overturned 20 feet (6 m) from shore. Two non-swimming pulp-cutters were swept away by the strong undercurrents. They drowned in about 15 feet (4.5 m) of water. They were so close to shore!

Ontario Provincial Police divers recovered the bodies, but a bush pilot refused to fly them out. We left the bodies in the water overnight and tied them to trees on the shore. Pulp cutters customarily shaved their heads while they worked in the bush. This prevented flies from getting in their hair, and cooled them down while they worked.

All I could see that night was their bald heads bobbing in the water in the moonlight. It was tough on all of us to stay there overnight knowing there were two corpses in the water. A few days later, we found a bush pilot who agreed to fly the bodies out -- for a price! (Snow G. 138).

My Father wrote to "Our Boys League." It had a prestigious letterhead that might have been sufficient to dissuade many British Home Children from asking questions about their backgrounds.

Dear Mr. Snow,   8th October, 1937

I was very interested in receiving your letter to note that you are happily married and have a little son, and am also glad to know that you are apparently doing quite well in Canada. With regard to your enquiry concerning your antecedents, I am afraid I can add nothing to the letter which was sent to you from this office on the 30th January, 1931.

In this letter it was mentioned that you were deserted by your father and mother before coming under the Society's care and when you were actually placed with us in October 1913, you were living with Mr. J. G. Snow, Dean Cottage, Dean Road, Croydon, Surrey. The only other thing I can tell you is that according to our records, you were born in September, 1909, at Larch Road, Balham, London, but as I believe you already know, we were unable to obtain a copy of your birth certificate, as your birth was not apparently registered. I am sorry I am unable to give you any more helpful information.

Yours sincerely,

J. C. Mason, Secretary

He may have lost the 1931 letter when he rode boxcars and did not have a fixed mailing address. They stated that his Parents deserted him, but they did not identify them by name. They did not explain how he became a ward, other than using euphemisms such as, "being placed with," and "coming under the Society's care." Was J. G. Snow his Father, Grandfather, Uncle, or friend of the family?

Did they really search for his Birth Certificate? This is apparently the only information they provided him from 1927-1937, when he was 18-28 years old.

This information must have been very disconcerting for him, as he may have received this letter while he was fighting forest fires. It must have given him much to think about while he was in the bush. Given this information, the words "illegitimate" and "abandoned" would reverberate through his mind all his life.

When he received this letter, he was a Father of one, and had a second on the way. My Brother Gary Frederic Snow was born on June 01, 1936. He may have been the first newborn my Father ever held in his arms. After years of being told that his blood was "tainted," he must have worried more than most about the health of his son. There were no Snow's anywhere in the world for him to notify about Gary's birth.

Chapter 5: Hard Times in the Bush, Peninsula, Ontario, 1938-1939

In 1937, my Father found work as a labourer for a few months at the construction of the Red Rock Paper Mill. He then found work at the CPR Peninsula Train Station. He was excited about the prospect of earning $100.00 a month and having his Family with him. My Mother was five month's pregnant and made baby clothes. Women were quite creative in the Great Depression. They knitted socks, mitts, scarves, and bleached cloth flour bags to make sheets, towels, and diapers.

Peninsula was located in a bay on the North-Western shore of Lake Superior. It owed its existence to construction of the CPR railway and it became a ghost town after the railway was completed. In the 1930's, logging operations revived it and in 1944, it was named Marathon after the construction of the Marathon Paper Mill. The climate of the region is extreme.[3]

Climate of Marathon, Ontario

Month	Mean Daily Max.	Mean Daily Min.	Mean Month Temp.	Rain	Snow
January	- 1.5 C	-36.5 C	-17.7 C	Nil	91.0 cm
February	6.0 C	-32.5 C	-10.9 C	.1 mm	36.0 cm
March	8.0 C	-25.5 C	- 4.7 C	13.5 mm	28.0 cm
April	22.0 C	-14.5 C	3.7 C	71.8 mm	10.0 cm
May	23.5 C	- 4.0 C	9.8 C	81.1 mm	3.0 cm
June	25.0 C	2.0 C	13.7 C	96.0 mm	Nil
July	25.0 C	3.5 C	14.3 C	68.8 mm	Nil
August	29.5 C	2.5 C	16.5 C	53.2 mm	Nil
September	21.5 C	- 8.0 C	9.0 C	119.5 mm	Nil
October	14.8 C	-10.5 C	4.5 C	116.0 mm	19.0 cm
November	9.5 C	-23.5 C	- 4.4 C	31.8 mm	63.0 cm
December	- 4.0 C	-34.5 C	-11.0 C	7.0 mm	59.0 cm

The train to Peninsula took six hours. They moved into two rooms beside the train office. The warehouse held supplies for the Relief Camps. After a few months, my Father confronted the "Walking Boss" with discrepancies he found in the inventory of supplies. It was impossible for him to keep the books straight because the Boss took supplies and traded them for liquor. The Boss swung at him and my Father wired the Head Office in Toronto. They sent a young clerk to investigate, but ignored the issue of theft. It was easier for them to replace my Father rather than deal with the theft. Rather than wait to be "let go," he quit.

The Train Station, Peninsula, Ontario, 1938

He was conscientious in his work no matter what position he had. This was neither the first nor the last job he had that he saw his choice as either keeping a job or keeping his integrity. He always opted to keep his integrity. There were those who might have thought he could ill afford this, when my Mother was eight months pregnant, and there was very little work available. There is a price to pay to look at yourself in the mirror and hold your head high. They moved out of the train station and rented a Section House.

My Sister Karen Victoria Snow was born on August 12, 1938. My Father cut a tire inner tube into narrow strips and laced them together to serve as springs for her bed. In the fall, he worked at Heron Bay on the wood flume that carried logs overland from the Pic River to Lake Superior. They floated huge log booms to paper mills in the US. To save the cost of staying in Heron Bay, my Father walked 32 km to work and back every day along the railway track. He walked up and down hills, through rock cuts, in the dark, in the cold, in the deep snow, and through blizzards -- with hungry wolves howling in the night.

When this work ended, they were in serious trouble. The local store did not give credit for groceries, so they and the remaining half-dozen residents applied for Provincial Welfare. When the wood supply dwindled, my Father cut green birch trees from the bush along the tracks. Technically, the bush along the tracks belonged to the railroad, and although he knew someone at the station wanted to catch him doing this, he did not care. They were desperate for fuel, so they collected bits of coal that fell off the train. He made a toy car garage out of wood washed up on the lakeshore. He hunted rabbits or partridge to supplement their meagre welfare food. Although fuel and food were scarce, they had each other, and an abundance of love.

There was no work in the spring. They had no money for train fare, so they sold their kitchenette set to a neighbour. This was the one my Father worked so hard at Jellicoe to save the money to buy. The $17.00 was enough for tickets for my Mother, Brother, and Sister. Villagers spirited their things one night down to the tracks just in time for the freight train. My Parents were concerned the landlord might keep their belongings in exchange for the few dollars they owed for groceries. They left their cook stove at the house to cover this debt. My Father stayed behind that night, as he was concerned someone at the station might burn the house down and blame it on them. He and a neighbour stayed in the house overnight with Husky dogs and a rifle. Nothing happened. The next morning, he hopped a freight train and rode to Port Arthur in the coal-tender.

Gert (25), Gary (2), Peninsula, Ontario, 1938

Section House, Peninsula, Ontario, 1938

The King and Queen of England visited Port Arthur in 1939. Men were paid $2.00 each to wear armbands and line the parade route. My Father was in the crowd but only got a glimpse of them when the entourage whizzed by. My Mother missed the parade because she had to take my Brother to a doctor after he had gashed his head when he fell against a radiator.

Gert (25), Fred (29), Gary (2)   Gert (25), Gary (2)

My Father received an effusive article from the Gibbs' Club that described the Royal Visit (Keeley 1-2). A number of British Home Children were mentioned in this article. These names may be important to a descendant of the British Home Children: Henry A. Gyertson, Joseph R. Moxon, Cyril Percival, Albert Rawle, Albert W. O. Saxtree, Albert E. Bance, Edward C. Leeming, Edwin Waldron, William C. Mattison, Richard Kilbourne, Edwin M. Baker, Henry W. J. Slater, Charles J. Williams, George A. Sharman, Alan Asquith.

The Waifs and Strays Society planned to expand their operations to Western Canada, but Canada restricted immigration because of high unemployment during the Great Depression. In 1935, the Gibb's Home was renamed the Gibb's Club, as it had become more of a centre for Old Boys rather than a Receiving Home. Eleven boys were sent in 1937, and only a few were sent in 1939. This marked the end of their child emigration to Canada (Stroud 194-195). The Waifs and Strays Society deported children to Australia and New Zealand after WWII.

GIBBS CLUB, SHERBROOKE, QUE.
Autumn Number - SEPTEMBER 1939.
CANADIAN NEWS

THE GREAT AND GLORIOUS 12TH (JUNE 1939). The greatest gathering that ever took place in our history is now a thing of the past and what a wonderful life memory it provided for those privileged to attend. It is fitting that it proved to be our biggest meeting as this was the first time British reigning sovereigns have visited Canada. From the time the King and Queen landed at Quebec the wave of enthusiasm and loyalty increased in volume until even the stolid people were submerged.

The lucky ones who could see their majesties twice or more, took full advantage of their opportunities and earned much good-natured envy. What a relief to forget the vulgarity and insanity of the totalitarian countries for a few weeks and revel in contemplation, talk and service, connected with one of the most wholesome emotional events of our lives. The tact, charm and downright good nature of our Royal Visitors was something to marvel at and they received our admiring sympathy for the extraordinary way in which they stood the strain of what we hope will be the most strenuous task of their lives.

. . . Old Boys came from all directions and provinces including the United States. Some traveled all night by car, bus or truck. Sweethearts, wives and children added colour and charm, decorating our large lawn with a happy, enthusiastic crowd. At 11 a.m., it was time to assemble the company of 100 men we provided to help line the route of the royal procession.

. . . Of course we all intended to strain our blooming hearts when the King and Queen passed, but strange to say we did not make all the noise we had planned. When the great moment arrived something gripped us that could not be interpreted by only wild cheering. A girl in the crowd explained this for us when she stated that as the Royal couple approached her vocal powers decreased, and she found tears of happiness upon her face. ...

Chapter 6: St. Anthony Gold Mine, Ontario, 1939-1940

Fred (20-31)   Gert (26-27)   Gary (3-4)   Karen (1-2)

There was still no work for my Father in town. Some good friends invited him to stay with them and do odd chores in exchange for his room and board until he could get a job at St. Anthony Gold Mine. It was 376 km West of Port Arthur. He hopped a train to Sioux Lookout, and then another to Savant Lake. He crossed Sturgeon Lake on a barge from Trapper's Landing. He mailed money to my Mother and she traveled there by train with their belongings and the children

Gert (26), Gary (4), Karen (2)   Fred (30), Gert (26)

Gary (4), Karen (2)   Karen (2), Fred (30)

They lived in a log cabin that was close to the mine and store. They carried water from the lake to do their washing in a tub with a washboard. The community had a bunkhouse for single men, schoolhouse, Hudson Bay Store, Post Office, and a General Store. They lived well, even if everything was expensive because of the cost of transportation to bring supplies into such a remote area. They used wood from dynamite boxes as building material for two 'potty chairs.'

My Mother had a bad toothache. A Doctor made periodic visits to the mine, and made a home visit. He carried a packsack and sterilized his instruments over a fuel lamp. He pulled her tooth and gave her two aspirins afterwards. One day, she took a short cut across the lake, and fell through an unmarked hole someone had cut into the lake. Fortunately, she threw her arms out as she fell. This prevented her from going completely under the ice. She pulled herself out and her clothes were frozen stiff by the time she went to a neighbour's house.

The single miners found mouldy meat in their lunches, and the bunkhouse meals unfit to eat. They went on strike. The married men had home-prepared meals, so did not strike. The RCMP forced the striking miners out of the bunkhouse and ordered them off the property. The strikers walked 56 km around the lake to get out to civilization. Two months later, the owners brought in a replacement crew. After the annual X-rays and medical examinations, my Father decided he had enough of underground mining, blasting, mucking, and tramming. There were serious health risks to this work. The "writing was on the wall," that the mine would close.

The men worked three shifts per day in the mine -- as timber-men, powder-monkeys, drill-men, muckers, and trammers. One shift drilled and blasted and the next shift 'mucked out.' They shovelled rock into tramcars they pushed along rails. When my Father smelled gas after a blast, he ran and signalled the hoist-man to send down the skip. Once above ground, he stretched out on the ground to get clean air into his lungs. He could not afford to take any time off for illness as this meant a loss of pay. It was a dangerous place to work deep underground. The roof of the mine constantly dripped water and the air was stale. Men were soaked daily and hung their clothes on hooks and hoisted them to the ceiling to dry in the work shed. One man was killed in a cave-in and another mutilated his hand. The mine had a forty-year history of sporadic production. It produced two tons of gold, permanently closed in 1941 (Barr 9).

My Father worked there over a year and decided that unskilled labour had a limited future. He continued with International Correspondence Schools to upgrade his limited education, but there was rarely money to pay for his courses. Providing for his family took priority. He quit before the mine permanently closed. He was again faced with an uncertain future. He had a Wife, two young children, a limited education, and no identity. They packed up their few belongings and took the barge across Sturgeon Lake and the long train ride to Port Arthur. My Father received a letter from his "Father" in 1939, when he worked at St. Anthony Gold Mine. It was written in pencil by a shaky hand. This was 26 years after the Waifs and Strays Society apprehended him in 1913, and 12 years after he was no longer under their care.

J. G. Snow must have contacted the Waifs and Strays Society to determine my Father's whereabouts. There must have been previous letters from my Father, because J. G. Snow referred to not receiving them. Did correspondence between them pass through the Waifs and Strays Society? Did they censor the mail? My Parents' calculations on the back of this letter showed that J. G. Snow was born in 1857 and was 53 years old when my Father was born in 1909. Was he my Father's Father? If he was not, why did he sign the letter as "Dad?"

Dear Fred & Gertie:

So very pleased to hear from you and hope that you are <u>all</u> in good health. I'm pretty fair -- can get about all right. Rather shaky. <u>82 last August.</u> Its [sic] so lonely here, small three-room house as myself. Do hope you and Gertie and children are having good health. I cannot understand not receiving your letters.

Jack is working for London Counties Council - in two weeks been there 12 months. Will then be permanent with pension to follow. He is a plumber. You know he is married, don't you but I don't see any family yet. How are you for work allright [sic] I hope.

God bless you and the children. Kiss them for me. Give my best respects to Gertie's Father and Mother -- all you can wish yourselves for the coming year. Dad.

They returned to Port Arthur and found a small house to rent. My Father found work at the grain elevators that paid $80.00 a month. Their rent was $20.00 a month, so there was not much money left for groceries for a family of five. My Sister Sandra was born on December 5, 1940. After the annual seasonal lay-off from the grain elevators, he found work at Canada Car and Foundry. They manufactured Hawker Hurricane airplanes during WWII. Every Christmas since they met -- no matter how tough things were -- my Father always bought my Mother a bottle of

"Evening in Paris" perfume. Often it was only a small 75-cent bottle, but he never failed to get some.

They rented another house that had two bedrooms, a living room, a kitchen with a sink, and a bathroom with a toilet but no bathtub. Shortly after they moved, my Father received this letter from his "Brother."

My Dear brother Fred: March 13, 1940

I hope, Fred, that you will take this bravely, but our dear father has crossed the border, Fred. I found Dad dead in his bedroom at 7 a.m., on Friday morning March 08, 1940. He passed out quickly and no pain from a stroke. He went on his last journey Fred, on Thursday March 14 at 1:45 p.m. There was George and wife, Amy and husband, my wife and I at the funeral. Just a few of us Fred, it was all very sad. I was with him on the Thursday morning and in the evening I was with Amy making arrangements for him to go and live with her.

Well, Fred, it wasn't to be for Dad to live with Amy. He often said he would not like to leave Dean Cottage until carried out. His wish was granted Fred. Dad lies buried in Croydon Cemetery. There is one consolation, old chap, dear old Dad was a good age (83) and he had led a good and interesting life. Now what do you make of this war Freddie - a devil isn't it. It's getting hot over here right now. I am due to register for military service next December (34's), but at present my trade (plumber) is on the reserved list so I may escape it. I am still working for the London County Council, have been with them since March 1938. I see Amy every week, am glad to say she is keeping well, also the children, but losing Dad upset her a lot at the time, but she is a lot better now.

Now a bit . . . (Rest of letter missing.)

Jack and Amy believed my Father was their Brother. Was George another Brother, Uncle, or friend? J. G. Snow lived on Dean Road for 27 years from 1913-1940 when he was 56-83 years old. Jack had previously sent my Father a picture of J. G. Snow. My Father tore it to pieces after he received news of the death of his alleged Father. Perhaps he felt there was no one left to give him information about his identity. He was 30 years old, married for 5 years, with a Wife and three young children aged 4, 2, and 3 months. He had many other things on his mind.

Following a lay-off at Canada Car and Foundry, he found work scaling timber for a timber operation in Mead -- 307 km East of Port Arthur. He was paid $165.00 a month plus room and board and this looked good to him at the time. He could not get weekends off to return to Port Arthur, so he was apart from his family for many months. The workday began at 6:00 a.m., and continued to all hours of the night. He scaled timber, kept the company's books, and was the Timekeeper. The living conditions were primitive.

In spite of the cost of rail fare, he returned home as often as he could. The war was in full swing, and the government enacted a law to ensure people stayed at their current jobs. There was a chance of his being 'frozen' in the bush job. He quit to be home with his Family and went to work at Canada Car and Foundry again. My Parents made sure every weekend had a picnic. Before we had a car, the whole family took three streetcars and then a bus to Chippewa Park. It seemed to take the entire day to make the trip, but it was always worth it.

The Sleeping Giant is a 32 km extension of the Sibley Peninsula that stretches into Lake Superior. The profile is one of a reclining man with folded hands across his chest 10 km across Lake Superior from Thunder Bay. The legend is that an Ojibway warrior named Nanibijou was turned to stone by the Great Spirit, because he revealed the secret location of a silver deposit to the White Man. In the late 1800's, a vein of silver was discovered at Silver Islet -- the tip of the Sleeping Giant. The mine was below water level and coal-fired pumps were used to pump out water that seeped into the mine. When a coal boat was delayed, the pumps stopped, and the mine was flooded. The Sleeping Giant is a quiet companion and silent sentinel to residents of Thunder Bay. The family made the occasional camping trip to Silver Islet. My Father stayed up one entire night to keep the fire going to take the chill out of the air in the tent.

Left: Karen (5), Sandra (2) Gary (7) Gert (29), Fort William, Ontario, 1942. Right: Fred (45), Karen (16), Gert (41), Gary (18), Roger (8), Perry (10), Silver Islet, Ontario, 1954

He worked at Canada Car and Foundry when he received a letter from the Gibbs' Club.

Gibbs' Club

20 Lawford Avenue, Sherbrooke, Que.   February 19th, 1942

Dear Mr. Snow:

In reply to your letter received today, I am enclosing a certificate covering your date and place of birth, and nationality. If any further guarantee is needed regarding your admission to Canada, I will write to the Immigration Department, Ottawa, asking them to certify that you were legally admitted to this country in April 1925, ex Cunard Steamship Andania."

I am glad to hear the good news that you have a chance to get a better job, and I trust that you will be successful. I am just leaving to attend a meeting and have hurried to get you a reply by return mail. With kind regards and best wishes.

Yours sincerely, Thomas Keeley, Superintendent

Gibbs' Club

20 Lawford Avenue, Sherbrooke, Que.   February 19th, 1942

TO WHOM IT MAY CONCERN:

This is to certify that according to our records in our possession, Frederick George Snow was born at Larch Road, Balham, London, England, on September 17, 1909. He is the son of John George Snow and Annie Snow, formerly Gifford. Both parents were of British Nationality.

I have known Mr. Snow for 17 years, and can personally vouch that his nationality is British by birth, and that I have been in touch with him during the seventeen years he has resided in Canada. Immigrated to Canada, April 17, 1925 on "SS Andania," Cunard Line. Berthed at Halifax, from Liverpool, England.

Thomas Keeley, Superintendent

This is the first record of my Father being informed of his date of birth. Thomas Keeley clearly identified J. G. Snow as his Father. When he received this letter, he was 33 years old, married for seven years, and the Father of three children ages 6, 4, and 2 years old. Until he had this letter, he had nothing to prove who he was. For the next 15 years, from the ages of 33-48, this note would be all he would have to prove who he was.

Chapter 7: War & Post-War, Fort William, Ontario, 1943-1949

Fred (31-40)   Gert (27-36)   Gary (4-13)   Karen (2-11)
Sandra (0-9)   Perry (0-5)   Roger (0-4)

In 1943, they rented a 'War-Time' house in Fort William that was to be their home for the next 20 years. The family consisted of three children, two adults, one bulldog, a cat, and three kittens. It was a 1½-story wood-frame home with hardwood floors. It had a living room and two bedrooms on the first floor. There were two bedrooms on the second floor. They felt they had come a long way, as this home had a three-piece bathroom! They took in boarders who worked at Canada Car and Foundry. It was a crowded, but happy home.

My Father tried to enlist in the Armed Forces in 1943, but was not accepted because of his bent arm and his 'key' position as an Aircraft Inspector at Canada Car. He was 34 years old with a Wife and three children aged 7, 5, and 3 years old. He had hoped that enlistment would allow him to get to England and possibly find his Family. This was the dominant motivation of many British Home Children who served in WWI and WWII.

CERTIFICATE OF MEDICAL REJECTION FOR
Service in the Canadian Army (A.F.)

1. The bearer hereof Frederick George SNOW, of Fort William, Ontario, Canada.

2. Description: Date of Birth: 17 Sept. 1909

IDENTIFICATION MARKS: Appendix Scar. Height: 5' 9" Complexion:__ Hair: Brown. Eyes: Blue. Weight: 143½ lbs.

3. Applied for enlistment in the Canadian Army (Active) on the 27 October 1943 at Port Arthur M.D. No. 10. 4.

He was eligible for enlistment but was found to be unable to meet the required military physical standards.

Signed by me at Port Arthur, Ontario this 27th day of October 1943, _____.

Countersigned by me at Port Arthur, Ontario this 27th day of October 1943, <u>Fred G. Snow</u>.

My Father's conscientiousness got in his way as an Aircraft Inspector at Canada Car and Foundry. They manufactured planes used in the Battle of Britain. Others adopted an indifferent attitude towards their work. My Father could not. He would not pass their work if it were not up to specifications. His coworkers ostracized him and treated him badly in other ways. This unnerved him, and he suffered a great deal of stomach distress. He stuck to his principles anyway.

I was born on Thanksgiving Day -- October 11, 1944. My Father walked home from the hospital to gather his scattered thoughts as he did after every birth. It had become a ritual for him -- as was making bread, and cleaning the house -- while my Mother was in the hospital.

He was laid off work from Canada Car and Foundry in 1945, when war production slowed. He worked briefly at a coal company delivering bags of coal on his back. He then found work at the Great Lakes Paper Mill woodpile. On his second day there, he was injured when a careless worker swung a 'pickeroon' to stick in the end of a log. A 'pickeroon' is similar to a small fire-axe. It has a pointed end but no blade on the other end. The 'pickeroon' grazed his head behind his ear. He was not seriously injured, but he could have been. He worked at the woodpile through the winter. My Brother Roger Maurice Snow was born on January 11, 1946. My Father was re-hired at Canada Car and Foundry.

In 1948, tenants of the Wartime Houses had the first option to buy. The down payment was $350.00, with a stipulation that the buyer had to put in a basement. All through the war, the houses rested on cedar posts 1.4 m above the ground with an open crawl space underneath. He borrowed money for the down payment from my Grandmother, who had inherited some money from her English Aunt.

237 East Christina Street, Fort William, Ontario, 1949

Gary (12), Karen (10), Roger (2), Perry (4), Sandra (8)

Right after he committed himself to buying the house, he was laid off Canada Car and Foundry. He then developed a swollen and ulcerated ankle, and was hospitalized for two weeks. I have vivid memories of the suppurating, painful, open sore on his left ankle. It was purple and so swollen that he could not walk. It may have been a form of cancer or early diabetes. The available medical treatments were very limited. He soaked his foot in a galvanized tub of hot water in the kitchen and sprinkled brilliant yellow sulfa powder all over it. He did not let on how painful it was. He bound it up in bandages, and awful fluids leaked through.

It did not completely heal. This wound and his misshapen toes caused him problems for years to come. When I asked him about his feet, he said a wagon wheel crushed his toes when he was young. I did not know, until 40 years later, that his feet were deformed because of wearing women's boots when he was in foster care in England. He made wall plaques using Plaster of Paris and jam-jar lids as moulds, just to keep busy. He put paper flower cutouts in the centre and trimmed the edges with lace. This project turned out to be quite useful as he revived this interest as a retirement hobby 30 years later. The neighbourhood Minister often visited our home. None of us children had been baptized, so he simply filled a glass of water from the kitchen tap and sprinkled it on us.

In the spring of 1949, our neighbours bought their houses, pooled their resources, dug their basements, and put in cement block walls. They all worked on one house until they finished before they began the next one. My Father missed this arrangement, as he had been incapacitated by his foot problems. He decided to put in his basement himself. He shovelled all the dirt by hand and moved it all by wheelbarrow.

By May 24, 1949 -- their special anniversary -- he carried away 200 cubic yards of earth from under the house. Some neighbours volunteered to help him raise the house on screw jacks under each corner. They added timbers until the house rested on pillars of wood. My Parents laid cement blocks for the basement walls until midnight. The next day, they hand-mixed the cement, dumped it by wheelbarrow, and hand-trawled the basement floor. They used 2.2 cubic metres of cement to cover 55.7 square metres of floor.

The first family car was a very old Essex. It was a cantankerous machine, but it was large enough to hold the seven of us. On many occasions the entire family piled into the car for a picnic at Oliver Lake. One of us sat in the front with our Parents and four of us crammed into the back seat. We lashed four inflated tire tubes on the roof. The entourage must have looked like a circus car, with an impossible number of clowns inside. We carried a supply of water because the Essex often overheated and blew off the radiator cap.

There was a very steep hill just before the lake and it would take the Essex many tries to make it up and over the hill. If it did not make it up the hill the first time, my Father carefully backed down the hill for another try. Six of us would get out of the car to make it lighter. If this attempt were successful, we would walk up the hill, and get back in the car again. The downhill road to the lake was as steep as the uphill and we held our breaths as we hurtled down the gravel road that ended abruptly at the lake. The days of swimming at Oliver Lake were memorable ones for the entire family.

The Essex, Fort William, Ontario, 1949

Fred G. Snow (39)

For a few years after WWII, the cycle was one of being recalled to Canada Car and Foundry for a few months of work and then being laid off for a few months. There were times when the spells of layoff were considerably longer than the periods of work. During one layoff, my Father painted a theatre lobby and a few homes in Port Arthur. He biked to the paint store and then biked uphill for 24 km to Port Arthur with gallons of paint in the carrier. He did all he could to work and provide for his family. The seven of us made a nostalgic trip to Peninsula, Heron Bay, and Ozone in 1950. We found the remains of their tent frame from 15 years earlier. They pulled a rusty spike from a rotted piece of wood and kept it as a memento. It helps to know where you have been, as well as where you are going.

Fred (41), Gert (37), 1951   Thomas Keeley (1949)

When my Father received the following letters from the Gibb's Club, he was 39 years old, unemployed, married for 14 years, and the Father of five children ages 13, 11, 9, 5, and 3. Keeley was described as a tall, handsome, personable bachelor, who worked for the Gibbs' Home from 1911-1951. He was called the children's guide and friend in Canada (Stroud 195).

Gibbs' Club,
20 Lawford Avenue, Sherbrooke, Que.   21st June 1949
Dear Mr. Snow:

In reply to your letter received today I was very much interested to learn you had three boys and two girls.

On the windowsill in the office we have some interesting pictures of children of Old Boys. It gives me a grandfatherly feeling to look at them, and they certainly are worth a look. I am making this short as I wish to give you quick service.

We have not got any details regarding your people, neither have we got a copy of your Birth Certificate. Since 1928 we have, or had copies of Birth Certificates for most of our lads who came to Canada since that year.

I have sent to Somerset House for one of the new type of Short Certificates which only cost sixpence. They bear the seal of the Registrar General so they are quite official.

It would seem that you had a stepsister named Amy Alice Snow and a stepbrother named John A. Snow. The last address we had of your people was dated October 3, 1913 which is the year the Society received you, at the age of four years.

You can send me 25 cents to cover cost of Birth Certificate and money order. With kind regards and best wishes.

Thomas Keeley, Superintendent

Seven years earlier, Thomas Keeley wrote that J. G. Snow and Annie Gifford were my Father's, Jack's, and Amy's common Parents. In this letter, he said Jack and Amy were my Father's Stepbrother and Stepsister. Did J. G. Snow have Amy and Jack with someone other than Annie Gifford? If she had them by a previous marriage, who was their Father?

Thomas Keeley once told him J. G. Snow was his Guardian. Twelve years earlier, they told him his birth had not been registered. Why did Thomas Keeley suggest he now apply for one?

Gibbs' Club

20 Lawford Avenue, Sherbrooke, Que.   August 2nd, 1949

Dear Mr. Snow:

Many thanks for your letter enclosing the splendid family group received yesterday. It certainly adds to the attractiveness of the photo gallery. Regarding the Birth Certificate. I thank you for sending the dollar bill, and would say we expect to get a reply from England in the course of the next two or three weeks. I sent the application to the Register General about June 25.

You referred to getting some news regarding lads you knew in Sevenoaks, and who came out with you in 1925. I am adding the names of a few fellows who came out in 1924, as we happen to be in touch with all of them, and it might happen you knew some of them better than those who came out in 1925.   1924:   Edwin J. MacDonald, Sidney W. Oaker, Robert Muir, Reginald M. Worby.

1925: Albert H. Barnes, Victor A. Barnes, Frank Howe, Arthur Catt, Alfred C. Britton, Cecil B. Racey, Ernest G. Roberts.

We have the addresses of some of them if you will please let me know which of them you would like to write to I will be glad to tell you where they live. Glad to know you are able to carry on a business of your own as a painter, etc. as there is always need for services in this connection.

I have enclosed the most recent photo of myself. Though I think it was taken about 1930.

With kind regards and best wishes for all,

Yours sincerely, Thomas Keeley, Superintendent

One winter, my Father built an elaborate snow slide. He constructed a wooden ramp from the roof of the house to the ground and banked snow to make an exciting luge run. He put a ladder alongside the house so we could climb upon the roof. We slid on pieces of cardboard almost 30 m down the length of our yard and onto the back lane. Other winters, he cleared the entire back yard of snow and flooded it to make a 6 m x 12 m skating rink. He ran extension cords to provide lights for night skating and speakers so we could play records. There was a public outdoor rink a few blocks away, but friends preferred to congregate in our back yard. He did not skate himself, but thoroughly enjoyed watching us. We enjoyed many nights of skating in the back yard under the Northern Lights.

Chapter 8: Middle age, Fort William, Ontario, 1949-1963

Fred (40-53)   Gert (36-49)   Gary (13-26)   Karen (11-24)
Sandra (9-22)   Perry (5-19)   Roger (4-18)   Wendy (0-8)

In 1954, my Father (45) had been unemployed for some time. On February 16, 1955, my Sister Wendy Anne Pamela Snow was born. He tried many times to obtain work at Canada Car and Foundry, and like many others, visited the neighbourhood Minister. One day, they both went there, and said a prayer before they got to the gate. He was hired that day and worked for three years until the final layoff in 1957 when the plant closed. Shortly after that, he wrote to the Police in Balham, London, England.

METROPOLITAN POLICE

"W" Division, Balham Police Station,

47 Cavendish Road, London, S.W. 12

Dear Sir: 24th October 1957[4]

With reference to your letter of the 8th October, 1957, a search has been made at the Register of Births at Somerset House, Strand, London, W.C.2, between 1906 and 1913, and no trace can be found of your birth having been registered.

Your letter has been forwarded to _____, Church of England Children's Society, Old Town Hall, Kennington Road, London S.E. 11, who will communicate with you in due course.

If _____ is unsuccessful, it is open to you to write direct to: Register of Births, Somerset House, or Register of Births, Strand, London, W.C.2, Edinburgh, Scotland, if born in England or Wales if born in Scotland.

Yours faithfully, A/Superintendent

It appeared that the Police actually conducted a search for his Birth Certificate. When my Father received this letter, he had been laid off Canada Car and Foundry. Groceries were often scarce, but somehow my Mother managed to make daily meals for all of us. My Parents often made sacrifices even with food to ensure that we got enough to eat. They could not always pay their debts on time, and bill collectors frequently turned up at the door. Those of us in school wore hand-me-down clothes that my Mother adeptly altered.

My Brother and I delivered advertising flyers' to 1,000 homes and were paid one cent for each flyer delivered, so we earned $10.00 for each load. This often included heavy Sears and Eaton's catalogues. My

Brother broke his arm when he slipped and fell on some ice. He was in the hospital for a few weeks, and had a cast on his arm for some time, so my Parents took his place on the route. Many carriers would stuff the flyers down a sewer and pretend they delivered them. Our employer once accused us of the same thing, and my Father was incensed he would think this of us. It did not occur to us to dump the flyers. Rain or snow, we delivered them. I did not fully appreciate how much they relied upon this income to buy groceries.

I helped my Father when he worked cleaning offices at night. One night I was quite tired after I waxed and polished an office floor. He came in and started to scrub a corner of the floor with steel wool. Sweat poured off his brow. I asked him, "Why bother? No one else has cleaned these corners in years." He replied, "No matter what the job, take pride in doing it, and do it well!" I helped him clean the corner. We knew we had left the floor better than we had found it. I learned something about the value of work, regardless of the nature of the work.

He next found work for a few months as a custodian at a Home for the Aged in Fort William. For a time, there were regular paychecks and more groceries. He came home one night and told my Mother that he could not work there anymore. He could not stand to see the old people being abused. He tried to report this, but his employers, "Did not want to know." I walked in on the conversation and blurted out, "Now what will we do for groceries?" He gave me a rare cold stare and replied, "There are more important things than food in your belly." I was too young to know about integrity and the price you paid to maintain it. Ironically, 37 years later, he would spend his final years at this very place.

Fred G. Snow (48), Prospecting for Gold, Beardmore, Ontario, 1957

While he was unemployed, he returned to the bush near Beardmore where he had prospected for gold 23 years earlier. He found a few traces, but nothing of any significance. He wrote again to the Children's Society. He received a copy of his Baptism Certificate. It did not have a date of birth and did not name his Father. He decided not to share this with his children aged 21, 19, 17, 13, 11, and 2. He must have felt very ashamed. He could not have felt very good about himself, as he was 48 years old, unemployed, and the sole provider for the family. I first saw this Baptism Certificate in 1994 shortly after his death.

CHURCH OF ENGLAND CHILDREN'S SOCIETY

Dear Mr. Snow,   November 11, 1957[5]

As you know your letter to the Chief Constable at Balham was forwarded to this office as you were once in the care of this Society. I have searched through your file and can find no other information than that supplied to you previously over the years since you left England. I did obtain a copy of your Baptism Certificate and enclose it herewith. You may already have a copy as one was sent to Thomas Keeley at the Gibbs Home, in December 1936. You will see that the Baptism Certificate gives your age as 4 years, this is because the exact date was not known.

I have tried the Registrar at Balham, and, as you know the Police searched at Somerset House and there isno [sic] trace of your Registration. As we had also searched in 1929 with no success, it seems that you were not registered. However maybe your Baptism Certificate can be accepted of proof of your age. You came to us in October 1913 and at that time you were not old enough to go to school. This means that you were under 5 years. I am sorry not to be able to send you your Birth Certificate but if there is any other way in which I can help please let me know.

Yours sincerely,

They again stated they had no other information about his family. They sent a copy of this Baptism Certificate to Thomas Keeley in 1936. Why did he not forward it to my Father, who wrote to him in 1936, 1942, and 1949? Why did Keeley give him a 'To Whom it May Concern' letter instead? Why did he tell him he was born on September 17, 1909, if his birth date was unknown? If they searched for his Birth Certificate in 1929, why did Keeley offer to search for his Birth Certificate in 1949? Why did he ask him for money to cover the cost of the search?

```
┌──────────────────────────────────────────────────────────────┐
│                    BAPTISM CERTIFICATE                         │
│ Baptism solemnized in the Parish of St. Peter's Croydon in the │
│ Diocese of Canterbury and County of Surrey in the Year 1913    │
└──────────────────────────────────────────────────────────────┘
```

BAPTISM CERTIFICATE

Baptism solemnized in the Parish of St. Peter's Croydon in the Diocese of Canterbury and County of Surrey in the Year 1913

Alleged Date of Birth	When Baptized	Child's Christian Name	Parents' Christian	Names Surname	Abode Dean Road
**** Years Old	8 Oct.1913	Frederick George	Annie	Gifford Snow	

By whom the Sacrament was administered. Arthur Reeve, Vicar.

I Certify, that the foregoing is a true copy of the entry of the Baptism of **Frederick George Snow** in the Register of Baptisms for the said Parish of St. Peter's Croydon. Signed: A. Reeve

If they had this in their possession for 44 years, why did they not give him a copy before this? Who scratched out his date of birth? It appeared to read as 4 years old, but underneath is a "½." Could he have been only 3½ years old when he was apprehended? His Mother was listed as Annie Gifford but his Father was listed only as "Snow." If John George Snow was his Father -- as Keeley told him in 1942 -- why was his name not listed? They gave him this information 30 years after he was in their care. This was the only piece of official identification he ever had that verified his name. For most of his life to date, he was not sure if "Snow" was actually his name. This must have caused him to reflect more upon his mysterious origins while he prospected for gold in the bush. This could only confirm him as illegitimate.

Each of us had a unique relationship with each of our Parents. For much of my childhood and adolescence, my relationship with my Father was one of Apprentice-to-Handy-Man. The entire family became known for its ability to fix almost anything with tape, glue, or wire.

I helped him repair the old Dodge one winter when I was 13 years old. He attached a tarpaulin to the house to make a roof over the car. He shovelled snow around the base of the car and crawled underneath. He did not have a "Trouble Light," so he used a pole lamp from the living room instead. He did not have a proper set of tools. If he needed a 13 mm wrench, and only had a 10 mm wrench, he used a screwdriver tip to take up the space. He was persistent and would not compromise by only doing a partial job. The job took hours and every repair seemed to coincide with a snowstorm and -34°C temperatures.

I do not know how he withstood the cold. I shivered so much I could not hold the light steady. He lay on the snow-covered ground underneath a car while the wind howled around us. I was too young to know he worked 16 hours a day in the winter on the farms in Quebec and wore only short pants and short-sleeved shirts.

Back: Karen (19), Fred G. Snow (47), Sandra (16). Front: Gary (21), Roger (11), Wendy (2), Gertrude Snow (43), Perry (12). Fort William, Ontario, 1957

He received a copy of his Baptism Certificate in November 1957. That winter was particularly difficult with brutally cold temperatures of -34°C that lasted for weeks. There was not much money around for the basics. That winter we ran out of coal for the furnace. My Father put an old 'pot-bellied' stove in the kitchen, cut a hole in the wall, and put pipes through to the outside. This wood stove was the only source of heat for the entire house. We shortly ran out of wood for this stove. He called me to the kitchen. I did not have to ask what he wanted, it was usually a given that he needed a hand with something. He just tilted his head to one side. I put my coat on and we walked down the driveway to the lane.

He said, "We need wood." We walked the length of the lane and picked up bits of wood along the way. There was not much as the snow was so deep. When we returned home, he stopped, lit a cigarette, and stood very still. I shivered from the cold as we watched the eerie Northern Lights flickering across the sky. He walked up to the neighbour's fence and ripped off a picket. I frowned and he said, "Give me a hand!" I tore off a few as well. He said, "That will do for tonight." My Mother did not ask where we found the painted wood. He had six cold children at home and the house needed heat. I would have willingly gone for more pickets. In the spring, he told the neighbour he hit his fence with the car, and replaced the pickets.

The "War-Time" houses were poorly constructed. I do not know how we all fit into such a tiny place. At one time, two boarders lived with us and shared one bedroom. My Parents had the other first-floor bedroom. Six of us children to shared the two bedrooms upstairs. My three sisters shared one bedroom, and my two brothers and I shared the other. The houses were inadequately insulated and had only wood shavings in the attic. The roofs were bare in the winter when heat loss melted the snow. The central furnace with its "octopus" pipes consumed over a ton of coal during the winter. The windows coated with a thick sheet of ice. We slept with socks on our feet and coats and blankets piled high upon us. The weight ensured that no one had a fitful sleep. Family love provided warmth when the furnace would not. Good-natured laughter circulated this heat. Others lived in better houses, but few lived in better homes.

My Father continued his International Correspondence School course he began when he worked at St. Anthony Gold Mine in 1940. His constant search for work and financial difficulties did not allow him to pursue this consistently. He enrolled in an Engineering correspondence course in 1959. He found work as a Construction Superintendent and supervised the building of a school, church, and highway extension to the United States border. Ironically, one project was the construction of a picnic area at Kakabeka Falls -- not far from the site of the Relief Camp where he worked 24 years earlier.

In the winter of 1958, I was 14 years old when I accompanied him on a trip to Gull Bay -- 192 km North of Port Arthur on the shore of Lake Nipigon. He had to inspect the construction of a new school on the Indian Reserve. There had been a heavy snowfall, and most of the road had not been ploughed. We made a trail for ourselves in the deep snow. Mostly logging trucks used the single lane, rough road. We came to a rickety bridge and I walked tentatively over it to guide him across in the blowing snow. He crept cautiously across the bridge and we heard ominous cracking sounds. The bridge sounded as if it was giving way to the weight of the truck. He "gunned" the engine and sped across the bridge. I jumped to the side. He could not stop because he would have stuck in the snow halfway up the hill, or slid back down the hill onto the bridge. He stopped at the top of the hill to let me back in the truck.

He reiterated his famous saying, "For every down, there must be two ups -- Right?" Neither of us mentioned how we would cross this bridge when we came to it on our return trip. We blazed a trail in the -30°F blowing snow. We stayed overnight in a log cabin. I could see the outside through the cracks in the logs. Wolves circled the shack and howled all night. The cook let the oil-drum "stove" go out overnight, and it was -30°C inside the shack as well by morning.

I was impressed with the way men treated him. It was different from the fear and fawning I had noticed when I worked on construction sites and "the boss" came around. He neither talked "up" nor "down" to these men. He treated them with respect, so perhaps, that is why they reciprocated.

When he finished his inspection, we headed back down the road. Neither of us said a word when we came to the bridge. He sailed across the bridge rather than slow down and creep across it. We both held our breaths when we raced across the bridge. Once over, we just smiled at each other and kept on going. When he returned for another inspection three months later, he was appalled to find the Indians had vandalized the new school. They broke windows, ripped tiles off the floors, and stripped paneling from the walls for firewood.

His next work was as a Construction Superintendent at the Keefer Seaway Terminal. At night, I helped him examine X-ray films of the welding joints from the overpass they built. Together, we did his "homework" from his correspondence course. A few of my friends in High School who were much better at Mathematics than me, sat at our kitchen table and helped him with his Algebra and Trigonometry. They admired his persistence and attempts to further his education at this age.

Fred G. Snow (52), Fort William, Ontario, 1960.

85

He found summer labouring work for me laying railroad tracks when I was 15 years old. I was underage, so they paid me $.85 an hour for a 10-hour day. Everything about the work was heavy. The railroad ties were soaked in creosote, and the 9.1 m rails weighed 453 kg. The labouring crew was composed of Italians, Croatians, Finns, Ukrainians, and Russians. Their English was limited to a few words. They were good, hardworking men. They had nothing more to look forward to in life, and were kind in their way. They reminded me daily to, "Go School!" Many were illiterate and signed for their pay packets with an "X." They asked me to read their important mail and check their pay packets. I discovered our employer was cheating them of their pay. I questioned the Timekeeper, who denied anything was wrong. The next week, I was laid off. This could have been a coincidence. Thirty years later, Revenue Canada charged my former employer with Income Tax Evasion and fraudulent withholding of Payroll Deductions. What goes around -- comes around. It just seems to take a while.

Back: Sandra (19), Karen (21), Gert (46), Fred (50).
Front: Roger (13), Wendy (4), Gary (23), Perry (15).
Fort William, Ontario, 1959

Chapter 9: Middle & Old Age, Thunder Bay, Ontario, 1963-1984

Fred (54-75)   Gert (50-71)   Gary (27-48)   Karen (25-46)
Sandra (23-44)   Perry (19-40)   Roger (18-39)   Wendy (8-29)

In 1963, my Parents bought a new house that was to be their home for the next 22 years. The landscaping took a lot of time and work. Our old cat refused to stay at the new house, and at every opportunity, ran off to our old home many kilometres away. She had problems other than being unable to settle into the new house and surroundings. She had developed sores of unknown origin and a rash around her eye. Other cats and dogs had torn off her fur in chunks while she made her treks to our old house.

We made several trips to pick her up, and finally had to put her to sleep. My Father selected me to help him take the cat to the Humane Society. We put her in a box and she must have expected the worst as she howled the entire trip in the car. It broke my heart to hear her struggle inside the box. My Father just drove on with his jaw clenched, and I saw he held back tears. We were in and out of the Humane Society as fast as we could. He had a soft heart for cats, dogs, and helpless animals of all kinds. He did not hunt or fish for sport.

Gert (50), Wendy (8)

Thunder Bay, Ontario, 1963.

My Father patiently persisted at his Engineering correspondence course from 1959-1964 while he was 50-55 years old. His self-education began 28 years earlier in the Relief Camp during the Great Depression. He completed the program and fulfilled the requirements of a Certified Engineering Technician. This helped him to obtain work with the Federal Government as Clerk of the Works.

In 1964, he supervised the construction of a school at Big Trout Lake -- 696 km from Fort William. It was a very isolated native community accessible only by bush-plane. He lived alone and kept house for himself. The Indians kept to themselves and shunned non-natives. During services, they sat together on one side of the church, and waited until the non-natives left after the service before they left the church. My Father's lifelong source of solace had been transformed into a stressful place.

The natives sabotaged the construction. They threw garbage into the lake to pollute the drinking water, stole construction materials, and broke newly installed windows. He was 55 years old when the isolation, alienation, and loneliness finally got to him. He could only communicate with us by radiophone. Atmospheric conditions interfered and disrupted the calls. After two months, he saw a Doctor in Fort William who gave him a letter saying that his health would be at risk if he continued to work at Big Trout Lake. At this age, he could not handle the ostracism and sullen hostility. He had experienced too much of this before. He was out of work for a while after that, and was quickly fed up with being idle. He went to local construction sites and applied for labouring work. The construction supervisors knew his reputation and were surprised to see him apply for labouring work. He could not get a job as a labourer because he did not belong to the Labourer's Union.

Fred G. Snow (56), Big Trout Lake, Ontario, 1965

He obtained work with the Government of Ontario Department of Public Works. I accompanied him on one of his trips to Red Lake. The 562 km drive was long and uncomfortable in his compact car that jarred our bones with every bump it hit on the highway. I developed an appreciation for the hazards of highway driving in the winter. We stayed two nights in the log cabin he rented, as it was much cheaper than the one motel. The cabin was quite primitive, and was similar to the shack we stayed in at Gull Bay six years earlier. The site inspections went well, and the contractors appreciated his thoroughness.

This trip allowed me to see my Father in a new light. He was 55 years old, married, and Father of five children ages 29, 27, 25, 21, 19, and 10. For the first time I saw him as aging. Until then, he always seemed to me to be strong and full of energy. On a miserable winter night in a shabby cabin, he tried to have a philosophical Father-to-Son conversation about Life. Our mutual effort failed, and we resorted to what had worked to date -- our silent understanding of each other. The cost of living-away allowance had not changed for 40 years and he managed on $5.00 per day for food and lodging. He lived in this cabin all winter -- isolated and alone in the cold bush. I felt he deserved much better than this, but for him to live comfortably in a motel would have caused financial hardship for the family.

He was then promoted to the position of Ontario Government District Manager, Buildings Management. At the age of 56, he finally had a secure and permanent position! He had not worked long enough at other positions to establish a pension plan. These nine years were the longest period of uninterrupted work he ever had. For the first time in his life, he did not have to worry about how long work would last. A few years later, they notice the following article in the local newspaper. My Father scratched out the word "WAIFS."

WAIFS:

I have been given the interesting assignment of preparing a history of the Church of England Children's Society - the second largest child-care organization in Britain. From its foundation in 1881, the society - then known as the Waifs and Strays helped a great many children to emigrate to Canada from England and, at one time, it ran homes at Sherbrooke, Quebec and at Niagara, Ont. I am anxious to hear from any Canadian who may have connections with the society and from anyone whose parents may have crossed the Atlantic this way, and may have talked to their children about their experiences. Many early records have been lost and I am therefore very interested in obtaining personal reminiscences. John Stroud

---

Dear Sir: April 21, 1969

Re: Advertisement relative to the Church of England's Children's Society

Having read the advertisement in our local paper, I have decided to answer it.   First, I emigrated to Canada in April 1925 at the age of 15 years from St. Augustine's Home for Boys at Sevenoaks, Kent.   There were 35 other Boys from all over England that came at the same time on the Cunard Liner SS Andania.   We all landed at Halifax and went from there by train to Gibb's Club, Sherbrooke, Quebec. Mr. Thomas Keeley was in charge at that time.

I do not wish to dwell on the intervals in between, at this time, as they are too lengthy and varied, but if you are interested, I have some tall stories to tell on life in Canada from 15 years to the present age of 60 years.   I am married with my Wife and children -- three boys and three girls.

One boy is 33 years with a BA degree from the University of Minnesota, now District Manager with General Motors of Canada.   One is attending Lakehead University in his third year with a BA and taking his Masters in Psychology.   The other lad is in Men's Wear as a Salesman in one of our exclusive Men's Stores.   One of my three girls is a Registered Nurse -- Assistant, Head Nurse at a local hospital.   One is a Certified Nursing Assistant -- now married with our first Grandchild. The last one is fourteen years old and is attending Grade 9 High School.

As you can see by my card, I am District Manager, Thunder Bay District, for the Ontario Government, responsible for all Government-owned buildings.   I will be glad to assist you in a more detailed account, if you would advise me of your requirements.   I have enclosed some material which may be of help to you.

I am, Yours very truly,

Fred G. Snow, Certified Engineering Technician

My Father (56) may have disclosed his true experiences as a ward of the Children's Society for the first time when he wrote to the author. He was dismayed to find only 12 pages of Thirteen Penny Stamps were about the British Child Deportation Scheme to Canada. The book undoubtedly activated his repressed memories. He may have been depressed to learn the true story of the British Home Children might never be told.

I first read this book 30 years later in 1995. It is a self-serving and farcical account of the scheme.

Dear Mr. Snow,   1st July, 1969

. . . Since I put my letter in the English and Canadian newspapers, I have heard from about two hundred Old Boys and Girls (some of them very old indeed): some of them went into the Homes before 1900. With their help, and with yours, I have been able to put together the first draft of my book and have delivered it to the Society. Now I have to wait and see whether they approve or not; but if they do, I hope the book will be published next year.

It has been a very interesting assignment and I have received so much information that I cannot do justice to it. On the Canadian end of the work, for example, I have been able to spare a little over one chapter, so of course that cannot cover the whole story. I expect that you have heard that Mr. Tom Keeley died at Christmas: he was over 90, I believe. He must have been a very fine man, everybody speaks well of him. I must say you have followed in a great tradition: Prebendary Rudolf, who was the founder of the Society, started out as a clerk in the English equivalent of the Public Works Department. Amongst other jobs he busied himself with the installation of electric lights in the House of Lords!

I expect you will want the documents you sent me, so I return them herewith with thanks for the loan of them. I was so pleased to hear from you and to learn what a wonderful family you have. With all good wishes, Yours sincerely,

John Stroud

He was depressed for a second time a year later, after he attended a Management Training Program in Toronto. When he returned home, I asked him how it went. He was more reserved than usual and said, "It was interesting." I asked him what he learned. He said, "I'm not sure. It was nothing like I expected." I became suspicious when he told me the program was held at a Lodge at a remote lake. I asked him, "What did they do to you?" His lip quivered, and he said, "What do you mean?"

I realized then that he had inadvertently participated in a Sensitivity Training Group. I told him what I knew of these "consciousness and awareness" groups. Untrained and unqualified amateurs operated on the premise that people needed to become "more honest with themselves and others." They compelled people to abandon their defences and become "more real." The group process was confrontational and could run 24 hours without interruption for food or washroom breaks. I told him how people could be damaged when they were rendered defenceless, and how honesty without kindness -- is simply cruelty. I described what I knew of coercive techniques and asked him how he handled it all.

Well, Per, they almost got to me. They accused me of living an isolated life because I had no friends. They said I was a 'social hermit' who was 'overly dependent' upon my family. That hurt.

They made us talk about our childhood -- and got on me for that, because I didn't say too much. They said unless I expressed my 'true feelings,' I would never be a 'whole person.' How did I handle it? The first two days I did not handle it very well. I thought there were some serious things wrong with me.

I was much older than everyone else there. I met a guy in his 50's, and as much as we could, we talked about our work, our wives, and our families. That helped us both. Whenever I could, I went for a walk. I had to sneak away sometimes because they didn't like you to be alone. I found a place where I could think my thoughts.

I thought of your Mother and you kids. I reminded myself you all loved me the way I am. I told myself, 'If I am good enough for my family, then who the Hell are these strangers to say I am not good enough?'

The third day was all right, because I played their game and knew it was only a matter of time until I was away from there. Some people were pretty messed up by the time they left. Like I said, they *almost* got to me -- but then others had tried.

Fred G. Snow (59), 1968

My Brother considered working in England in 1971 and wrote to search for our Father's Birth Certificate. He may not have known of previous attempts. The General Register Office informed him that no record of my Father's birth was recorded between 1907-1911 and he received a letter from St. Peter's Church in Croydon.

92

I attended Post-Graduate Studies at Strathclyde University, Glasgow, Scotland in 1971-1972. Family history was of little interest at the time, as I had simply accepted by then the unvarying story of my Father's life. I had no knowledge how someone would go about looking for a lost family. My paternal Grandparents existed only as names. I was oblivious to the correspondence between my Parents, Amy, and Jack.

Fred G. Snow (64), 1973

My Father (64) became a Canadian Citizen on September 23, 1973. It was a momentous day, as he finally had some proof of his identity. It was always difficult for him to cross the US border without official identification. He retired at the age of 65 in 1974 and needed proof of his identity to qualify for an Old Age Pension. His Baptism Certificate with his estimated year of birth and his "To Whom it May Concern" letter would not have been sufficient.

93

My Parents started a ceramic business they called The House of Snow, with an igloo as a logo. My Father discovered he had a talent for teaching, and held classes three evenings a week. They could freely travel to Duluth, Minnesota, USA to attend training courses and obtain supplies that were not available in Thunder Bay. My Father poured the moulds and my Mother painted the fine details on them. It was a busy time for them and they thoroughly enjoyed their hobby. They kept the ceramic classes going for two years until his health deteriorated.

House of Snow Ceramics, 1974

"Smiley" Hockey Players

Thirteen Penny Stamps was published in 1971 but was difficult to obtain, and was quickly out of print. Apparently, the author did not notify the hundreds of British Home Children who wrote to him when the book was published. My Parents wrote the author in 1976, and the Children's Society in an attempt to learn how a copy might be obtained. They tried to solicit his help in obtaining information from the Children's Society.

Dear Mr. & Mrs. Snow,   17 August, 1976

Thank you for your letter. I am so pleased to know you have been able to obtain my book and I hope you enjoy reading it.

. . . I have asked the Society if they can help Mr. Snow with his enquiry about other boys who came out to Canada with him in 1925 but I am not sure if the records are sufficiently detailed.

One of the problems is that a lot of old records were destroyed during and just after the last war. If Mr. Snow could rack his brains for the names of the boys he met on the voyage, we might be able to trace them from the old papers.

With best wishes to you both, Yours sincerely

John Stroud

Dear Mr. & Mrs. Snow,   20 September, 1976

. . . I write to say that I pursued Mr. Snow's enquiry with the Society and have just heard back from them. They have very kindly searched through the old records and have sent me the following list of names of boys who were at St. Augustine's and who sailed to Canada with Mr. Snow on the SS Anderia [sic] in 1925:

Victor Barnes   Albert Barnes   Alfred Britton

Frank Howe   Arthur Catt   Leonard Knell   Cecil Racey.

Unfortunately none of these boys ever wrote back to the Society so we do not know where they may be now.

I can only suggest that perhaps you both might like to consider putting advertisements in one or two of the Canadian papers asking for "the lads" to contact you.

However, you know the local scene and some other idea might occur to you e.g. Using radio services. I am very sorry I am unable to send you any further information.

With best wishes to you both, Yours sincerely, John Stroud

With the exception of Ernest G. Roberts, these were the same names Thomas Keeley gave my Father 27 years earlier.

Back: Roger Snow (29), Perry Snow (31), Logan D. (37), Roger M. (36), Gary Snow (39). Centre: Marion M./Snow (29), Bonnie B./Snow (30), Karen Snow/D. (37), Sandra Snow/M. (35), Wilga H./Snow (26). Front: Paul P. (22), Wendy Snow/P. (20), Gertrude Snow (63), Fred G. Snow (66). Thunder Bay, Ontario, 1975

My Father (68) became very ill in the spring of 1977, after a callus on his left foot became infected and would not heal. No one knew whether the infection caused his diabetes or vice versa. He had not been in a hospital or seen a doctor in 20 years. The infection quickly developed into gangrene and they admitted him to the hospital where I worked as a Psychologist. As the day wore on, his condition deteriorated. He first said in a very dispassionate way, "I may lose my toes." An hour later, he said, "I may lose my foot." His entire leg was black, and he was in considerable pain. He said, "They can take my whole leg -- as long as it stops the pain." He was quite unemotional about it all. He was fine until a nurse came in and announced his left leg would be amputated below the knee. He stared off into space, raised his chin, and said, "Fine."

Fred G. Snow (69), 1978

96

My Parents developed an attitude I call the "Next-Best Scenario." The best possible scenario was he would not require any amputation. The "Next Best" was to lose only his toes. The "Next Best" was a below-the-knee amputation, as it was harder to fit prosthesis to an above-the-knee amputation. They counted their blessings all their lives. They were grateful for the medical help, and were glad they were in a city, rather than a small town in the bush. Others might focus upon losses, but they concentrated on what they had rather than what they had apparently lost.

A Nurse took a marker pen out of her pocket and drew a dotted line on his leg below his left knee. Only then did tears come to his eyes. When she left, he asked me why they had to mark his leg. I had tears in my eyes as well, and could not speak. I just shrugged. I could not tell him they did this to minimize Surgeon error. He recovered quickly from this gaffe.

My Mother leaned over and kissed him just before he went into the operating room. She said, "See you soon, Dearie!" He smiled and winked at her. I asked her if she wanted to wait in my office with me but she declined. She went instead to a window at the end of a hallway and looked out over Lake Superior at her beloved Sleeping Giant. I anxiously waited in my office. The operation went well and they saved his upper left leg. He spent the night in Intensive Care. They transferred him to a semi-private room the next day.

I walked into his room and found him struggling to get out of bed. My first thought was he was not aware of the amputation. Before I could say anything, he gave me a sharp look and said, "I know my leg has been cut off! Come here and help me out of bed!" I went to him and asked him why he wanted out of his bed. He said, "I am a man who has for 68 years of his life stood up to pee. I do not intend to lay in a bed and pee in a bedpan!" I put my arm around him, and held the bottle while he urinated. The Surgeon walked in just then and was angry that my Father was out of his bed. My Father just smiled a contented smile. I was never more proud of him.

He was in a hurry to recover and get out of hospital. He felt the whole hospital atmosphere was not conducive to his healing and recovery. He asked me if he had to "be depressed" before he was discharge him from hospital. I hesitated before I answered, but I could not lie to him. I nodded and explained the nursing staff had a checklist. They expected people to "grieve for their losses" in a particular way. I suggested he convince them he was a typical patient who was recovering in a typical way -- by "grieving for his lost limb." He acknowledged that he was uncomfortable with letting strangers know how he felt. I encouraged him to tell the staff how much he missed his leg. He replied, "Well, I was rather attached to it."

He was most atypical in his recovery. Once when I visited him, he stared at a picture on the wall. I asked him what was special about the picture. He replied, "I am not looking at the picture, I am looking through it!" Perhaps this is what he learned to do while he was in the foster home for eight years, Boys' Home for four years, and hospital for one year as a young man. He was eager to get home to familiar surroundings and home-cooked meals. He pestered the staff to accelerate his prosthesis fitting and crutch-training. They reluctantly discharged him three weeks after he lost his leg. Most amputees were in hospital at least three months.

I went to his room and found him on his crutches, kicking his prosthesis around the floor. I asked him what he was doing. He said, "I can accept this, but I do not have to like it!" He explained he had read a book written by the Canadian radio announcer Norman DePoe. He had a leg amputated, and advised amputees to do this to their prostheses. It appeared to work. The staff had emphasized that people "had to accept their condition." Anything other than "acceptance," they considered "denial." It seemed their version of "acceptance" required patients to "smile all the while." Mr. DePoe's suggestion seemed much more appropriate. My Father accelerated his recovery when he was home. My Parents had overcome many challenges in their lives. This one was different -- but just another.

Almost a year later, they flew to California to visit my Brother. I found out my Father was ill when I phoned my Mother in San Diego. She minimized his condition by saying he had "a touch of the flu," as she did not want the Family to worry. When I called the San Diego Hospital for information, they put me straight through to him! I asked him how he was, and he said, "Fine." He paused and then said he had tubes in his arms and nose. I told him I intended to escort them home. He said "O.K." This surprised me, as I expected him to say this was unnecessary. This convinced me that that his condition was quite serious.

My flight was a series of hops through Ontario, Manitoba, North Dakota, Colorado, and California. When I got off the plane, my Mother and I went straight to the hospital. He had pneumonia and a spot on his lung. Our flight from San Diego was delayed and we had very little time to catch the flight from Duluth to Thunder Bay. I pushed him in a wheelchair as fast as I could through the airport and hollered at people to get out of the way. My Mother rushed along behind us, with his prosthesis under her arm. He could not wear it, as he had lost weight in the hospital, and it chafed his stump.

When we arrived in Thunder Bay, he was immediately admitted to hospital. They wanted to operate and biopsy his lung. He was very apprehensive about this, as his strength was diminished from the trip and hospitalization in California. His diabetes was out of control. He told me he simply was not up to an operation. He just wanted to go home and regain his strength. He signed himself out of the hospital, "Against medical advice." I took them home and helped them settle back in after the strenuous trip. A few weeks later, his X-rays showed that the spot on his lung had inexplicably disappeared.

They continued with the ceramic business but it eventually became too much for him and he switched to hydroponics gardening in 1980. They made a nostalgic trip to Savant Lake and had dinner in the same hotel they stayed 41 years earlier on their way to St. Anthony Gold Mine.

Fred (71), Gert (67), St. Anthony Gold Mine, 1980

The only correspondence my Parents had with Amy and Jack were the occasional exchange of Christmas Cards. One Christmas card dated 1979 from Amy (74), mentioned that her Niece Eileen Snow lived in Kamloops, BC. In 1956, Eileen hitchhiked across Canada, and called my Father from a phone booth in Thunder Bay. The call was interrupted when she ran off to catch a ride, and there was no other contact with this potential Niece or Step-Niece.

One letter from Amy (75) provided the first and only account he had from anyone, how he came under the care of the Waifs and Strays Society. He was 71 years old when he read this.

Dear Fred & Gertie: 23 Sept. 1980

Jack didn't seem to remember as much as I do. You are right about Mother's name Anne Gifford, and Father John George Snow. I do not know what transpired in Fred's first four years, we lived in Parker Road, South Croydon. I remember one day my Mother and Father were rowing. My uncle Bill was there, he was Dad's Son by his First Wife. There was also uncle George, also by Dad's First Wife.

As children, Jack and I would go to Uncle George and his Wife Aunt Nance and our cousins, a girl and a boy. I forget the girl's name but young George, Jack, and I went to Archbishop Tenison's School.

I recall the row, I was about 4 years old. I don't remember Jack being around, he probably went out to play, he never liked rows. I think the argument was over my (our) Mother and Uncle Bill. Freddy, as I always called him, was about two years old, he was toddling. The next thing I remember Jack, Dad, and myself were living at Dean Cottage, Dean Road, Croydon. I have been round once or twice to look at our old place, but it makes me cry. Dad was such a wonderful Father he did his best for us all.

One day Mother came back with Freddy, he was about 3½ years old. So far as I can make out, Dad had been looking after Jack and I and Mother had Freddy. I can't remember whether Mother stayed at all, but I remember she was gone, and left Freddy with Dad. Whether she and Bill had parted or what happened I don't know.

Jack and I had to take Freddy to school with us as my Father had to go to work. Of course Freddy wasn't old enough for school, I still remember him calling out in classes and my saying 'Shoo.' We all three sat in the front row. How long we did this I can't remember but I suppose the authorities must have told Dad they couldn't have Freddy at school.

Dad had to go to work to keep us so he couldn't stay home. Jack says he remembers my Father had a girl about 14 years to come daily to look after Freddy. I don't know what happened except I remember some people being there at home and somebody saying she (meaning me), ought to go as she is a girl. But I suppose Dad had me all along and had managed because we were at school.

I didn't see Freddy go, maybe they didn't let me, but I remember asking Dad repeatedly where he was and when was he coming back. I must have asked all over the years as I knew Fred had gone to Canada. I met Mother a couple of times at Tooting at Mother's Sister's house. I don't know if Mother is alive or not. She was younger than Dad and liked a gay life whereas Dad was quiet. Mother also played the piano well. She was a cashier at Selfridges in London. Dad ran away to sea on the sailing boats when he was 14. He was also a guard on the trains later on. He jumped ship, as the living was terrible in those days. Dad did his best but we went hungry many times.

Dad had Jack and I to go into a cook shop to have a hot dinner. Even at that age I was embarrassed at sitting having a dinner with working men around. Previously, Jack and I had been going to the back of the Church to a room and getting a jug of soup and a hunk of bread. The only reason I can see why Fred was fostered out was that he was not old enough for school and Dad couldn't get anyone to look after him through the day. Best Wishes, Amy

J. G. Snow was previously married and had two sons named Bill and George. They would have been 31 and 28 years old in 1913 when they apprehended my Father. At the time of the argument, Amy was four years old and my Father was two. About what was the argument? Was Uncle Bill my Father's Father? Why did Thomas Keeley tell him J. G. Snow was his Father? Annie Gifford/Snow apparently may have left my three-year-old Father with J. G. Snow in 1912. Amy and Jack took him to school with them, even though he was underage. The authorities may have told J. G. Snow they could not have him in school. He hired a girl to look after my Father. Amy was almost apprehended along with him.

119 Churchill Drive, Thunder Bay, Ontario, 1975

Fred G. Snow (75), Thunder Bay, Ontario

In the spring of 1983 my Father (74) bought a 6 m greenhouse that could be disassembled for the winter. He became quite ill that summer and had to be hospitalized because of ulcers. He went on insulin and faithfully followed the ulcer and diabetic diet. Five months after he was released from the hospital, he was off both medication and insulin. He sold the greenhouse and ceramic kiln, as both had just become too much work. The next spring, he bought another greenhouse so he could continue gardening on a smaller scale.

He kept busy with gardening, and as he sat in his living room, a truck pulled up in front of the house. A man jumped out and took some photographs of the house. My Father had no idea what this was about. A month later, he received a letter from the City of Thunder Bay's 'Beautification Committee.' He had been chosen, along with 30 others to receive an award for his gardening efforts! It was an unexpected surprise, as he simply did what he enjoyed, and was unaware of any competition. He did not make the papers for discovering gold in his prospecting days, but he was pleased with this all the same.

In 1984, my Parents again wrote to the Children's Society.

The Children's Society.

Church of England Children's Society

Dear Mr. & Mrs. Snow,   2nd March 1984

Thank you very much for your interesting letter with the fascinating story of Mr. Snow's journey from England to Canada.

I am unsure if we will be able to help you but I have passed your letter on to _____ in the hope that _____ will be able to sort out some background for you.

> ... it is wonderful to hear that your husband made such a happy life in Canada and have such a lovely family as witness to it.
>
> I wish you and your family all the very best for the future and I hope that we will be able to help in some way with your queries. Yours sincerely

The Children's Society.
Church of England Children's Society

Dear Mr. & Mrs. Snow,   13th March 1984

Your letter has been passed to me from _____. I was interested to read that you are planning to write about your younger days and would be very interested to receive a copy upon completion. The Society would of course pay postage.

... I have taken it upon myself to go through the Society's magazine, 'Our Waifs and Strays' and extracted all information on Emigration. However, the cost of pack is quite considerable at 20£ plus postage * of which the latter to Canada would be quite considerable.

I do have a photograph and others ... of Tom Keeley. The cost of these photos is 2£ for a print if there is an existing negative or 3£ 90p if there isn't.

... I would be most interested in hearing about Mr. Keeley and life in the Home in Canada, so if you have anything that you feel would be of interest to me I shall be very interested to hear from you. All good wishes and good luck with the writing. Yours sincerely.

* It is possible to loan for cost of postage.

My Father wrote his final letter to the Children's Society in 1984. He was 74 years old, married for 48 years, and the Father of six children ages 48, 46, 44, 40, 38, and 28.

Dear Madam: 31st March 1984

Thank you for your prompt reply to my letter. .... The photostats are good for my records, it's a good one of the Home, but I am not familiar with the boys in the sailing pictures. I wish now to give you some information regarding my background. I have enclosed a copy of my Baptism Certificate. I am at a loss to know why, with all the investigations, no one has checked with St. Peters' Croydon Church! I do not know how long they keep records, but I would think it would be a considerable time.

To gloss over quickly my movements, as I can remember, from the time I was four years old, to the time of emigrating to Canada on April 17, 1925 on SS Andania berthed in Halifax Canada from Liverpool, England. At age 4 years I was placed with Mr. & Mrs. Smith at Rumburgh, Suffolk, England. I remained with them to age 11 years. I was sent to St. Augustine's Church Home for Boys, at Sevenoaks, Kent. From there I emigrated to Canada at age 15 years, where I still am.

Enclosed, please find letters relevant to my quest for a Birth Certificate, and family connections. I wish to state here all the time I was in England I never had any contact with any of my relatives. To this day I have never seen one of them. I am enclosing some money to defray costs of photostats and mailing. I have no idea of costs. If you have no use for the enclosed letters and Baptism Certificate, would you please return same and I will pay any additional costs.

Thanking you for your time and cooperation.

Yours with gratitude, F. G. Snow

The Children's Society.
Church of England Children's Society

Dear Mr. & Mrs. Snow,   18 April, 1984

Your letter to _____ dated March 31st 1984 has been passed to me. In answer to your enquiry concerning The Parish Church of St. Peter, Croydon, I would imagine that the reason behind the investigations not been carried out there would be because that someone would actually have to go to the Church to plough [sic] through their records. Maybe you have a friend in England who could possibly do this for you.

From your correspondence, I am not clear whether in fact you have received information from our records relating to the time you spent in our care. If not, and you would like to avail yourself of this information, please let me know so that I can retrieve the records.

I look forward to your reply,

Who in England might my Father have as a 'friend?' They stated they were "not clear" whether he received information from them and asked him if he would like to "avail" himself of information. What other reason did he have for writing to them? This was beyond bureaucratic ignorance -- it was cruel. He gave up his search of 55 years in 1984.

Gert (72), Fred (76), Thunder Bay, Ontario

In 1985, they sold their house and moved to an apartment that had an elevator, as he found it increasingly difficult to climb stairs with his artificial leg. Their third floor apartment was only a few hundred yards away from their home. They had the same view of Mount McKay as they had from their house. My Father gardened on the patio deck. The house sale provided them with enough to keep them comfortable until the end of their days. They were happy. They had each other, and that is all either of them ever needed.

The Children's Society returned copies of my Father's Baptism Certificate and previous correspondence from two years earlier.

The Children's Society.

Church of England Children's Society   31 May 1986

apologies for not return [sic] this to you with our letter of 18 April 1984.
With compliments

Chapter 10: The Final Years, Thunder Bay, Ontario, 1985-1994

Fred (75-85)   Gert (71-81)   Gary (48-58)   Karen (46-56)
Sandra (44-54) Perry (40-50)   Roger (39-49)   Wendy (29-39)

Fred (76), Gert (72), Thunder Bay, Ontario, 1985

Many elderly lifelong friends attended my Parents' Golden Wedding Anniversary. There was the occasional tear in the audiences' eyes when my Parents danced to <u>The Anniversary Waltz</u>. My Father was a wonderful dancer in spite of his artificial leg, and it was always a special joy for my Parents to dance together. Throughout their lives, they were truly grateful for all they had. They believed they always had help along their way. They believed they were never alone. In times of adversity,

106

they relied on this phrase from the Bible: Trust in the Lord with all thine heart; and lean not unto thine own understanding; In all thy ways acknowledge Him; and He shall direct thy paths (Proverbs 3:5,6).

In 1988, my Father (79) and my Mother (75) flew to Calgary to visit my Family and then to Los Angeles to visit my Brother. We had a wonderful time. We toured the Rocky Mountains and enjoyed the magnificent scenery. My Mother related to the environment as an artist and saw every vista as a potential oil painting. My Father recalled a few memories of the "Boxcar Years."

On August 13, 1989, my Daughter Elizabeth (12) developed Hodgkin's Disease -- a form of lymphatic cancer. She weighed only 24 kg and we were anxious whether she would survive an operation. The Surgeon split her sternum lengthwise to obtain a biopsy sample. It was held together with metal ties after the operation. She took up very little space in the adult hospital bed in Intensive Care after the operation. She had intravenous tubes in her arms and drainage tubes in her stomach. She sat up in her bed and said she had to go to the bathroom. She ordered me to leave the room. While I waited in the hallway, my Wife pushed her down the hall in her wheelchair. I could not believe she had gotten out of bed only a few hours after such an operation.

I rushed after this apparition of wheelchair, intravenous pole, and balloons. I asked them where they were going. My Daughter stuck out her lip out and said, "I am going to the bathroom, -- I am not going to use a bedpan!" That sounded familiar. When she was released from hospital a week after surgery, she still weighed so little. Legally she qualified to ride strapped into a child's car seat -- even though she was about to celebrate her 13th Birthday. She underwent six weeks of radiation treatment and recovered fully. We were grateful she did not require chemotherapy.

My Daughter Charlotte (16) developed some unusual symptoms a year later. She and I discovered we have a rare condition called familial hypobetalipoprotenemia. We both have abnormally low levels of cholesterol. While most people are concerned with lowering cholesterol, we have to raise ours to normal levels. This genetically determined condition is associated to some extent with longevity. I most likely inherited the condition from my Father, and she inherited it turn from me. The need to know family medical history became more of a priority.

From 1989-1991, my Father's health declined further and his vision and hearing were problematic. His diabetes became more difficult to control. He was very conscientious about following his exercise, and diet regime, but he developed a stomach ulcer and circulation problems in his right leg. My Parents moved to another apartment that allowed for easier wheelchair access. It was obvious he could no longer adequately care for himself, and my Mother reached her limits as to her ability to look after the two of them. In 1991, he was admitted to hospital for an operation to improve the circulation in his remaining leg. There was a risk he could lose it. At the time, the procedure of inserting a balloon into the veins was quite new. This was a major operation and he did not recover as quickly as he had in the past. My eldest Sister felt that the end was drawing near, and phoned to tell me, "This is it."

It was difficult to arrange a flight from Calgary to Thunder Bay, and the only one available short notice was from Calgary-Winnipeg-Toronto-Thunder Bay. It was very much the long way around. All through the flight, I dreaded I might arrive too late, and find that he had died while I was *en route*. He knew I was coming. My Sister picked me up at the airport and we sped away to the hospital. When I walked into the room he said, "Well, its Perry -- my Guardian Angel, or the Angel of Death!" He made a remarkable recovery while I flew many anxious hours. This was his pattern. When his health deteriorated, he was admitted to hospital in very poor condition. With a minimum of care, he rapidly recovered. After this operation, he required more intensive and extensive care.

He was reluctantly transferred to a Home for the Aged where he slowly regained his health from 1991-1992. It was a frustrating year for the entire family because his health was too good for this Home and not good enough to qualify for the other Home. I saw him only once at this home. It was heart-breaking for all the family to see him there, but there were no other choices available, and he made the best of it. My Mother moved into a Senior's apartment nearby and faithfully visited him every day for the final three years of his life at both Homes.

In 1992, I flew to Thunder Bay for the weekend to attend the funeral of a good friend. I arrived on Friday night and met with my grieving friends before the funeral on Saturday. I saw my Mother briefly and visited with my Father on Sunday. I tried to see all of my Family, but there was so little time.

On Monday, a Nurse at the Home called me and said my Father was crying inconsolably. He wanted to see me. She had deliberated whether to call me or not, but I was so glad she did. I went to see him. He dressed himself in his suit and tie, as he always did for a special occasion. We had a cup of tea together. I took him out in his wheelchair for a stroll around the grounds and along the river. He insisted on getting out of the wheelchair and walking with his cane. We did not talk of any "weighty things." He was as anxious as I, that this might be the last time we might ever see each other. It was not, but it could have been

My Mother-in-Law died at Easter, 1993. My Wife flew to Thunder Bay and was there for a month before her Mother died. I arrived the day after. When my Brother drove me to visit my Mother, I noticed an impressive new building. I asked him what it was and he said it was to be a new Home for the Aged. We stopped and toured the building. It was lovely, and we encouraged our Mother to put in an application. She was accepted and has been at this Home ever since. She has a comfortable apartment in aesthetically pleasing surroundings, and a magnificent view of Lake Superior and the Sleeping Giant.

I borrowed a car and went to the Home to take my Father on an outing. He dressed in his sport coat and tie. He was quite frail, and we took his wheelchair along. We picked up some of his favourite fast food to take with us on our drive to Mission Island. When he commented on the pussy willows at the side of the road, I stopped the car and went into the ditch to pick them. I stepped in the water and soaked my shoes. I managed to pull some pussy willows and bull-rushes from the bog. He was very pleased, as this was a long-standing spring tradition. Part of this tradition included my getting my feet wet. We parked the car at the bird sanctuary on the shore of Lake Superior. He insisted he walk, rather than sit in the wheelchair. We held his arms as he manoeuvred himself out of the car. He took his cane and carefully walked to the water's edge and stared at the Sleeping Giant. We were all silent on the return trip to the Home. He and I knew we would not see each other again. My Wife had just lost her Mother, and she knew I might lose my Father in the next year. He and I silently made our peace with each other, and gave each other our silent blessings that day. We had -- in our way -- let each other know that we loved and respected each other. He knew I was proud to be his Son, and I knew he was proud to be my Father.

Two images come to my mind when I think of the last time I saw him. One is a picture of him standing, leaning on his cane, and gazing over Lake Superior. His chin is raised and he has a contented smile on his face. The other less preferable picture is one of seeing him hunched over in his wheelchair, holding himself, and weeping at the Home, when I left him. He could not help himself. Our Family tends to "whimper" when overcome with emotion. It comes from hearts that ache with love. It is our "way." When I think of the last time I saw him, I try to concentrate on the former picture rather than the latter. He and I were not inclined to write to each other, and I treasure the few letters we exchanged. Whenever we spoke on the phone, we "choked up," lost our voices, broke down with tears, and could not speak. We were similar in many respects. When others say, "You are just like your Father," I take it as a compliment.

DEATH ON A BIRTHDAY

My Father died peacefully on his alleged birthday -- September 17, 1994. It could be a simple coincidence that he died 12 days later -- on what he believed was his birthday. The simple funeral service was attended only by his immediate family. After the service, we cried, laughed, and renewed our love for each other. He was cremated and his ashes interred in the Perry family plot in Thunder Bay. There were no "Snow" relatives to notify of his passing. His obituary read that he was born in Croydon, Surrey, England in 1909 and was the Son of John George Snow and Annie Gifford/Snow. I was angry his death went so unnoticed except by his immediate family. I knew that with his death, my siblings and I were unrelated to any other "Snow's" in the world.

Who were his Parents? Why was he apprehended? Does he have any Brothers or Sisters? I vowed I would find the answers to these questions. Shortly after his death, my Mother gave me my some of my Father's personal effects. His passports were his most prized possessions because they proved he was a person with an official identity. His was too ill at the age of 84 in 1993, to obtain a sixth passport.

1968: Age 59   1973: Age 64   1978: Age 69

1983: Age 74   1988: Age 79

I began my search for his identity in earnest following his death. It would take four years to piece together the enigma of his life in England, reclaim his stolen identity from the Children's Society, and find his Family.

PART II: DISCOVERING THE TRUTH (1993-1998)
Chapter 1: An Inherited Mystery of Family Origins

I began my search in a limited way, a year before his death. I was quite ignorant of how to conduct a search for familial roots. All I had was the alleged names of my Grandparents -- John George Snow and Annie Gifford. I did not know where they were born, where they lived, how old they were, or if they were married when my Father was born.

The Calgary Family History Centre has excellent research materials, but these were of little use to me. It was difficult to find what I was looking for with such sparse information. I collected addresses of other organizations involved in the British Child Deportation Scheme (Appendix). I was surprised to find so many still existed.

I wrote to the Salvation Army and inquired about their Family Tracing Service.

The Salvation Army

Territorial Headquarters

20 Salvation Square, Toronto, Ontario, M5W 2B1

Dear Mr. Snow   RE: Your Inquiry   October 28, 1994

Please be advised it is the policy of The Salvation Army that a request for a search is received by The Family Tracing Service office which is responsible for the community in which the inquirer resides.

For this reason your inquiry has been forwarded to our office for response.

We regret to inform you that we are not able to accept your inquiry since the purpose of our Family Tracing Service is to reunite family members so that broken ties can be restored and relationships may be renewed.

To this end we do not conduct an investigation where the inquiry relates to genealogical purposes.

We regret that we cannot be of service to you. May God bless you.

I was not conducting an idle genealogical search! I was trying to locate living relatives. Amy could be in England, Jack in Ireland, and his Daughter in British Columbia. I felt I was trying to put together a jigsaw puzzle that consisted of disparate pieces of information. All the important pieces were in England. There was no complete picture on a box to guide me.

I first wrote the Children's Society in October -- a few weeks after my Father died.

The Children's Society.

A VOLUNTARY SOCIETY OF THE CHURCH OF ENGLAND AND THE
CHURCH IN WALES

Dear Mr. Snow   17 October, 1994

Thank you for your letter of 5th October 1994. I am sorry to hear that your father has died. I can confirm that he was in the care of the Children's Society.

The date of birth on the record card only says September 1909. The record card shows that he was placed in a Child's Receiving Home on 31st October 1913 and was boarded out on 6th December 1913.

He moved to Sevenoaks on 12th October 1921 and emigrated on 3rd April 1925. I have passed your letter on to _____ who may have further information.

We have no trace of any brothers or sisters in our record cards. I hope this brief information is helpful.

Yours sincerely

If they had "no trace of brothers or sisters" on their record cards, then who were Jack and Amy Snow? The Children's Society once identified them as his Brother and Sister, and once as his Stepbrother and Stepsister. Even though searches had apparently been made for his Birth Certificate, I wrote to the General Register Office and requested another. They did not find a record of his birth between 1907-1911.

I phoned the Children's Society for clarification of their note and received two replies.

The Children's Society.

A VOLUNTARY SOCIETY OF THE CHURCH OF ENGLAND AND THE
CHURCH IN WALES

Dear Mr. Snow   3 November 1994

Further to our telephone conversation on 2 November 1994, I am writing to confirm that your enquiry regarding your late father has been passed to _____ . . . who holds all the records relating to people who were in the Society's care before 1930. A copy of this letter has been passed to _____ who will be in touch with you directly in the near future. . . . Yours sincerely

---

I sent them a fax to advise them that my search for his Birth Certificate was unsuccessful.

Dear _____   November 16, 1994

. . . I am very curious as to what exactly constitutes 'the contents of the file.' I would be most grateful to receive any/all information that is available as to his past, since so little is known. If there are any costs involved in photocopying, postage, etc., please advise me, as I am very willing to pay such costs.

Recently, however, I did discover that his Father was John George Snow (August 1857 - March 8, 1940), and his mother was Annie Gifford, and that he had a Brother John A. Snow (1905-?) and a Sister Amy Alice Snow (1903-?). St. Catherine's House has not been able to locate a Birth Certificate as per his alleged d.o.b. of September 17, 1909. It appears this date is incorrect. I look forward to hearing from you soon.

Sincerely, Perry Snow

Someone sent me a newspaper clipping that described the British Child Deportation Scheme to Australia. This was the first time I heard of this. The revelations of the Child Migrants Trust in England in 1989 exposed the scandal of the scheme. In Empty Cradles, Humphreys described how the organizations sent 15,000 children to Australia, New Zealand, and Africa from 1947-1967. Most people believed the scheme had ended before WWII.

The organizations changed children's names and birth dates in case files. They told children they were orphans, when they were not. They told Parents families in England adopted their children. Instead, they shipped them to Australia where the Christian Brothers physically and sexually abused them. They stymied the children's efforts to obtain information and lied about the existence of records. The Child Migrants Trust researcher kindly conducted an unsolicited search for my Father's Birth Certificate.

The only Fred Snow born in 1909 was Frederick Thomas G. Snow. Even though this name was dissimilar, I decided it was worth the effort to obtain this Birth Certificate. It was not the right one. I was very disappointed.

The Children's Society initially stated I could expect a reply from them in two or three weeks. I finally received a reply from them -- two months later. They ignored my first request to release "any/all information that is available as to his past." I had hoped they would send me his entire case file. At the very least, this letter confirmed the existence of a comprehensive case file! The information they provided validated his recollections. I did not doubt his account, although it crossed my mind on occasion, that he was free to invent any explanation of his past. I wonder how many British Home Children did? It might have been easier for many of them to say their parents were killed in WWI, or died of illness. I was ecstatic when I read their letter.

The Children's Society.
A VOLUNTARY SOCIETY OF THE CHURCH OF ENGLAND AND THE CHURCH IN WALES

Dear Mr. Snow   4 January 1995

Your enquiry concerning your father, Frederick George Snow, has been passed to me. Below are details of his time in care with the Society that have been drawn from his case file.

According to Frederick's admission form, dated 2 October 1913, he was taken into the Society's care on 31 October 1913 when he was admitted to our former receiving home at Clapham in south London. He remained there until 8 December 1913 when he was boarded out with a foster parent, Mrs. A. Smith of Rumburgh, Halesworth, Suffolk.

A report dated September 27, 1920, noted that this foster home was: . . . a very good home and contains 3 bedrooms, sitting room and kitchen. The foster mother's husband is a labourer. The foster mother is an exceptionally nice woman.

In 1921, Frederick was transferred to the Society's former boys' home at Sevenoaks in Kent, St. Augustine's. At the beginning of 1925 Frederick was recorded as being "very anxious to emigrate to Canada". On 13 January 1925 the Society's Emigration Committee sanctioned his emigration and he traveled to the Society's Gibbs' Home at Sherbrooke, Quebec, Canada, on 3 April 1925.

From the Gibb's Home he was found work on a farm at East Angus in Quebec. His file contains two letters written to the master and matron at Sevenoaks that give quite a graphic description of life on a Canadian farm during the 1920's; enclosed are photocopies of each.

Two letters from your father dated January and February 1929 bearing a company letter head would seem to indicate that he was employed by the Canadian Ingersoll-Rand Company at this time.

His admission form contains a number of personal details. He was born at Larch Road, Balham, south London, in September 1909. He was baptised at St. Peter's Church, South Croydon, on 8 October 1913. His mother was Annie Gifford, who was aged 39 when the admission form was completed in 1913.

The information given about your father's parents is sketchy having been compiled by the local clergyman at St. Peter's Croydon, who referred the case to the Society.

From the evidence it is clear that Annie Gifford was the second wife (as described in the admission form) of John George Snow, by whom she had two children, Amy Alice Snow (aged 6 in 1913) and John Allen Snow (aged 8 in 1913).John George Snow had an adult son by his first wife, called William Henry Snow, who was nine years younger than Annie Gifford. The detail given in the admission form then goes on to suggest that Frederick was the son of Annie Gifford and the son of, John Snow's first marriage, William Henry Snow. Annie and William Henry cohabitated [sic] after Frederick's birth, during which time Annie left Frederick with John Snow.

In 1913, John Snow father was living at The Stables, Dean Road, Croydon. He is described as having "very uncertain employment, often being out of work. At best, he has about 30 shillings (£1.50) per week for 8 months out of the 12 months."

Please contact me if you have any queries regarding the above. Equally, if you would like me to search for a photograph and details of St. Augustine's Boys Home at Sevenoaks, please let me know. Copy photographs can be supplied at £5.00 ($11.15) each, plus postage and packing. Yours sincerely,

They stated they "admitted" him to their care on October 02, 1913. His recollection was that the Police forcibly removed him from his Family. He did not remember being in their Clapham Receiving Home from for six weeks after they apprehended him. They described the foster home in positive terms and the foster mother as "exceptionally nice." He described the home as impoverished. They said he was "very anxious to emigrate to Canada" in 1925. He recalled being told to choose between deportation to either Canada or Australia. The sailing dates indicated the ship took two weeks to cross the Atlantic. They gave me copies of two letters he wrote to the Master and Matron at St. Augustine's. They referred to two letters he wrote in 1929 on Ingersoll-Rand letterhead, but did not give me copies of these.

The second half of the letter contained a number of surprises. They said he was born at Larch Road Balham, London, in September 1909. Where did the date of September 17, originate? They said he was baptised at St. Peter's Church, South Croydon, on October 08, 1913. I had sent them a copy of this Baptism Certificate. There was no explanation why the local clergyman "referred" him to the Children's Society.

They identified his Mother as Annie Gifford. If she was 39 years old in 1913, then she was born in 1874. Was this not too old for a woman to have children? This letter explained she was the Second Wife of John George Snow. Amy was born in 1907, and Jack was born in 1905. This information made Amy his Half Sister and Jack his Half Brother. Why did they tell him in 1949 that Jack and Amy were his Stepbrother and Stepsister? The letter identified William Henry Snow as J. G. Snow's Son by his First Wife. If he was nine years younger than Annie Gifford was, he was 30 years old in 1913, and born in 1880.

They said William Henry Snow was my Father's Father! In 1942, they told him he was "the son of John George Snow and Annie Snow, formerly Gifford." Why did they do this? This letter said Annie and William Henry Snow lived together after he was born, and he was then "left" with J. G. Snow. Does this constitute "abandonment" as they previously told him?

They offered to sell me photocopies of St. Augustine's Home for Boys for £5.00 ($11.15). I simply asked the same questions of the Children's Society that he asked for over 55 years. Why did they release this information to me now? Was his death a prerequisite to this? This information contradicted other information they gave my Father.

For the first time -- 82 years after he was in their care -- they clearly identified the relationship between William Henry Snow and J. G. Snow as Son-to-Father. Why did they tell him on one occasion that J. G. Snow was his Father, and on many other occasions, his Guardian?

While I was grateful to receive this information, I shuddered to think of what might have transpired had I not persisted in requesting more information. In 1929, he was legally an adult, and kept the Ingersoll-Rand Company letterhead for 65 years. It must have been the first record of his attempt to find out about his background. There was a letter missing between the two mentioned in the Children's Society letter.

When I fitted these pieces of the puzzle together, I had a new account of my Father's origins. It was one he never knew because they never told him. His Grandfather J. G. Snow was born somewhere in England about 1857. He likely first married about 1877 and had two sons -- George Snow born about 1879 and William Henry Snow born about 1881.

This marriage ended or perhaps his First Wife died. My Father's Mother was Annie Gifford. It was not clear whether "Gifford" was her maiden, or previously married name. She was born about 1874, which would make her 17 years younger than J. G. Snow. They may have married about 1903 when George Snow was 24 years old and William Henry Snow was 22 years old.

In 1909, it appears that Annie Gifford (35) became pregnant by her stepson William Henry Snow (26). She may have left J. G. Snow (52), Jack (4), and Amy (2) to live with William Henry Snow and my Father. Apparently four years later in 1913, she returned to Croydon and left him with J. G. Snow, Jack, and Amy.

J. G. Snow was apparently impoverished and having a difficult time trying to care for three young children on his own. The Vicar of St. Peter's Church may have been responsible for his apprehension. She applied for his admission to the Waifs and Strays Society.

They placed him in a receiving home in Clapham for six weeks and then a foster Home for eight years. In 1921, they transferred him to St. Augustine's Church Home for Boys in Sevenoaks, Kent, where he stayed for four years. On 3 April 1925, they deported him to Canada.

He wrote one letter to St. Augustine's Home for Boys and another to a British Home Child friend in England shortly after he arrived in Canada.

East Angus, Quebec, Canada   May 01, 1925

Dear Master and Matron:

At last I have found time in writing a little letter to you after having a busy three days (which Mac. calls very easy). Well, after journeying over water and land I have at last reached my destination which as you see is in Quebec. I expect Master can tell you more than I can about our voyage. How did you get on with the boys while Master was away? I guess the boys behaved themselves all right [sic]. I hope Master had a better voyage home then [sic] he did when he went. We all fed the fishes except myself.

Now as regards the farm I am on, I like it very much. We have five horses, thirteen cows, seventy hens, about fifty young chicks, three pigs, about 8 calves, [sic] two steers, one dog, two cats; - this is not a bad farm. I can milk. I have milked two cows and and [sic] trying three tomorrow.

I guess this is very different from the Old country. We get up at five weekdays, quarter two [sic] six Sundays. No eight o'clock Sundays here we are always up before the sun. We are just over two miles (3.2 km) from the nearest town which is East Angus. I walked to church with Mac on Sunday.

Our bosses [sic] name is _____. He is brother to Fred Allen's boss. We are about 3 mls [sic] from him and two mls [sic] from Leonard Knell.

I hope you got he card I sent you. It is rather cold here, but ever since I have been out here I have been working in my shirts [sic] sleeves. This is as Master has said this is no place for playing the fool, we have got no time for it, we get about a quarter of an hour for meals. Then we are out again in our shirtsleeves at work.

Now I think is all for this time as I would like to go to bed and get ready for morning. I will ask you please to excuse writing this time as I am in a hurry.

I still remain an Old Boy of St. Augustine's Home England.

Fred Snow PS. Please write soon.

I was moved to tears when I read these letters written by my 15-year-old Father. His letters appeared to say that he was happy and well. Had I not read about the children's lives on the farms of Ontario and Quebec, I would have simply accepted these letters at face value. He was up before the sun at 4:30 a.m., each weekday morning and up at 5:45 a.m., Sundays. He was fortunately allowed to go to Church on Sundays. He was allowed a 15-minute break for lunch. He worked 16-hour days in shirtsleeves, regardless of the weather, and worked until 10:00 p.m., each weekday. Farmers brought him into their kitchens and humiliated him in front of their neighbours because of his accent.

The organizations routinely tampered with British Home Children correspondence. They removed their return addresses from their letters. They censored offensive passages such as pleas to return to England, and intercepted correspondence from British friends. They placed children far from post offices. Children had little time to write and few had paper, pencils, or money for stamps. They collected the children's' letters of complaint and did not deliver them. These letters still lay in the agencies' files. They isolated the children and severed their familial ties (Parr 72-76). The children had no one to whom they could complain.

Corbett noted that many children were victims of sexual assaults, beatings, neglect, and "accidents" with pitchforks. They were immobilized by fear and physically isolated in a foreign country (58). They were very much at the mercy of the Canadian farmers.

C/o Mr. _____, East Angus, Quebec, Canada   May 28, 1925

Dear Len:

I am at last answering your most welcome letter which I received quite safely. Well I will tell you who I am working for and who I am with, first of all I am with Edwin John ☐Head and I'm working for Fred Allen's Boss' Brother so am pretty lucky Knell lives two mls [sic] of me.

Will you write as often as you can because its all the news we get of the old Country, we look forward to the Mail like we do our dinner when we have been working hard.

We have been very busy getting in Springs work. I can harrow with a team of three and also drive a single team in the buggy. I can also milk eleven cows and separate in one and a half hours, you have to move some.

We rise with the sun at half past four, sometimes we forget the alarm (accidentally of course) and sleep overtime. Sundays we get a special treat get up at five weekdays we go to bed half past nine (not eight o'clock), which I (with) wish it was.

We buchered [sic] three pigs on Thursday and I went to town with them on Friday. The only thing that is wrong with Mac and I he pinches all the clothes and I pinches his pillow. There is lots more news but I am so tired I can hardly see to write so I will wind up.

I remain yours sincerely "Akela"

PS. Ask Mr. French for me if he will send me the Pathfinder.

I am writing him a letter. Take my tip and come out here you will never regret it, Thanks to Mr. Jago.

I could have ended my search here, and could have been satisfied with this still incomplete account of his origins. Perhaps they expected me to be satisfied with what they provided me, and yet did not provide my Father. I was salivating for more information and I made my second request for the release of his entire case file.

Dear _____   18 January 1995

Thank you very much for the information you provided . . . You can't imagine just how important it was to receive <u>any</u> information regarding my Father. As I may have mentioned, he and my Mother corresponded for over 50 years with the Society in an attempt to obtain information about his background.

I only discovered after his death that their efforts persisted up until 1984 when he was 75 years old. It is very gratifying to receive this information. It doesn't really matter whether his Father was John George Snow or <u>his</u> Son William Henry Snow. What matters is knowing versus not knowing.

. . . I am very interested in obtaining <u>any</u> additional information that you are in a position to provide. If this information exists, I am certain that it is of no use to anyone other than my siblings or me. Conversely, it is of inestimable value to my siblings and me. Like our Father, who lived his life never knowing whether he had brothers or sisters, uncles, aunts, etc., all of us also lived without ever knowing grandparents, uncles, aunts, etc. I would like to review whatever you are able to provide from his file - ideally the entire file.

. . . I have enclosed a postal order in the amount of £15 ($33.45), which I hope is sufficient to cover the costs of photocopying and postage/packing. Sincerely, Perry Snow

It took the Children's Society four months -- and some prompting on my part -- to reply to my second request for his complete case file. In the meantime, I tried to find a Birth Certificate for my newly confirmed Great Grandfather J. G. Snow and Grandmother Annie Gifford. The General Register Office wrote they could not find Birth Certificates for either J. G. Snow from 1857-1861, or Annie Gifford from 1872-1876.

I joined the East Surrey Family History Society in February 1995 and listed what family information I had in their publication. I hoped someone, somewhere, had researched the genealogy of the Snow's. I obtained a microfiche entitled <u>The British Isles Genealogical Register Index</u> from them. It contained a list of family surnames being researched by people all over the world. It had the addresses of people who either had, or were seeking information about specific families. I held my breath as I scanned the microfiche. I hoped there just might be listings for "Snow." There were only a few but I wrote to them anyway and decided to include potential "Gifford" sources in my search.

Everyone to whom I wrote responded quickly, but no family links were established. My curiosity rapidly transformed into an obsession. I no longer just hoped that I could find a family history -- I was convinced that somehow I would find his family. I spent many hours at the Calgary Family History Centre searching their records to no avail. In March 1995, I submitted an article to the local newspaper.

Man's quest took a lifetime[6]

Fred Snow was an immigrant who died a few months ago in Canada after trying unsuccessfully for more than 50 years to discover who his father was, and what relatives he might still have back in England. This is the sorry legacy of an emigration scheme that saw thousand of British children 'orphans, waifs, and strays' as they were classified, plucked from their homeland, and shipped across the sea to the supposed bright promise of a new country.

Fred Snow was a ward of the British child welfare system, allegedly deserted by his parents at age four, though this was likely untrue, raised in British foster homes and institutions until he was 15, then exported to Canada as cheap farm labour, likely without his family's knowledge or consent. There were thousands like him - homeless and abandoned children from the streets of London - shipped to Canada, Australia and other parts of the Empire, from the 1860's to the 1920's, as part of what author Kenneth Bagnell calls "one of the most Draconian movements in the history of emigration."

For Britain it was a cheap way of dealing with the problem of surplus children, and populating the colonies with good British stock. For the colonies, it was a cheap way of building the work force.

When Fred Snow was in his 20's, and had escaped from the southern Ontario farms where he was first indentured, he began to search for his identity and roots. Who were his parents? Did he have any siblings? Why was he placed in the care of an agency at age four? Why did he not hear from his family?

He wrote to England, but received few answers. Fifty years later, he was still seeking answers. He had settled in the Thunder Bay area, married and raised a family of six, worked at different jobs, and written many letters to England.

Fred's children didn't become aware of his lifelong quest until after his death, last year, at age 85. His son Perry Snow, a clinical psychologist in Calgary, took up the search, and has now managed to obtain information never available to his father.

Fred Snow died without ever knowing that he may have had other family. Why was the information kept from Fred Snow?

His son might learn the answer if there were an organization in Canada similar to the Child Migrants Trust in Nottingham, working since 1987 to uncover information on the thousands of British 'orphans' shipped to Australia as recently as 1967, decades after the child deportation program supposedly ended.

. . . If there is such an organization in Canada, says Perry Snow, "I will be relieved to know that I am not alone in my search, and I would contact them." If not, he would like to know why. Failing all else, he would like to start one.

There may be as many as 1-3 million descendants in Canada of the estimated 90,000 child immigrants shipped here from the 1860s onward, and many more in Britain who don't know what happened to their children after they were deported.

I received a few phone calls and letters from people who read this article. One woman called to tell me someone named Barnardo sent her Father to Canada. She asked if I ever heard of him. Another wrote of how her Mother wrote to an English child-care organization all her life and never found out anything about her family. All I could do was give them addresses of current child-care organizations in England. Why is there no organization in Canada to help us?

I read Humphrey's Empty Cradles. It provided a disturbing and disheartening account of the British Child Deportation Scheme to Australia. Until I read this, I had assumed that the scheme had beneficent motives and regarded it as a historical anomaly. The duplicity of the child-care agencies had finally been made public.

Parr wrote that only 6% (1,800) of the 30,000 Barnardo children deported to Canada were actual orphans, who had lost both parents. Half of all of these children (15,000) were children of widows or widowers and as such, were 'half-orphans' (65).

A woman in Calgary sent me this newspaper clipping.

Young child's torment in a long voyage[6]

. . . Britain has a long, sad history of solving its social problems by transporting the causes elsewhere. . . . Britain may have ceased shipping its convicts to colonial Australia in 1868, but by 1880 the British Government had again given the go-ahead for the transportation of Britons - but this time it was a very different type of human cargo. Instead of petty thieves and hooligans, the British Government had sanctioned the transportation of its very lifeblood - its children.

. . . Targeted were those children from poverty stricken backgrounds, broken marriages and illegitimacy, who had been placed in the care of English charities and churches. These were children who were given no say in their future, who without their parents' knowledge or permission, were placed onboard ships and sent to a supposedly 'new and happier life' on the other side of the world. But instead of the happy future they had been promised, many of the children suffered the most profoundly damaging physical, sexual and emotional abuse at the hands of their supposed caretakers.

'Many children's names, dates and places of birth were altered.'

Even the opportunity to be adopted into loving, caring families was denied as permission had not been obtained from parents for their children to be adopted, let alone leave England, and the British Government was not about to admit it had acted illegally by transporting children without their parents' knowledge or consent. Deception became rife. Not only were children told their mothers had abandoned them at the hospital or had been killed in an accident, but many parents who later returned to collect their children were told they had either been adopted in England or had died. Many children's names, dates and places of birth were also altered.

All the major British child-care agencies were involved in these schemes - Dr. Barnardo's, the National Children's Society, Fairbridge Society, Salvation Army and Quarrier Homes along with a variety of social welfare groups operating under the umbrellas of the Catholic Church, the Church of England, Presbyterian Church and Church of Scotland . . . Little if any thought was given to the long term consequences of such schemes. . . . For many it was a sad and miserable childhood, completely devoid of love and affection. So deeply ingrained was the psychological hurt that many former migrant children found it impossible to speak to anyone about their experiences. And who would believe them anyway? . . . but the scheme was abandoned in 1954 because the 'right type of children' were unavailable. 'By this they meant children under 10 years of age, girls aged 15 to 17 or boys old enough or strong enough for farm work.'

. . . Margaret (Humphreys) . . . approached all the major charities involved, including the British Department of Health, and asked each to open its files to make it easier for former child migrants to trace their families. All refused. . . . the experiences of child migrants, particularly those men, who as boys were institutionalised at the Catholic Church's Bindoon and Clontarf in Western Australia, were nothing short of soul destroying. Many former child migrants told of repeated sexual abuse by the Christian Brothers. . . .

I compiled a fax and mail campaign to Canadian Federal and Provincial Government organizations in March 1995. I naïvely assumed there must be some organization in Canada that concerned itself with British Home Children. Why was this aspect of Canadian history so unfamiliar? Why did I not come across any reference to my Father's experience in my Canadian education? Surely 100,000 Home Children could not have simply disappeared in Canada. Surely some of the millions of their descendants had formed an affiliation of some sort. I thought that it would be a simple matter to locate a long-established Canadian organization.

I contacted almost 100 Federal, Provincial, and other organizazations: Prime Minister of Canada, Premier of Alberta, Leader, Reform Party of Canada, ACCESS Alberta, Minister of Human Resources, Minister of Health, Family and Social Services, Minister of Veteran's Affairs, Minister of Foreign Affairs, Minister of Citizenship & Immigration, Minister of Canadian Heritage, Toronto Globe and Mail, Queen's Privy Council for Canada, Child Welfare League of Canada, Secretary of State, Information Commission of Canada, Canadian Senate, Human Rights Directorate, Canadian Heritage, Humanities Research Council, CTV Television Network Ltd., National Archives of Canada.

Most of the people I wrote had no idea what I was talking about. Some did not bother to reply. Others were helpful in providing other sources to contact. Some of the responses conveyed messages such as, "I do not know" along with, "I do not want to know." The Federal Government Ministers replied in a predictable way. They "appreciated being made aware of my concerns." They assured me that my "account of this unhappy chain of events" had been carefully noted. The most disappointing response was from the Information Commission for Canada. They were interested and tried to be helpful. Unfortunately, their mandate is restricted to Canada. I had hoped they might be able to facilitate the release of information from the British child-care organizations.

The organizations have always been protective of the children's files. On the one hand, they argued that the information belonged to the children and yet when the children themselves requested information, they were denied. The Canadian Council for Child Welfare tried to get information about the children in 1927. The child-care organizations argued their records were kept to protect the children, and refused to disclose the records to anyone (Wagner 1982 220). In the past, no one in Canada could question the British child-care organizations. They determined their own policies for child placement, education, medical care, inspection, and welfare. They took all the children's records to

England, and in some respects, erased their presence in Canada. The current Canadian responses of helplessness made me set aside the idea of creating a Canadian organization to advocate for release of information. The prospect was overwhelming and my personal search took priority. We descendants are very much on our own, as were our Parents.

After months of writing letters, I found the address for the Heritage Renfrew Home Children Canada Committee. David and Kay Lorente seemed to be the only people in this country concerned about the British Home Children issue. Their small, volunteer organization is very under-funded, and yet they have helped more than anyone else has. They pay for their trips to England and receive no assistance from the Canadian Government. Barnardo's once donated £250 ($557.50) to help defray the costs of their trip to talk to the British Parliament. We corresponded for the next three years, and I was fortunate to meet these remarkable people in 1997 in Calgary. The Lorente's have tirelessly assisted over 12,000 inquirers of British Home Children and compiled a database of thousands of British Home Children.

David organized the first known reunion of British Home Children in 1991. At a later reunion, he asked the Governor General of Canada to write an open letter to the audience. This was perhaps the first public acknowledgment by a Canadian government official that some of the British Home Children were removed from their homes in England against their will, and were not all "orphans." David told me a chilling story of how he read a newspaper article many years ago about an unmarked grave of an unidentified number of British Home Children in an Ottawa Roman Catholic cemetery. How could this have occurred in our nation's capital? He has identified all the children. The Nugent Care Society of Liverpool, England gave him a grant of £250.00 ($557.50) to erect two plaques at the graveside.

As Governor General of Canada, I am honoured to extend my warmest greetings to all those attending the national reunion of the 'Home Children.' Of the many stories which newcomers to Canada have to tell, there are few more heart rending than those that are told by the 'Home Children.'

Removed from their homes in England, frequently against their will or as 'orphans,' these children arrived in Canada without their families and, indeed, without their history. These young pioneers were sent to farms throughout Canada and courageously began to build new lives, make new friends and to discover new dreams.

Despite their often tragic circumstances, the 'Home Children' grew into proud and productive Canadians. Their contributions to our society and the strength of their spirit are a unique part of our Canadian heritage.

I have no doubt that, as we learn more about their history and their accomplishments, the 'Home Children' can become an inspiration for many Canadians seeking a better world for themselves and their communities.

On behalf of all Canadians and as Her Majesty's representative in Canada, I send my best wishes to participants in the national reunion of the Home Children' as they gather to share their stories and successes with people who have lived through similar experiences.

Ramon John Hnatyshyn, Governor General of Canada

Margaret Humphreys of the Child Migrants Trust interviewed aging British Home Children in Canada. She told them of the deportation scheme to Australia. They unselfishly encouraged her to help those children to find their families (Humphreys 133).

I learned my search was far from unique. John McGillion was 50 years old before he learned he had a twin Sister. They had both been placed in the same Catholic Home in Ireland as toddlers and then were separated. His Sister stayed in the Home while he was sent to Australia when he was 10 years old. His search took 30 years from 1958-1988. He finally obtained a Birth Certificate that confirmed his full name and place of birth. When he again wrote the organization, they told him they had "reason to believe" he had a twin Sister. He cried for a week. Why did they not want him to know this? He located her in Ireland and met her after 50 years (Bean & Melville 155-157).

British Home Children described the alienation they felt as adults. They felt they did not belong to anyone. They regarded themselves as "nobodies" and "nothings," because they did not have an identity. They rarely felt safe or secure, and lived with an emptiness. Something important was missing inside them. Marriage and families of their own did not fill the void. They felt alone, rather than lonely. They wanted someone who belonged to them, and someone to claim them as "theirs." They knew they must have relatives somewhere. They wanted to know who they were, and where they came from. They were embittered and traumatized when they learned the organizations withheld information from them (Bean & Melville 152-155).

I waited three months for a reply from the Children's Society. I sent them a fax and made my third request for his entire file. They replied two weeks later.

I believe they had not intended to voluntarily release information to me, and only complied following my demand.

Dear _____   24 April 1995

I last wrote to you on 18 January 1995 and at that time requested a copy of my Father's entire file and sent a money order in the amount of £15 ($33.45) to cover costs of photocopying and mailing. I have been patiently waiting 3 months now for a reply. Is there a problem? If you require a formal Release of Information to send the entire file to me, enclosed please find the appropriate Release of Information. This is usually sufficient authorization for me to release my client records to appropriate requests from doctors and other professionals. My solicitor has advised me that it should be sufficient to allow you to release my Father's complete file to me. If there is anything else you need to send the complete file to me, I would appreciate hearing from you. Sincerely, Perry Snow

RELEASE OF INFORMATION REQUEST

I, the undersigned, do hereby authorize and direct you to release to: Perry Snow . . . any and all information he may require, including but not limited to all documents, medical records, school records, correspondence, inquiries, progress notes, reports of all diagnostic tests and assessments, medical/professional opinions, case notes, and/or other knowledge or information in your possession, power or control relating to his father Frederick George Snow (1909-1994) who was under the care of the Children's Society from 1913-1925, and for doing so, let this be your good and sufficient authority. Dated at the City of Calgary, in the Province of Alberta, in the country of Canada this 24th day of April 1995. Perry Snow

I wrote to Barnardo's to find out their policies regarding the release of information. They said they were committed to providing family background information to adults formerly in their care and their relatives. They received 300-400 inquiries per year from Canadians, but stated "to date," they had "not received any enquiries from British relatives searching for child migrants."

I found it hard to believe the hundreds of thousands of British relatives *never* inquired about their Sons, Daughters, Brothers, and Sisters -- the British Home Children. They said they were not legally bound to release information, and did not withhold information unless a child migrant had requested this.

In 1995, the Child Migrants Trust video, The Leaving of Liverpool, set off a flood of 1,400 inquiries to Barnardo's in eight months. In 1998, they were still processing inquiries from 1995.

By comparison, David Lorente's volunteer organization routinely received 2,000 inquiries per year from British Home Children and their descendants. Their cumulative number of inquiries over the years is 15,000. The Child Migrants Trust received 20,000 enquiries in their first four years of operation.

While I waited for the Children's Society to copy my Father's case file, I wrote to the Metropolitan Police in Croydon, as my Father had written to the Police in Balham 38 years earlier. I hoped they might have an incident report regarding his apprehension in 1913. They did not, and replied they did not keep "records of this nature" for more than seven years. The Children's Society replied by fax a week after they had received mine.

The Children's Society.
A VOLUNTARY SOCIETY OF THE CHURCH OF ENGLAND AND THE CHURCH IN WALES

Dear Mr. Snow   5 May 1995

Thank you for your recent fax message regarding your father's case file. The Release of Information Request is useful and I will keep it on file.

As you may have gathered by now, the copying of these files is a fairly time consuming process. The file itself is fragile and has to be copied carefully to ensure that it is not damaged. The work is in progress, but may take another week to two weeks to complete. Yours sincerely

---

Why did it take weeks to photocopy a file? Someone sent me this newspaper clipping.

A childhood rediscovered and a 'family' reunited[7]
According to Michael (not his real name) he was just nine years old when he arrived in Sidney . . . on October 13, 1954 . . . sent by . . . Dr. Barnardo's. For the next six years of his life he remained at Greenwood. . . . not only was he sexually abused by a group of older boys, but also a senior Protestant clergyman. The same clergyman would later describe Michael as a boy who would 'never be much good until he gets rid of his self-pity and faces up to life.'

'I'll never forget him,' Michael said. 'Do you know this man is still held in high regard within the organisation?'

Anxious to trace his background he approached Barnardo's on a number of occasions for access to his personal file, but his requests were always refused. It would take another 39 years before Barnardo's would see to send the information to him.

... For Michael, not only had his file revealed a mother, but somewhere in England, Michael now knew he had a brother.

... Michael is still hoping that his mother will eventually make contact with him. 'She has been told of my existence, but hasn't replied as yet,' he said.

In the meantime, he hopes to try and find his brother Nigel, which Michael said could be difficult, as Nigel might not even be aware that he was adopted, let alone had a brother.

The Victoria Day weekend 1995 marked the 60th Anniversary of the day my Parents met. Coincidentally, the long-awaited information from his case file arrived that weekend. There were more surprises.

The Children's Society.

A VOLUNTARY SOCIETY OF THE CHURCH OF ENGLAND AND THE CHURCH IN WALES

Dear Mr. Snow   5 May 1995

Please find enclosed copies of the documents from your father's case file.

This material represents key documentation that has a bearing on your father's time in care with the Society.

Routine notes and letters dealing with purely administrative and internal Society matters have not been copied in an attempt to save on cost and staff time.

Please contact me if you have any queries relating to these papers. Yours sincerely

Chapter 2: A Review of Waifs and Strays Case File # 18264

I held the thick envelope and stared at it for a few moments before I opened it. I was a little apprehensive what it might contain. I ripped it open and resisted the temptation to skim through it. I intensely studied every word on every page. They gave me 61 photocopied pages from his case file. Fifty-five of these pages had tiny numbers written on them ranging from 4-74. What information is on the missing pages? If the pages they withheld contained "routine and administrative matters," I could decide if they were useful to me. The first page was a hand-written letter from the Vicar of St. Peter's Church to Prebendary Rudolf of the Waifs and Strays Society. I needed a magnifying glass to decipher it.

S. Peter's Vicarage, South Croydon
Dear Mr. Rudolph [sic]   24 September 1913
We are most anxious to get a small boy - by name Freddie Snow into a Waifs & Strays Home. He is about 4 years old, and a fine grown little fellow. We have been paying for him to be kept in a Convalescent Home in Croydon for over four months past now, not knowing what else to do with him, but our poor funds will not allow of our doing this any longer.

I was telling my mother . . . about this case, a few days ago and she says she was recently trying to get a child in herself to one of the Waifs & Strays Home, but that her child had been withdrawn, & she thought perhaps this child we are interested in could take the place of hers. It is a very sad case indeed, the mother having run away from home twice, this last time she probably will not come back again. She left this child behind this time, together with her two elder children and their father. It is hard to say who the father of this little Freddie is. The father of the elder ones has been very good, and tried hard to scrape up 6s or 1£ now and again to keep this poor waif 'Freddie' but he is often out of work and can hardly make both ends meet for himself and his two older children. I don't know what will happen to this child unless we can get him into a nice Home. If you wish us to fill up a form, will you kindly send it to Mr. Reeve or myself. We want to get this settled as quickly as possible. Yr. Sincerely, V. Inez Reeve

---

Why did the Children's Society not include these pages in their first response to my inquiry? Why was he in a hospital from May - September 1913? Why did the Vicar pay to have him kept there when free hospitalization was likely available in Croydon? Did my Father completely repress memories of his being in this hospital?

Church of England Society for Providing Homes for Waifs & Strays
Otherwise Known as "WAIFS AND STRAYS."
Patrons - Their Majesties the King & Queen
Patron of the "Children's Union" - H.M. Queen Alexandra
Presidents - His Grace the Lord Bishop of Canterbury and His Grace the Lord
Archbishop of York
Secretary - Rev. Prebendary Rudolf   Secretary's Assistant - H. M. Fowle, Esq.

MEDICAL CERTIFICATE: A medical certificate signed by a duly qualified practitioner replying to the following questions is <u>absolutely necessary</u>. Consequent upon many recent cases of ringworm and skin disease, very special attention must be given to questions 2, 4, 5 and 7, and the slightest signs of any such complaints (whether at present existent or traces of them having existed at some previous date) must be notified.

1. Child's name and age: *Frederick George Snow*. Age: *3-4 years*
2. Has the child any organic disease, any affection of the limbs, joints, ears, eyes, or skin? *No*
3. If so, will they have the effect of preventing her or him from entering domestic service? ---
4. Has the child any trace of tuberculosis? *No*
5. Has the child any trace of heart disease? *No*
6. Has the child any albumen or sugar in the urine? *No*
7. Has the child ringworm or any other infectious disease? *No*
8. Has the child enlarged tonsils or adenoids? *No*
9. Please state when last vaccinated. *May 23, 1913 (Did not take)*
10. If boy, has he been circumcised? *Yes*
11. Is the child's general health good? *Very*
12. Height? *3 ft. 2 in.* **(96 cm)** Weight? *2 stone 10 lb. 8 oz (17.5 kg)*
Girth (in nipple line with lungs moderately inflated) 23-½ *in. (59 cm)*
13. Is he mentally up to the average? *Yes*
14. Is the child subject to fits, or has he ever had one?
If so, please state its nature. *No*
15. Is the child subject to incontinence of urine?
If so, state its frequency/probable cause. *No*
16. Has the child had Scarlet Fever, Whooping Cough, Measles, Diphtheria, Smallpox? *German Measles two (unreadable) ago and (unreadable).*
I hereby certify that I have this day *personally* examined the child.
Doctor's Signature: W. T. Dunpsler
Address: 94 Brighton Road, South Croydon, Surrey.
Date: Sept. 29/13

They estimated his age as 3-4 years old in September 1913. Is this where they first decided he was born in September 1909? He had German measles twice before the age of four years old, and some other illnesses that were unreadable. He was vaccinated on May 23, 1913, in the hospital, but it "did not take." The next six pages in the package were copies of an intake form completed by the Vicar. The originals had broken and blackened edges.

Church of England Society for Providing Homes for Waifs and Strays
Otherwise Known as "WAIFS AND STRAYS."
Patrons - Their Majesties the King & Queen
Patron of the "Children's Union" - H.M. Queen Alexandra
Presidents - His Grace the Lord Bishop of Canterbury and His Grace the Lord Archbishop of York
Secretary - Rev. Prebendary Rudolf   Secretary's Assistant - H. M. Fowle, Esq.

APPLICATION FOR THE ADMISSION OF A CHILD

NOTE: This form, when filled up and certified by a Clergyman of the Church of England, should be returned with the medical certificate to Rev. Prebendary Rudolf, Secretary, Waifs and Strays Society,

QUESTIONS TO BE REPLIED TO.

1. Give the child's christian names and surname in full. **Frederick George Snow.** N.B. - In the event of an application being made on behalf of more than one child, separate forms should be asked for.

2. State the exact date and place of birth: Please forward birth certificate if possible. **September 1909, Larch Road, Balham. No.**

3. Legitimate? (Yes or No): **Probably no (See Letter)**

4. State exact date and place of baptism. **St. Peter's Church, South Croydon, October 1913**

5. Are parents living? **Yes**

6. If either or both are dead, state nature of disease and give date of death: **No**

7. If living, give their exact places of abode, how long they have resided there, and rent paid. Mother ___ Father ___ **(See Letter)**

8. Give the christian names and surnames of parents in full, and state their ages. Mother: **Annie Gifford Age 39.** Father: **(See Letter)**

9. What was, or is, the nature of the father's occupation and the amount of his weekly earnings? Give the name and address of his present or last employer. **(See Letter)**

10. What was, or is, the nature of the mother's occupation and the amount of her weekly earnings? Give the name and address of her present or last employer. **(See Letter)**

11. Have the parents or guardians ever received parish relief? If so, to what extent? **No**

12. Give the names, addresses, and ages, of all the brothers and sisters of the child and occupations and earnings (if any). Replies to this question must be very full and exact. No application can be received without full enquiry as to earnings having been made, and result stated. The name of the child upon whose behalf this application is being made should not be given here. **Probably sort of step brother and sister. Name: Amy Alice Snow Age: 6. Name: John Allen Snow Age: 8**

13. At what address and with whom is the child now staying? **C/o Miss Westoby, Children's Convalescent Home, Brighton Road, South Croydon.**

Give in full the names, addresses, occupations, and earnings of each living relative the child is known to possess, either on the father's or mother's side, such as grandparents, uncles, aunts. Replies to this question must be very full and exact. No application can be received without full enquiry as to earnings of relatives having been made, and result stated.

Please see letter. It is impossible to answer this question correctly as will be seen from the letter, only the mother's own rightful husband (on whom the child has no claim) has very uncertain employment, often being out of work, at best he has about 30 shillings per week for

8 months out of the 12 months. He is Mr. Snow, the Stables, Dean Road, Croydon.

15. State whether any of the child's relatives are, in your judgment, in a position to maintain the child or to contribute in any degree? **No**

16. Can payment for the child be guaranteed from any source exclusive of the relatives? If so, by whom? State full name and address. **No**

17. Has the child ever been convicted? Has his or her character been affected in any way by exceptional knowledge of evil? **No**

18. Ever attended day school? If so, where and for how long, and in what standard? **Too young.**

19. Ever attended Sunday school? If so, where and for how long. **No**

20. Ever been in the Workhouse? If so, where and for how long. **No**

The consent for emigration was known as the Canada Clause. A child-care organization could make a child's admission contingent upon the parent signing the consent to emigration.

---

21. I, **J. G. Snow** of **Dean Cottage, Dean Road, South Croydon** (guardian) of **Frederick George** do hereby commit him wholly to the care of the Society, and promise to obey the rules in force, and to permit the said child to be brought up in the Faith of the Church of England, and when fully trained to be sent to any situation in the United Kingdom, which may be obtained for **him** by the Committee.

Signature: **John George Snow.** Date: **October 3, 1913.** Signature of Witness: **V. Inez Reeve** Address: **St. Peter's Vicarage Croydon**

22. I also hereby give my consent to the child being emigrated to Canada, if he or she is found suitable and if the Committee consider it advisable.

Signature of Witness: **V. Inez Reeve** Signature: **John George Snow.**

(If consent to emigration is not given, this space should be left blank)

N.B. - Preference will be given to those cases in which consent to emigration is expressed.

I certify that the foregoing questions have been correctly replied to, to the best of my belief. Name: **Arthur Reeve** Address: **St. Peter's Vicarage, Croydon.** Incumbent of **St. Peter's, Croydon.**

Date: **October 2nd, 1913.**

There was no Birth Certificate when he was apprehended. His Parents were alive, so he was not an orphan. Where did he get the idea that his Mother was dead when he was apprehended? Vicar Inez Reeve stated that his parents' address, occupation, employers, and earnings were unknown. She identified Annie Gifford as his Mother but did not identify his Father, and wrote, "It is hard to say who the father of this little Freddie is." She identified J. G. Snow as Annie Gifford's "own rightful husband," and yet later called him my Father's "Guardian," when obviously he was his Grandfather. She identified Jack and Amy as, "Sort of stepbrother and sister." Surely, a Vicar knew the difference between a Step sibling and a half sibling. Even though the application form twice stated an application would not be processed, "without full enquiry as to earnings of relatives," they made an exception in my Father's case.

Barnardo's apparently conducted meticulous family investigations of the child's extended family. This was to ostensibly keep children with their families as long as they could provide bare subsistence (Parr 66). There was nothing in my Father's case file to indicate the Waifs and Strays Society made any attempt to assess either his immediate or extended family's circumstances or resources. Barnardo's took photographs of children and noted their height, weight, and general health. They listed the names of siblings, addresses and occupations of the child's immediate and extended family (Wagner 1979 303). Perhaps Barnardo's kept better records.

He was in a hospital when the Vicar applied to have him admitted to the Waifs and Strays Society. J. G. Snow (56) was unemployed and tried to look after his two young children himself. Did he really have any choice but to sign? Was my Father, "Held hostage?" What would have happened to him had J. G. Snow refused to sign the application? There were no temporary provisions when Parents or Guardians signed over care of their children. They were to be *permanently* in care until they were, "Fully trained for service." The minimum training period was to be six months, but some children were deported within weeks of coming into care. The earlier the organizations rid themselves of children, the more money they could save -- and earn.

Fortunately, they did not deport my Father immediately to Canada at the age of four years old. The "Child-Savers" publicly portrayed families as neglectful, cruel, abusive, improvident, and immoral. The children's families were actually affectionate and cohesive. The prejudiced attitudes of their caretakers pervaded every aspect of the children's treatment. They misrepresented children and their families to justify their actions.

The Secretary of the Waifs and Strays Society -- Edward Rudolf -- described the children in his care as "rolling stones." He felt they did not have the intelligence or physique required to create careers for themselves (Parr 63 137). British Child deportation to Canada was interrupted because of WWI, but only after two ships with British Home Children cargo were stopped and detained by German destroyers (Bagnell 1908a 215). Somehow, four children were shipped to Canada in the second year of WWI in 1915 (Stroud 154).

The next pages of the intake form revealed more startling information.

IMPORTANT:

This page must be filled up (as concisely as possible) with a full and particular account of the child, its parents, family, etc. Details should be added here if Question 17 is answered in the affirmative. The guarantee for payment (if any) should also be written here. When signing this page please state permanent address and whether "Rev.," "Mr.," "Mrs.," or "Miss."

The mother of Frederick George Snow, is the second wife of John George Snow, by whom she had two children, Amy Alice Snow & John Allen Snow. Her husband had a grown up son by his first wife, called William Henry Snow - who is nine years younger than his stepmother Annie Gifford.

Annie Gifford turned out a very bad woman, & behaved very disgracefully with her stepson, in such a manner that when Frederick George was born, this woman's own husband did not own this child, but says it undoubtedly is his eldest son's child.

Shortly after this the woman ran away with her stepson, taking only Frederick (the baby) with her. About a year ago the woman returned, bringing Frederick with her, and another baby William Henry born 29/8/1912 (hers and her stepson's).

She stayed with her own husband, and her two eldest children for a month or two, and ran away again to join her stepson again, this time taking only her baby with her and deserting Frederick - leaving him to the mercy of - not his own father, but his wife's legitimate husband, John Snow.

This man was very good to the child, although it was not his, and he had been so wronged, but having the two children of his own to work for & feed & clothe, and having very little work to do, they were almost at starvation's door.

The Reverend A. Reeve, Vicar of St. Peter's Croydon, then sent this deserted waif to the 'Children's Convalescent Home', Brighton Road, South Croydon, where he has been ever since. This is such a drain on St. Peter's Poor Fund, that Mr. Reeve finds he can do it no longer.

Please see other additional paper.

Please do not write on page 4.

Any additional particulars of the case should be written on foolscap. Acknowledgment of the receipt of this application will be sent, but the Committee's decision will be forwarded with the least possible delay.

UNANSWERED QUESTIONS:

7. It is not known where the father and Mother of Frederick George Snow are?

9. Nothing is known about the child's own father.

10. It is not known as to whether the Mother earns anything or not. She took to drinking dreadfully, & the short time she was home last, she tried to pawn everything she could, to buy drink.

12. The only real brother (or sister) is a tiny baby.

14. Being an illegitimate child it is difficult to answer all this question, but the Mother's Mother is known to be dead, and the Mother's Father is a very old man, receiving Old Age Pension.

21. The Mother having deserted the child, has no right to say where the child shall now go or not go, & as she has run away & it is not known where she is, it would not in any case be able to ask her.

The poor man with whom the child was left, is only too thankful for the child to be taken care of anywhere in England or abroad, & he naturally never wishes to see it again, for although he is a most kind man with children, (& was to this one too) this Frederick, naturally only causes him pain. **N.B.** It has only just been found out lately that this child - Frederick - has not been baptized, but he is going to be next week when the Matron, who is now away, returns home. He will be baptized in the name of Frederick George.

The Vicar wrote, ". . . this woman's own husband (J. G. Snow) did not own this child, but says it undoubtedly is his eldest son's child (William Henry Snow)." J. G. Snow named his Son -- William Henry Snow -- as my Father's Father. This is clear enough. Why did they not tell my Father this? The Vicar stated that J. G. Snow "naturally never wishes to see it (my Father) again" because "this Frederick, naturally only causes him pain."

In 1980, Amy confirmed that her Father did all he could to care for her, her Brother, and my Father. This included hiring a baby-sitter to look after him during the day, while she and Jack attended school. The Vicar implied that J. G. Snow was responsible for his becoming a ward, when the initiative clearly came from her. In my Father's case, the clergy acted as procurers of children for the British Child Deportation Scheme.

It suited the purposes of the organizations to portray families as disreputable. The Vicar described Annie Gifford as "drinking dreadfully." She wrote that she was, "a very bad woman," who "behaved very disgracefully with her stepson."

She clearly identified their relationship with each other. William Henry Snow and Annie Gifford had "a tiny baby" named William Henry Snow. His date of birth -- August 28, 1912 -- was written in the margin of the paper as an afterthought. When I read this I cursed and then cried. My Father has/had a Brother! My mind raced that this Brother could still be alive and 83 years old. Why did they never tell my Father?

Vicar Arthur Reeve did not just "send" my Father to the hospital. It is very likely he had the Police apprehend him. The Vicar claimed that Annie Gifford deserted my Father. Why did she return to her Husband J.

G. Snow in 1912, when my Father was three years old, and his newly identified Brother was a few months old? Why did she leave my Father with his Grandfather? Did she intend this to be temporary or permanent? Were her whereabouts really unknown?

The next page in the case file was a copy of his Baptism Certificate. Why did they not give it to him when he first wrote to them in 1929 when he was 20 years old? They could have alleviated the 28 years of anguish he suffered about whether the surname Snow was really his own.

Church of England Society for Providing Homes for Waifs and Strays
NOTICE OF BAPTISM
Full Name of Child: **Frederick George Snow**
Place of Baptism: St. Peter's Church, S. Croydon
Date: October 13, 1913
Date of Baptism: 8th October 1913   Signed: Arthur Reeve
To be returned to the Head Offices.

Yes, Vicar, there are indeed many, "Unanswered Questions!" My Father's lifelong questions were now mine.

Why did they never inform him of the circumstances of his "coming into care?"

Who provided the information for the Vicar's application? Obviously, it was not his Mother or his Father. It may not have even been his Grandfather J. G. Snow.

Whomever the informant, this information turned out to be inaccurate.

How did the Vicar know baby William Henry Snow's birth date and yet not know my Father's birth date?

Why did they initially not volunteer this information to me?

Had I not persisted in asking for the entire case file, I never would have learned of my Uncle's existence. I submitted all the information I knew of the Snow's in my first letter to the Children's Society. They did not volunteer information as to the identity of my Father's Brother. This discovery about my Uncle's existence led to unravelling the mystery of the Snow family.

Church of England Society for Providing Homes for Waifs and Strays

Otherwise Known as "WAIFS AND STRAYS."

Dear Mrs. Reeve, <u>Re: Frederick G. Snow:</u>   10 October 1913

It is with much pleasure I write to inform you that my Committee yesterday decided to accept the above-named boy, for admission under the Society's care.

You may rest assured there will be no avoidable delay in endeavouring to arrange for Frederick's reception, and I will communicate with you further as soon as possible.

I should like to have full details as to the lad's baptism at St. Peter's Church, South Croydon, on the enclosed red slip.

Needless to say, I am most pleased to send you a favourable decision, and feel confident that you will continue to help forward the Society's interests as opportunities occur. Yours sincerely. (Rudolf)

S. Peter's Vicarage, South Croydon   Oct. 13/13

Dear Mr. Rudolf

We heard your good news for us with great relief and thankfulness. It is been good of you to have taken so much trouble & I am truly glad that poor little Freddie Snow will now be taken care of for the rest of <u>his life</u>.

The enclosed slip has been filled in as you wished. I trust that we do not have to buy clothes for him, as we have already had to buy or give him a good many things.

We shall be glad to hear as soon as possible where you can have Freddie, & where we have to send him to.

With Kind regards.

Yr. Sincerely. V. Inez Reeve

Rudolf saw the children of the poor as "opportunities" and the clergy as those who could help "forward the Society's interests." The Vicar was pleased that, ". . . poor little Freddie Snow will now be taken care of for the rest of his life."

There was no ambiguity as to the fate of children once in their care -- they deported them. They put my Father on a train alone with a name-tag pinned to his shirt, and shipped him to their Receiving Home for six weeks.

On November 7, 1913, he had a second Medical Examination.

There were five weeks between these Medical Examinations. They must have assumed a birth month of September 1909. Did he lose 6 cm in girth, and lose .67 kg in five weeks?

Church of England Society for Providing Homes for Waifs & Strays Otherwise Known as "WAIFS AND STRAYS."

Mrs. Green   11 November 1913

Rumburgh, Halesworth   re: Frederick G. Snow

I have to thank you for your letter informing me that Mrs. Smith is prepared to receive the above child. As soon as we hear from the Authorities of our Receiving House that he is ready for boarding out, I will then appoint a day and hour for him to be sent to your kind supervision. I will see that a cheque in payment of your claim, as well as the expenses incurred in arranging for George Sabine's removal, is forwarded in due course. I note with many thanks that you have not included all the incidental expenses entailed in the transfer. Yours very truly, (Rudolf)

Church of England Society for Providing Homes for Waifs & Strays Otherwise Known as "WAIFS AND STRAYS."

Vicar Inez Reeve re: Frederick G. Snow   November 18, 1913

In reply to your card I beg to say that if you will kindly forward this boy's Baptismal Certificate to me at this office, I will then see that it is placed with the other papers. I may take this opportunity of informing you that I have this morning received medical reports from the Society's Doctor, in which it is stated that Frederick has enlarged tonsils and adenoids and requires vaccinating. In these circumstances I shall be glad if you can kindly see the father as soon as possible with a view to obtaining his consent to the necessary operations, and forward a letter to this effect direct to: Dr. Rose Turner, St. Elizabeth's Home, 7 Victoria Road, Clapham Common, London, S.W. As desired, I herewith have pleasure in enclosing a 'C.U.' Receipt book. Yours sincerely, (Rudolf).

S. Peter's Vicarage South Croydon   November 19, 1913

Dear Mr. Rudolf

Many thanks for the C.U. Receipt book. Enclosed is Freddie Snow's Baptismal Certificate. I have written to Dr. Rose Turner, as you wished. The child had been vaccinated, as I took him myself to Dr. Beard, but it never took. I had to give Dr. Turner permission to do anything necessary for Freddie, as there is no one to ask anything about him, or to give permission for anything. You had his story from me in the first place, & I have not gone into it all again with Dr. Turner. With Kind Regards, Yr. V: Sincerely, V. Inez Reeve

---

Vicar Reeve took it upon herself to appoint herself as his Guardian because there was "no one to give permission for anything." There is nothing in his case file to indicate if his tonsils and adenoids were ever removed, or if he was ever vaccinated. His Grandfather J. G. Snow lived a few hundred yards down the street from the Church. Perhaps because he opposed his apprehension, the Vicar was reluctant to seek his permission for medical operations.

The Waifs and Strays Society had 87 children in foster care in 1884, 702 in 1900, and 916 in 1914. The practice of 'baby-farming' plagued the foster care scheme. Women insured babies and then killed them (Stroud, 66). Children in foster care were to have a minimum of two Medical Examinations per year. My Father was in foster care for eight years and his case file should have contained 16 Medical Examinations. There were only two. One was when he was 11 years old in 1920 and the other a year later when he was about to be sent to St. Augustine's Church

Home for Boys.   If there were more, why did they not provide me with copies?

Church of England Society for Providing Homes for Waifs and Strays
Otherwise Known as "WAIFS AND STRAYS."

Mrs. Green   December 3, 1913

Dear Madam, Unless you hear to the contrary, the above child will be brought to your kind supervision on Saturday next, the 6th, by the train leaving Liverpool Street at 11:40, due to arrive at Halesworth at 3:30, where I shall be glad to hear you will kindly have met him upon arrival. In the meantime, I enclose two forms of undertaking to be filled in by the foster mother, one of which should be retained by her, and the other returned to me at this office as soon as the child is received under her care. The box containing the little one's outfit will be sent in advance, so as to be in readiness for him on arrival. Yours very truly, (Rudolf)

CHURCH OF ENGLAND
Incorporated Society for Providing Homes for Waifs and Strays
Otherwise known as "Waifs and Strays"
Form of Undertaking by the Foster Parent.

I, *Anna Maria Smith* of *Rumburgh, Halesworth, Suffolk,* foster parent, do hereby engaged in consideration of receiving the sum of five shillings per week to bring up Frederick George Snow as one of my own children, and to provide him with proper food, lodging, medical attendance, and washing, and for the proper repair and renewal of clothing, and to endeavor to train him in habits of truthfulness, obedience, personal cleanliness, and industry; as well as in suitable domestic and outdoor work; to provide the said child with a *separate bed* to take care that the said child Frederick George Snow shall attend at church, and shall, while boarded out between the ages of four and twelve years attend Day and Sunday Schools, unless prevented by sickness or other urgent cause, during all the usual hours for instruction thereat: in the case of the illness of the said child to report to **Mrs. J. V. Green**, Rumburgh Suffolk and at all times to permit the said child and home to be visited by any person specially appointed for that purpose by the Executive Committee, which will include a medical examination of the child by a lady doctor twice a year or more frequently if deemed necessary; to acquaint the supervisor immediately of any improvement in circumstances of the relatives of the said child that may come to my knowledge.

Witness: **J. V. Green**   Signature: **A. M. Smith**   Date: Dec. 8/13

Children under four years old could not be boarded out with foster parents. Did the Waifs and Strays Society simply *make* my Father four years old when they apprehended him, so they could place him with foster parents?

Supervisors of foster children were supposed to provide quarterly reports. His case file should have contained 32 such reports, but there was only one dated in 1919. If there were more, why did they not give them to me?

The agreement stated foster parents were supposed to report if they knew of any changes in the child's family circumstances. This implied that the foster parents had contact with the child's family. The organization did not provide foster parents with any information how children came into care. There was no contact between children and their families while in foster care, so how could foster parents ever learn anything of the child's natural family? Families were not told where their children were.

The organizations irrevocably severed family ties so that emigration could go on without interference. They did not board out children with their relatives.

CHURCH OF ENGLAND
Incorporated Society for Providing Homes for Waifs and Strays
otherwise known as "Waifs and Strays"
BOARDING OUT
Foster mother's undertaking with regard to the Child

Name of Child: Frederick George Snow   aged __ .

Address of Foster mother: Mrs. A. M. Smith, Rumburgh, Halesworth.

Address of Supervisor: Mrs. J. V. Green.

I, **Mrs. Anna Maria Smith** of Rumburgh Halesworth hereby acknowledge I have this day received **Frederick George Snow** aged Four - last Sept. years from the Church of England Incorporated Society for Providing Homes for Waifs and Strays on the terms and conditions contained in the rules supplied, and I undertake to hand over the said child to the Society when called upon.

Dated this 6th day of Dec. 1913.   Signed: A. M. Smith.

Witness: J. V. Green   Address: Rumburgh, Halesworth

Re Frederick Snow   December 8, 1913

Dear Mr. Rudolf:

This child arrived quite safely last Sat. Dec. 6th. I had previously been informed by you his box would be sent in advance. It was not at the station where I went to meet him and we were informed there that a day is not long enough before hand for luggage to arrive the same time or rather before the passengers as it is so often delayed to Liverpool Street.

It is a pity the box was not sent with the child. I think you are aware we are 4 miles (6.4 km) from a station and there is no regular carrier.

I had to pay 2 shillings for the little boy to be met and now there will be further expenses in getting the box here. The box arrived this morning by post; The Station Master at Halesworth thought the box would most likely be here today.

Frederick Snow seems a very bright little fellow and is quite happy at his new home.

I have not put the date of birth because I have unfortunately destroyed the letter I received from you when you asked if Mrs. Smith could receive the little boy. I believe the date of birth was in that letter.

With the other children, I had an account of their parentage. I do not know if you usually send this kind of thing with the children. J. V. Green

My four-year-old Father rode the train alone for three hours to Rumburgh. The Social Worker paid someone to meet him. There was much "to-do" about the box, incidental expenses, and bureaucratic trivia.

Church of England Society for Providing Homes for Waifs and Strays
Otherwise known as "Waifs and Strays"

Mrs. Green, Rumburgh, Halesworth   9th December 1913

I have to thank you for your letter and enclosure in regard to the above boy.

I am very sorry to hear the trouble and expense which you have been put to in sending for the box containing his outfit, and if you will kindly include the amount in your next claim for maintenance, I will kindly see that it is refunded.

The date of the boy's birth is September 1909, but unfortunately the day of the month is not given. We have recently decided not to send the full particulars of a child when arranging for it to be boarded out, as we have found from past experience that it is not always desirable that the foster parent should know the family history.

However, I have pleasure in sending you the case paper copy of the child in question, and shall be obliged if you will be so good as to return the same to me as soon as you have taken what information you require.
You will, of course, treat the particulars, as confidential.
Yours very truly, (Rudolf)

Dear Sir: Dec. 15, 1913
I was not of course aware of the recent decision not to send full particulars of children when arranging for them to be boarded out or I should not have asked for them.
I am _very_ much obliged to you for sending them and under the circumstances I take it as a great favor to me.
If I may be allowed to express an opinion on the subject I think the decision a very wise one. I have always thought it a great pity that anyone should have the chance of casting any stigma on these unfortunate little mites in a few years.   *
Truly the history of this little boy is too awful for words and one that certainly ought not to be made public for his sake.
I note in one of the letters this little boy had not been baptized but was going to the following week when the matron returned home. I presume this was done.
The only charge I shall send in my weeks claims for maintenance is the trap hire for _fetching_ the boy.
Again thanking you, I am, Truly, J. V. Green.

Church of England Society for Providing Homes for Waifs and Strays
Report of visit to Fred Snow 11. At home of Foster Mother Mrs. Harry Smith. At Rumburgh. Date of last visit Nov. 12/19
1. What are the circumstances of the Foster mother, and your impression of her character? Foster Mother's husband has a little private means. This is an exceptionally good home containing 3 bedrooms sitting room and kitchen. The foster Mother was out but her daughter who lives here was at home. Another of our boys - Ronald Young is boarded out here.
2. What is the state of the child's health? He is in good health. He has some bad teeth which should be attended to. Ht. 4 ft. 7¼ in. (138 cm) Girth 24½ in. (62 cm)
3. Is the clothing suitable and how is it provided? Yes, by foster mother.
4. Is sufficient care given to personal cleanliness? Yes.
5. Have any complaints been made by the Foster mother? No.

6. Has the child made any complaints? No.

7. Is the child in your opinion properly cared for and happy? Yes.

8. Has the child attended school regularly? Yes. In what standard? III.

9. Does the child attend Church and Sunday School? Yes.

10. Is the sleeping accommodation satisfactory and has each child a separate bed? Yes.

11. Remarks of School Teachers, &c., &c. Yes.

12. General remarks. (If child is of an age to be transferred, do you recommend the same?) Yes. R. Turner September 27, 1920

If there was a previous inspection made a year earlier, there was no copy of it in the case file. There was nothing in the case file to indicate they did anything about his bad teeth.

The Smith's were too poor to buy him shoes and he wore Mrs. Smith's boots. Perhaps Dr. Turner did not notice this. This was the first or possibly second visit by someone from the Waifs and Strays Society in his seven years of foster care. What boy in these circumstances would complain?

An issue of supervision pay arose. Mail appears to be have been delivered quite quickly. I am amazed that the head of the organization -- Prebendary Rudolf -- routinely dealt with such trivia.

To. The Secretary C. of E. Waifs and Strays Society   Nov. 28, 1920

Dear Sir: As supervisor of the two waifs and strays Fred Snow and Ronald Young I should be glad to receive the extra pay which I understand has been sent to other Supervisors in the Parish for some time. You will be able to tell me how much is due to me no doubt and you will also be able to say whether this omission is due to my not having claimed the amount when writing for the last quarter's pay. I would have written before had I not been prevented by a great sorrow in the loss of my dear husband. Yours faithfully, J. V. Green

Church of England Society for Providing Homes for Waifs and Strays
Otherwise Known as "WAIFS AND STRAYS."

Dear Madam, Re Frederick G. Snow & Ronald B. Young 1 Dec. 1920

In reply to your letter, I beg to say that as the Committee has recently decided to increase the payment for boarded-out children to 10 shillings a week, per head, which is inclusive and covers the grant of £1. a quarter for clothing.

Perhaps you will claim accordingly in future on behalf of the above-named boys. I am afraid, however, we cannot see our way to make a retrospective payment.

The Committee only decided to increase the allowance on receiving the first application from the respective Supervisors.

As I find we already have many children boarded-out at Rumburgh, under the supervision of the Rev. W. Linton Wilson and it is not unusual, unless there are special circumstances connected with the same, to have two Supervisors in the same district, I am venturing to write and ask whether you would have any objection to handing over the supervision of the two boys in question to this gentleman, in which case I will write and let him know, so that he can include the children together with those already under his charge.

I should like to take this opportunity of expressing my sympathy with you in the great sorrow you have recently sustained in the loss of your husband.

Yours faithfully, Rev. W. Fowell Swann

To. The Sec. Homes for Waifs, Rev. W. Fowell Swann M.A. 12/12/20
Dear Sir:

Thank you for your letter and your kind sympathy therein expressed.

I am glad to know that the Foster Mothers are to be allowed more children in the future.

I am relieved also to know that you can dispense with my supervisorship. I have today seen the Vicar - Rev. Linton Wilson and he has agreed to take over my two little charges.

It has always been a great pleasure to do this for you but as there is no longer any need . . .

(Next page missing). J. V. Green

> **Church of England Society for Providing Homes for Waifs and Strays**
> **Otherwise Known as "WAIFS AND STRAYS."**
>
> Dear Madam, re Frederick G. Snow & Ronald B. Young   6 Dec 1920
>
> Thank you very much for your kind letter with regard to giving up the Supervision of the above two boys. Let me assure you that my only reason for this suggestion was that I thought you might like to be relieved, whereas the additional Supervision would not add much to Mr. Wilson's labours. I need not say how grateful I shall be if you will kindly carry on the work of Supervision as you have done hereto. I have written to Mr. Wilson and I hope you will quite put out of your mind that I have any desire to hurt the feelings of a very good helper.
>
> Rev. W. Fowell Swann

> Rev. W. Fowell Swann   Sept. 12, 1921
>
> Dear Sir: Fred Snow is now almost 12. If he is to be removed for definite training I should be glad to know. Mrs. Smith does not desire another in his place, she is getting into years and past it. W. L. Wilson

> **Church of England Society for Providing Homes for Waifs and Strays**
> **Otherwise Known as "WAIFS AND STRAYS."**
>
> The Rev. W. Linton Wilson   14 September 1921
>
> Dear Sir, re Frederick G. Snow. I have to thank you for your communication received respecting this lad and as I gather that neither you nor the foster mother have any suggestions to make as to his future, I shall be glad if you will be kind enough to have the enclosed report form filled in as fully as possible on his behalf with a view to his being transferred to on of our ordinary Homes for further training. We are shortly opening a new Home at Sevenoaks and if the lad is suitable I am hoping that arrangements can be made for him to be sent there.
>
> Yours faithfully, Rev. W. Fowell Swann

This foster home was in a small village in Suffolk. What suggestions could the foster parents or the Minister have made regarding his future? They planned to transfer him to a Home "for further training." The only training he had to date could be called "Waif Training." Stroud described how Dr. Edith Green and Dr. Rose Turner provided Medical Examinations for every child in their care in all of England. They made unannounced visits to the villages and saw children at their schools. They inspected the children's heads, eyes, ears and measured their height and girth. They noted how happy were the children. They inspected the foster home, looked at the beds, and made sure the children had nightshirts. They met with the Parson, Lady of the Manor or Retired Teacher Supervisors and wrote reports at night in the hotel (72-73). The Waifs and Strays Society may have had well over a thousand children in foster care by 1920, when Dr. Rose Turner inspected my Father. Her report was almost identical to the one a year before.

Church of England
SOCIETY FOR PROVIDING HOMES FOR WAIFS & STRAYS
Otherwise known as "Waifs and Strays."

Report of visit to Fred Snow 12. At home of Foster Mother Mrs. Harry Smith at Rumburgh. Date of last visit Sept. 27.20

1. What are the circumstances of the Foster mother, and what is your impression of her character? This is a very good home and contains 3 bedrooms sitting room and kitchen. The foster Mother's husband is a labourer. The Foster Mother is an exceptionally nice woman. Another of our boys - Ronald Young is boarded out here.

2. What is the state of the child's health? He is a healthy boy. Ht 4' 11" (147 cm) Girth 25 3/4 in. (64 cm)

3. Is the clothing suitable and how is it provided? Yes, by foster mother.

4. Is sufficient care given to personal cleanliness? Yes.

5. Have any complaints been made by the Foster mother? No.

6. Has the child made any complaints? No.

7. Is the child in your opinion properly cared for and happy? Yes.

8. Has the child attended school regularly? Yes. In what standard? IV.

9. Does the child attend Church and Sunday School? Yes.

10. Is the sleeping accommodation satisfactory and has each child a separate bed? Yes.

11. Remarks of School Teachers, &c., &c.

12. General remarks. (If child is of an age to be transferred, do you recommend the same?) Yes. R. Turner September 20, 1921

There was no mention whether his teeth were repaired, as she recommended in her 1920 report. Perhaps she did not examine his malformed feet. He apparently grew 9 cm in height and 2 cm in girth in one year. He had four Medical Examinations from Dr. Rose Turner during the 11 years he was a ward of the Waifs and Strays Society. The first occurred when he was four years old in 1913, when he was apprehended. The second occurred when he was six years old in 1915, and had been in the foster home for two years. The third and fourth occurred when he was 11-12 years old in 1919-1920, and had been in the

149

foster home for 7-8 years. These last two were in preparation for his transfer to the Home.

REPORT OF A CHILD

THE CHURCH OF ENGLAND SOCIETY FOR PROVIDING HOMES FOR WAIFS AND STRAYS

Name: Frederick G. Snow Age: 12 Home: Mrs. H. Smith

1. EDUCATION: 1. In what Standard? IV. 2. If backward, give reason. He is sharp.

2. DISTINGUISHING CHARACTERISTICS: 1. Disposition. *Cheerful and obliging. 2. Intelligence Fair. 3. Health. Excellent. 4. Height. ___ 4a. Weight. ___ 5. Conduct. *Good. 6. If over twelve years of age, please state for what occupation the child appears suitable. * These should be answered *fully*.

Signed Rev W. Linton Wilson.

Church of England Society for Providing Homes for Waifs and Strays
Otherwise Known as "WAIFS AND STRAYS."

The Rev. Linton Wilson re Frederick G. Snow   4th October 1921

Dear Sir, Adverting to my communication of the 14th. ult. I write to inform you that arrangements have now been made for the above boy to be transferred to the Society's St. Augustine's Home, Sevenoaks. Will you, therefore, please see that he is sent to London on <u>Wednesday the 12th inst.</u> by the train leaving <u>Halesworth at 8.28 a.m.</u> due to arrive at <u>Liverpool Street</u> at 11.22 am. where he will be met by a member of our staff and seen into the train for his future Home.

The boy should be allowed to leave with his complete outfit, and the enclosed blue form of medical certificate should be filled in on his behalf and accompany him. Any expense which you may be put to in effecting the foregoing will be refunded, if you will charge for the same in your next claim for maintenance. Please let me have a line to the effect that the foregoing will be carried out.

Yours faithfully, Rev. W. Fowell Swann

They again put him on a train alone for a three-hour ride into London. Some stranger met him sometime during the two-hour layover at Liverpool Street Station. They put him on another train for another hour ride to a "Home" where he spent the next 3½ years of his life.

Church of England Society for Providing Homes for Waifs and Strays
Otherwise Known as "WAIFS AND STRAYS."

The Master, St. Augustine's Home   4th October 1921

Dear Sir,   re Frederick George Snow.

I have to thank you for you communication of the 1st. inst. enclosing a report of George Hodgson.

I take this opportunity of enclosing particulars of the above lad, and, unless you hear to the contrary, will you please expect him on Wednesday the 12th inst. by the train leaving Charing Cross at 1.45 p.m. due to arrive at Sevenoaks (Tubs Hill) at 2.23 p.m. where I shall be glad if you will kindly see that he is met.

In accordance with instructions received from the Homes' Committee, I shall be very glad if you will be so kind as to let me have a report of the boy in question.

I should like to have a report as to his health, attainment, and the outfit which accompanied him, and any such other details as appear advisable.

Yours faithfully, Rev. W. Fowell Swann

Church of England Society for Providing Homes for Waifs and Strays
Otherwise Known as "WAIFS AND STRAYS."

Mr. J. G. Snow, S. Croydon re Frederick George Snow   21 Jan. 1925

I am sorry to trouble you in this matter, but the above-named boy is very anxious to emigrate to Canada, and it is proposed to include him in a party of boys we are sending out in a month or two's time.

You may remember that when application was made for his admission under our care you signed an agreement for him to be sent to Canada should the Committee consider it advisable, and I shall be glad, therefore, if you will kindly sign the enclosed form and return it to me at your earliest convenience.

Yours faithfully, Rev. A. J. Wescott, D. D.

He was not given the choice of staying in England. No one wanted him there. He had to choose between "emigration" to Canada or Australia.

> **Church of England Society for Providing Homes for Waifs and Strays**
> **Otherwise Known as "WAIFS AND STRAYS."**
>
> **Form of Consent** to be signed by the Parent, Guardian, or nearest Relative, in cases of Children Sent to Canada. *I,* **John George Snow** *residing at* **Dean Cottage, Dean Road, South Croydon** *do hereby declare that I am the** **Guardian** *of* **FREDERICK GEORGE SNOW** *and that I hereby of my own free will give* **him** *up to the Committee of the above Society to be sent to one of their Canadian Distribution Homes, and thereafter to be provided with a suitable home in such manner as the said Committee shall see fit.* Signed: J. G. Snow *in the presence of* Lilian Keers, 296 Franciscan Road, Tooting *Dated* Feb. 2nd, 1925.

What "suitable homes" did the Waifs and Strays Society ever provide for the children they deported to Canada? Were any of the 100,000 children ever adopted or placed in foster homes in Canada? Who was Lilian Keers and why did she sign as a witness? Was she Annie Gifford's married Sister Lilian Gifford?

> **CASE SUMMARY SHEET**
>
> Diocese of: Canterbury.
>
> Application Number: 27426.
>
> Accepted Number: 18264.
>
> Name: **Frederick G. Snow**. Decision of Committee: Accept. Vide Case Agenda 9.10.13. Informed Mrs. Reeve 10.10.13. October 31, 1913. Admitted Clapham Receiving House 41 Days. December 6, 1913: Supervisor Mrs. J. V. Green, Rumburgh, Halesworth. December 8, 1920: Supervisor Rev. Linton Wilson, Rumburgh Vicarage, Halesworth. October 12, 1921: Transferred St. Augustine's Home, Sevenoaks. Informed Mrs. Reeve 13/10/21. January 13, 1925: Passed by Emigration Sub-Committee. Informed Mrs. Reeve 31/03/25. April 3, 1925: Emigrated to Gibbs' Home, Sherbrooke, Quebec, Canada

This information provided invaluable pieces of the puzzle. His Parents' identities had been confirmed as William Henry Snow and Annie Gifford. J. G. Snow was his Grandfather, and Jack and Amy were his Half Brother and Half Sister. He has/had a natural Brother named William Henry Snow Jr. While I was overjoyed to learn so much from his file, at the same time, I was indignant that they never provided my Father with this information. I sent them a fax and made my third request for the release of his entire file.

Dear _____   Re: Frederick George Snow (1909-1994) June 1, 1995

I received the copies of documentation from my Father's case file. I note that you included his first letter of inquiry . . . January 17, 1928, when he was 19 years old. What was not included was a letter of response to this inquiry. You should know that I have in my possession copies of most of his correspondence to and replies from the Children's Society. . . . I want copies of all such correspondence in order that I have a complete record of his 56-year-old search for his identity. I also want any and all school records from the time he was at St. Augustine's (1920-1925). Also, there may be records of his time in Canada at Gibbs' Home, Sherbrooke, Quebec.

From the records you sent, it is quite apparent that his actual parents were Annie Snow (née Gifford) and William Henry Snow. Since this information was withheld from my Father, in spite of his unremitting attempts over 60 years to elicit such information, he died believing that his Father was J. G. Snow and that John Allen Snow and Amy Alice Snow were his Brother and Sister, when in fact they were his Grandfather, Half Brother, and Half Sister, respectively.

I now discover that he has/had a Brother named William Henry Snow Jr., who was born on August 19 1912. You neglected to mention this in your letter of January 04, 1995. . . . I need to know if William Henry Snow Jr. was ever in the care of the Children's Society. . . . While I can understand why this information was withheld from him while he was a child in the care of the Children's Society, I cannot understand why it was continued to be withheld from him for over 65 years of his adult life.

Again, I must insist that you release the entire contents of his file as per my request of April 24, 1995. I believe the £15.00 ($33.45) I sent you should be sufficient to cover costs of photocopying and mailing. I sincerely hope to prevail upon your sense of integrity and humanity in complying with my request. For over 65 years, the Children's Society ignored my father's requests for information, implied that they had no information, provided inaccurate information, and withheld information. I believe that two weeks should be sufficient time for you to decide whether to comply with my request. I expect to hear from you before June 15, 1995. Please phone me collect, fax, or write your reply. My solicitors have advised me to make one more attempt to have his entire file released to me. If I do not hear from you in the next two weeks, I will have to assume that you intend to perpetuate the Society's tradition of withholding information. If that is to be the case, I will reluctantly have to seek legal advice as to what alternatives are available to me through Canadian/British courts.

Sincerely, Perry Snow

They sent a lengthy, defensive, and evasive letter the day after they received my fax. They gave me a few more pages from his case file. These were clearly not "routine notes and letters dealing with purely administrative and internal Society matters." They stated they had conducted thorough and time-consuming research on my behalf. Perhaps they felt I was ungrateful. They explained they did not include post-1929 correspondence as this "did not offer any further perspectives" regarding his time in care. They cited a letter they sent to my Father identifying his Father as William Henry Snow.

In 1938, they incorrectly (?) sent him a copy of their 30 January 1931 letter instead. It did not mention William Henry Snow. Thomas Keeley of the Gibbs' Home told him that J. G. Snow was his Father. The Children's Society made no comment about this in their latest letter.

Even though they knew the relationship between William Henry Snow and J. G. Snow was one of Son and Father, they never once clarified this for my Father. They continued to refer to J. G. Snow as his Guardian rather than his Grandfather in this letter. They listed his correspondence between 1931-1957, as he "pursued the issue of his past," and noted their attempts to find his Birth Certificate. They wrongly stated he did not identify his "Brother" by name, when he clearly named him as Jack Snow, in his 1938, letter. They acknowledged they sent him his Baptism Certificate in 1957, but did not explain why they did not give it to him 30 years earlier.

They asked the Croydon Local Studies library to search the Electoral Registers and found that Jack lived on Dean Road from 1938-1951. While I appreciated their effort, this information was not vital. They suggested I could retain their Post Adoption and Care Project researchers. They did not have his school records, but gave me the address for the Kent Archives Office. They insisted they had operated "in the full spirit of cooperation" and provided me with information that was "in excess of the level of detail" they are required to give under their "Interim Policy and Guidance Re: The Ownership of User Records." They reminded me the case files were confidential and their property.

They did not refer to his last letter to them in 1984, and their offer to release information from his Case File. They did not acknowledge the fact they knew his natural Brother's name and date of birth for 82 years and yet never informed him. They did not even mention William Alfred Snow's name in this last, long letter. They maintained they did not have any records from the Gibbs' Home at Sherbrooke, Quebec. In 1995, David Lorente found an index of over 3,000 names and a Sailing List from 1886-1915. He notified the Children's Society of his find, and donated copies to the Archbishop of Canterbury, National Archives of Canada, and The Church of Jesus Christ, Latter Day Saints.

Did their policy allow them to *not* inform my Father of his Brother's existence? Did their guidelines allow them to mislead him as to his Parents' identities, tell him his Grandfather was his Father, and withhold his Baptism Certificate from him until he was 48 years old? Why did they not provide these latest pages in the first package they sent me? They either "did not get it," or "did not want to get it." I would not correspond with them for five months. The back-and-forth would be futile, and I had more documents from his case file to examine.

I decided to "pursue the issue" of my Father's past with added zeal. Perhaps they did not read the material they first sent me, and inadvertently revealed the existence of his natural Brother William Henry Snow Jr. My Mother felt vindicated, as she always suspected they withheld information. She was excited by the prospect that my Father has/had a Brother, and may have/had more siblings. The first piece of correspondence in this package was a letter my Father wrote when he was legally an adult and no longer under their care.

Canadian Ingersoll-Rand Company Limited
SHERBROOKE, QUE.

Dear Sir: Re: Fred G. Snow   Jan. 17th 1929

I am writing to ask you if it would be of any inconvenience to you if I asked you to look up my birthplace and also my past history.

I have been living in Sherbrooke the past five years, and certain things have occurred that under the circumstances I would very much like to know where I was born, and also if I have any parents living at the present time. I was in St. Augustine's Home in Kent before I came to Canada, I also know that I was in Rumburgh for a while befor [sic] going to Kent.

If you could inform me as to these matters I would be more than oblidge [sic] to you. Trusting that you will help me out in this matter, I am, Yours truly,

F. G. Snow

This letter was not included in the first package of correspondence they sent me. He obtained work with Ingersoll-Rand after he had been in the hospital for a year. His comment that "certain things have occurred" might have referred to prejudice he met with in the small, French-Canadian community of Sherbrooke. Perhaps he began to date, and was informed of his "tainted origins." He was 19 years old. He did not know

155

when or where he was born and did not know who his Parents were. He had nothing to prove who he was. When he was laid off this job, he joined the Reserve Army Service Corps.

I believe the following letter was lost when my Father's landlady kept his traveling trunk in Winnipeg in 1929. In all the correspondence over the years, this is the *only* time they told him William Henry Snow was "believed to be" his Father. The intake form quoted his Grandfather J. G. Snow naming his Son William Henry Snow as my Father's Father.

They led him to believe J. G. Snow was his Guardian, and 13 years later, Thomas Keeley told him J. G. Snow was his Father. He believed him. They requested a search for his Birth Certificate, but did not give him a copy of their request. If they had, he may have been satisfied, and not pursued this over the years. He did not believe them. They could have given him a copy of his Baptism Certificate in 1929. They could have informed him that he had a natural Brother, William Henry Snow Jr., who would have been 17 years old in 1929.

Church of England
SOCIETY FOR PROVIDING HOMES FOR WAIFS & STRAYS
Otherwise known as "Waifs and Strays."

My dear Snow,   7th February, 1929[8]

In reply to your letter asking for information as to your birth, I write to inform you that one of our representatives called at the General Register Office in London, to obtain these particulars for you, but unfortunately could find no entry of your birth.

According to the information we possess at this Office, your full name is Frederick George Snow, and you were born at Larch Road, Balham, sometime in September, 1909, the exact day being unknown.

Your mother's name is Annie Gifford Snow, and your father is believed to be William Henry Snow.

I am sorry it is not possible for me to give you any more definite details, but it may be possible for your former guardian, Mr. John George Snow, Dean Cottage, Dean Road, South Croydon, Surrey, England, to furnish you with further particulars.

With every good wish for your continued happiness and success in Canada, Believe me,

Your sincere friend,

Secretary's Assistant.

He immediately wrote back to them.

> **Canadian Ingersoll-Rand Company Limited**
> SHERBROOKE, QUE.
>
> Dear Sir: Re: Fred G. Snow   Feb. 21st/29
>
> In reply to your letter received here the 21st inst; I write to thank you for your trouble and also to tell you how much I apreciate [sic] your generosity in giving me the information you did concerning my parents.
>
> I am writing immediately to the address you informed me of, and am trusting to luck that I will be able to trace a little of my past history.
>
> Thanking you again for you [sic] kindness, I remain,
>
> Yours sincerely, F. G. Snow

He rode boxcars, and lived as an itinerant labourer, when he next wrote them. He wrote an impassioned plea in fountain pen and flowing script.

> Box 10, Hatzic B. C.
>
> Dear Sir: January 11, 1931
>
> I am writing to you, at the advice of Mr. Keeley, Gibbs' Home, Sherbrooke P. Que. requesting you if possible, to advise me, as to the whereabouts of my parents (if any).
>
> My name being, Frederick George Snow, age 21 years, Born Sept. 17th 1909.
>
> As far as I know, I resided with a Mrs. M. Smith, Pleasure Ground, Rumburgh, Suffolk, England at the age of 4 years, from there I was transferred to St. Augustine's Home, Sevenoaks, Kent, until the age of 15 years, when I imigrated [sic] to Sherbrooke, PQ Can.
>
> I would more than appreciate your kindness, if in any way you can throw light on this matter for me, and by doing, help one who has been in darkness, and ignorant as to who he is.
>
> I am, Sir,
>
> Yours most Respectfully,
>
> Fred G. Snow

They replied with a rather terse note -- "My dear Snow." They told him he was "left" with "a Mr. J. G. Snow." They could have told him he was his Grandfather, and identified his Father.

In 1931, Prebendary Rudolf was appointed Commander of the Order of the British Empire and awarded an Honorary MA Degree from the University of Oxford (Stroud, 174-175).

Prebendary Edward de Montjoie Rudolf died at the age of 81 on May 29, 1933. The Waifs and Strays Society changed its 55-year old policy of handing second-hand shoes from one child to another in 1935. Each child was provided with new shoes (Stroud 198).

Five years passed before my Father wrote to Thomas Keeley. He prospected for gold and cut lake ice for a year before he married. He and my Mother lived in a tent, while he worked in the gravel pit at Ozone. When they moved back to Port Arthur, there was little work available, and the unemployment rate was 15%. He shovelled snow from the streets in the winter, and washed dishes in a bush camp in Mobert in the summer. He had a seven-month-old Son. Keeley wrote to Secretary Vaughan of the Waifs and Strays Society. The letter had a boastful letterhead.

Dear Mr. Vaughan: re. Fred G. Snow   Dec. 8th 1936[10]
I shall be obliged if you will kindly secure a copy of the Birth Certificate of Snow, if it happens to be obtainable. I am expressing doubt, because of the meagre details contained in the Case-paper. It would also be helpful if you would kindly send us a copy of page three of the Case-paper, as we have only got half of the form on file.

We heard from Fred this month after a silence of two years. He states he is married and has a son seven months old. In his letter he asked for his Birth Certificate and details regarding his family history. I will be responsible for the cost of the Birth Certificate and or other charges.

Yours sincerely,

Thomas Keeley

Church of England
SOCIETY FOR PROVIDING HOMES FOR WAIFS & STRAYS
Otherwise known as "Waifs and Strays."

Dear Mr. Keeley, re Frederick George Snow   23rd December, 1936[11]

In reply to your request for a copy of this man's birth certificate I should mention that application was made for this at Somerset House in February, 1929, but no trace could be found that his birth was ever registered, so that it is impossible to obtain a certificate, and we informed Snow of this at the time.

I am now enclosing copy of the third page of the casepaper relating to Snow and we will leave it to your discretion as to how much of this information you pass on.

Yours sincerely, W. R. Vaughan, Secretary.

PS It has occurred to me that Mr. Snow's Certificate of Baptism might be of use to him, and I am, therefore, sending it herewith.

It "occurred" to Secretary Vaughan that his Baptism Certificate "might be of use" to my Father, who had been in Canada for 11 years without any form of identification. The "third page of the casepaper" contained an explanation of how my Father came into care, and identified his Father, Grandfather, and Brother. Thomas Keeley chose not to pass on *any* of this vital information and did not forward a copy of his Baptism Certificate to him.

My Father next wrote to St. Augustine's Home for Boys and J. C. Mason, Secretary of the "Old Boys League."

Dear Sir,   September 14, 1937

I am writing this letter as you will notice to Mr. Jago, as I am under the impression he is still Master, if I am mistaken I do hope sincerely that whoever reads this will do me a great favour, and try and find out for me the little information I am about to ask you.

First my name is Frederick George Snow, I came to Canada in 1925, but what I really would like to know is have you any official data on me or my life concerning where I was born, my parents, if any, are still living, or anything regarding me personally.

I do hope you can help me in this matter.

I am married and have a son 15 months old so for his and my wife's sake, please help me.

Sincerely, Fred G. Snow

Dear Sir,   September 14, 1937

I take this opportunity as a member of our great organization to ask you if you can help me in a matter that is of great importance to me and my family.

I have been in touch with communication with [sic] Mr. Keeley at Sherbrooke but he has been unable to do much for me, and I thought perhaps you being closer to the place than us, you might have a better opportunity to communicate with the parties concerned.

I would like you to get any data you can on me or any of my relatives and let me have the same.

I don't know much about any of them and I thought you could help. The address is Dean Cottage, Dean Road, Croydon, Surrey, my father is supposed to live there, I have no prove [sic] of anything my league number is 207 and I came out here from St. Augustine's, St. Johns Rd, Sevenoaks, Kent. Mr. Jago was Master at the time, 1925.

My Mother was Miss Annie Gifford before she married I think. I was born in London in 1909.

Can you help me Sir to get some legal information of some kind, I will be forever grateful to you. I am doing well in Canada here, have a lovely home and all modern conveniences, and I sure like the country.

Trusting I may hear from you Sir, at your earliest, I remain,

Anxiously waiting, Fred G. Snow

My Father believed his entire life, what Thomas Keeley had told him -- that his Father was John George Snow. They never told him otherwise.

Church of England WAIFS & STRAYS SOCIETY
ST. AUGUSTINE'S HOME FOR BOYS

Dear Mr. Vaughan,   29th September 1937[12]

Herewith letter received on the 28th. inst. from Mr. Fred G. Snow, one of our old boys, a former inmate of this Home and who is anxious to obtain some information regarding his antecedents. Submitted for your information and necessary action.

Yours sincerely, J. Frost, A/Warden

In the fall of 1937, my Father fought forest fires in Northern Ontario. He was 28 years old, married for two years, and had a 16-month-old Son. They moved to Peninsula where they would have the most difficult winter of their lives. He received a Christmas card from Jack Snow, who signed it "Brother." In January 1938, he wrote again to the Old Boys' League. He had quit his job, subsisted on intermittent labouring work, and hunted small animals for food. My Mother was a month pregnant with my Sister.

Dear Mr. Mason: January 23, 1938

. . . I was very surprised at receiving a letter from you so promptly, and I must apologize for not answering it sooner than this. With regard to the information I enquired about, I am sorry to say I have no knowledge nor can I recollect hearing from your office on January 30, 1931. It might possibly have gone astray in the mail somehow but if you have a copy on our files at the present time and it has any bearing on this matter I would be very grateful if you could forward a copy of same to me. Speaking for myself, I am under the impression that the name Snow, I am at present using is not my own and I feel it is only fair to my Wife and child that this be in some way proven, true or false.

At time of writing, I am in receipt of a Christmas Card sent to me from, (as he calls himself) my brother, he is at present living at No. 3 Churchill Road, S. Croydon, Surrey, England. If, Mr. Mason, you thought we could gain anything by contacting him, in regards this matter, would your Office be willing to undertake the task? I am grateful for your interest in this matter and trust you will inform me if anything new turns up.

Yours very Sincerely, Fred G. Snow.

PS My brother's name is Jack Allen Snow.

He still had serious doubts that his surname was truly "Snow." He had nothing to verify this. The only way Jack (33) could have located my Father was by writing to the Waifs and Strays Society. Where are the copies of this correspondence in his case file? Why did they claim my Father did not identify his "Brother?"

Church of England
SOCIETY FOR PROVIDING HOMES FOR WAIFS & STRAYS
Otherwise known as "Waifs and Strays."

Dear Mr. Snow   8th February, 1938[13]

In replying to your further letter received this morning I am now enclosing copy of our letter to you dated the 30th January, 1931, as I note you have no recollection of ever receiving the original of this.

I hope this information will be of help to you and as you received a Christmas card from your brother I see no reason why you should not write to him direct as it is possible you might be able to obtain some further particulars from him.

Yours sincerely, J. C. Mason,

Secretary "O.B.L.

Their 1929 letter suggested that William Henry Snow was his Father. They gave him a copy of their 1931 letter instead, that did not identify his Father. Was this an innocent example of bureaucratic ineptitude or a deliberate attempt to confuse him? In 1995, they repeated the same mistake (?), when they gave me a copy of the 1931 letter instead of the 1929 letter.

Barnardo's made their last shipment of 21 boys and 7 girls to Canada in 1939. The Waifs and Strays Society deported eight boys to Canada in June 1939. They may have been the last of their shipment of children to Canada. The Waifs and Strays Society admitted Child Number 50,000. They had 6,000 children in their care in 1941 and had been in operation for 60 years (Stroud 212). In 1949, W. R. Vaughan retired as Secretary of the Waifs and Strays Society and was replaced by Colonel E. St. J. Birnie.

Almost 20 years later, my Father wrote to the Balham Police, London. He had been laid off work at Canada Car and Foundry when the factory closed. It was a very difficult winter. It was hard for him to keep the family supplied with groceries and the house supplied with heat. This was the winter we gathered wood, and took pickets off a fence for fuel for the house.

My Father had been married for 22 years and had six children ages 21, 19, 17, 13, 11, and 2. Two of us were in Elementary School, and two were in High School.

He was anxious he might not be allowed to cross the border without a Birth Certificate to attend my Brother's Graduation at the University of Duluth, Minnesota, USA. He still had nothing to verify who he was. They could have given him the Baptism Certificate that lay in his file for 44 years.

Dear Sir: October 08, 1957

I should like to make enquiries regarding records we have from Our Boys League, Old Town Hall, Kennington Road, London, S.E.11 referring to myself, Frederick George Snow, that I was born at Larch Road, Balham, London in September 1909.

Would there be any means of obtaining a birth certificate from hospitals, church records, or your department?

We also have records that I am supposed to be the son of John George Snow (deceased) and Anne Snow (née Gifford) formerly of Dean Cottage, Dean Road, South Croydon, Surrey, England.

I am now married with a family of six children, been in Canada since 1925 and this birth certificate is essential to me regarding property and legal transactions and also permission to enter the United States if the occassion [sic] arises.

Hoping you can throw some light on this matter it will be greatly appreciated by myself and family.

Yours truly, Fred G. Snow.

PS Trusting all matters are strictly confidential.

The Police apparently searched for his Birth Certificate at Somerset House but with no success, and forwarded his letter to the Children's Society. In 1949, Secretary Vaughan retired and was replaced by Colonel E. St. J. Birnie. Vaughan then became Secretary of the Fairbridge Society, that was devoted to child emigration (Stroud 224, 227).

Instead of simply giving my Father their copy of his Baptism Certificate, they obtained a photocopy from St. Peter's Church in Croydon. They also searched for his Birth Certificate at Wandsworth under the name "Snow" and "Gifford," without success.

Church of England
SOCIETY FOR PROVIDING HOMES FOR WAIFS & STRAYS
Otherwise known as "Waifs and Strays."

The Revd. The Incumbent,

St. Peter's Vicarage, South Croydon, Surrey   29th October 1957[14]

Reverend and Dear Sir,   Re Frederick George Snow born? September 1909.

We are experiencing great difficulty in obtaining a Birth Certificate for the above named, who was once in the care of this Society.

He is now in Canada and has written for details of his history and Birth Certificate.

On our file we have a record that he was Baptized at St. Peter's on the 8th October 1913.

We have found in the past that sometimes the date of birth is quoted on the Baptism Certificate and would be most grateful if you would let me have a copy Certificate of Mr. Snow's Baptism.

As he was in the Children's Convalescent Home, Brighton Road, South Croydon, at this time his parents had deserted him, it is quite possible the correct date of birth was not known.

If you can let me have the information I shall be grateful. I understand from our file that Mr. Snow was being maintained at the Home in Croydon by St. Peter's Poor Fund.

I enclose a stamped envelope for reply.

Yours sincerely,

Col. E. St. J. Birnie, Secretary

St. Peter's Vicarage, 55 St. Peter's Road, Croydon
                    30 October, 1957[15]

Dear Sir,

With reference to your letter of yesterday's date, I enclose herewith an exact copy of the entry in our register of the baptism of Mr. F. G. Snow. Unfortunately, the entry does not show the precise date of his birth.

I suppose this was not known at the time, hence the appropriate column gives only the information as stated on the enclosed copy.

I regret that no more definite information is to hand.

Yours sincerely Rev. _____

WANDSWORTH REGISTRATION DISTRICT
(COMPRISING THE METROPOLITAN BOROUGH OF
WANDSWORTH)

Col. E. St. J. Birnie   8th November 1957[16]

Secretary, Church of England Children's Society

Dear Sir,   <u>Frederick George Snow or Gifford</u>

With reference to your recent enquiry about a Birth Certificate in respect of the above-named, I regret that I am unable to trace in the registers in my custody an entry agreeing with the particulars given by you.

Your remittance of *4/6d* less the appropriate fee of *3/9d* is therefore returned herewith.

Yours faithfully, Superintendent Register

My Mother (63) wrote to them in 1976.

Dear _____   Aug. 1, 1976

Just a letter to thank you for your help in getting us the book

. . . We received our copy last week and will enjoy reading it.

I am writing on behalf of my Husband, Frederick George Snow.

During the 41 years of our very happy marriage we have tried at various times to trace something of his past.

I am enclosing a copy of a baptism certificate that we managed to obtain. He has had correspondence from a Brother whose last address is in Ireland and a Sister in England.

We were never able to obtain a birth certificate, or any information except what Mr. Snow remembers of his childhood.

. . . Now, my Husband would like to find out if some of these boys . . . are still alive in Canada.

We figure, that so many people answered Mr. Stroud's enquiry, that some of them from St. Augustine's might like to get in touch.

Yours sincerely, Mr. & Mrs. Fred G. Snow

No one wrote to her. My Father wrote his final letter to them eight years later in 1984. They replied they "were not clear" whether he received any information from their records, and asked him if he would like to "avail himself of this information." This ended my review of his file.

The fall of 1995 marked the first anniversary of his death. I wrote the Kent archives in hope of obtaining his school records, and possibly those of his Brother William Henry Snow Jr. Their records listed a Frederick George Snow who entered the school on 13 October 1921, and left on 17 April 1924.

His birth date was September 09, 1909. His previous address was given as Dr. Barnardo's Homes, St. John's Road, Kent. His previous school was listed as Ebury Bridge LCI School, St. George's Road, London. The Waifs and Strays Society sent him to Canada. I had some doubts this was his record. I wrote for clarification and they replied their records were incorrect in listing St. Augustine's as a Barnardo Home. Given this error, it was probable that his previous school attended was incorrect as well.

The Sevenoaks Council School records contained the names and birth dates of eight other British Home Children who were deported to Canada along with my Father. Someone may just be looking for these names and dates of births of these British Home Children: George Hodgson (20 October 1908), William Mason (29 October 1909), Cornelius Van Loon (09 February 1908), Thomas Maynard (03 April. 1909), Frederick Van Loon (09 February 1908),   Stephen   Mildred (03 May 1911), Reginald M. Worby (21 September 1909), Robert Muir (15 March 1909)

This was the first record of his complete date of birth. From where did this originate? Did someone at the school decide that the ninth day of the ninth month of 1909 was a convenient date of birth for my Father? In 1942, Thomas Keeley told him he was born on September 17, 1909.

His last day at school was April 17, 1924. Where was he for a year until he was deported from England on April 03, 1925?

A year had passed since I first contacted the Children's Society.

I was not entirely satisfied with their explanation, "The left hand did not know what the right hand was doing."

Dear _____   October 4, 1995

It has been exactly a year since I first contacted the Children's Society regarding information about my Father's origins.

_____ wrote to me on October 17, 1994 and stated "We have no record of brothers or sisters on our record cards." This turned out to be most inaccurate.

. . . After much correspondence with _____, I now discover from these records, that my Father did indeed have a Brother named William Henry Snow (August 29, 1912 -?), Son of Annie Gifford, and William Henry Snow.

This information was withheld from my Father, and would not have been provided to me had I not been persistent.

. . . My Father died not knowing with any certainty whom his parents were, and without knowing he had a Brother.

After 60 years of correspondence with the Children's Society, none of this information was provided to him.

His Brother . . . may still be alive at the age of 83 . . .

_____ has suggested that you may be of some assistance in tracing members of this family.

. . . In order to begin a search for he and his descendants, I need to know if he was ever under the care of the Children's Society (or Barnardo's).

I will write to the Archivist for St. Augustine's school records.

It would also help if you could tell me what school my Father might have attended in Rumburgh, Suffolk, from the ages of 5-11 (1914-1920).

Yours sincerely,

Perry Snow

The Children's Society.

A VOLUNTARY SOCIETY OF THE CHURCH OF ENGLAND AND THE CHURCH IN WALES

Dear Mr. Snow   17 October 1995

I am writing to thank you for your letter of 4 October 1995, which gives a good summary of the information you have gathered so far.

I am aware of the correspondence between yourself and _____ and _____ on this matter.

I apologize if you felt that the information sent to you by _____ was inaccurate. It was perhaps not made clear that only the record cards are held at this office. They were checked and no brothers or sisters were identified.

The fuller records (pre 1930) are held . . . at Headquarters, hence the passing of your enquiry from one office to another.

However, I will arrange for the record cards to be checked again with the names you supplied to see if any further information is found.

We do have the services of a researcher. I would appreciate it if you could complete the enclosed authorisation form and I will then ask the researcher to undertake some work.

I will also make enquiries regarding schools that your father might have attended.

I hope that the enquiries may lead to some answers for you, and we will be in touch as soon as we have information to give you.

Yours sincerely

I wrote the Children's Society and made my fifth request for the release of his entire case file.

Dear _____
                            October 27, 1995

In your last letter of June 01, 1995, you neglected to make any reference to William Henry Snow Jr., my Father's heretofore-unknown Brother. You neglected to make mention of his existence in your letter of January 04, 1995.

This information lay in the records for over 82 years, and yet the Children's Society never informed my Father of his Brother's existence.

Since you did not answer my questions, . . . I again have to ask you if William Henry Snow Jr., was ever in the care of the Children's Society.

. . . At any time over the past 82 years, my Father could have been informed of these details.

When I first contacted the Children's Society a year ago, I could have been informed, but was not. Again, I need to remind you of my Release of Information request of April 24, 1995.

… If you refuse to comply with this request, please be so kind as to notify me in writing of your refusal. Should this be the case I will have to seriously consider my lawyer's advice regarding my options of filing suit. … Sincerely, Perry Snow

I was tempted to end my search. I wrote to a man in England whose name I found on a <u>British Isles Genealogical Register Index</u>.

Dear Perry: 28 October 1995

Very many thanks for your most interesting letter dated 14 October 1995 re the Snow's. It was fascinating to read and aroused my interest. I will try to help if I can.

However, I regret to say that Annie Gifford is not (as far as I can see) related to me -- unless in some convoluted way, which goes back several generations. I will, however, be very pleased to research some of your missing links which, as you have names and approximate birth years, may be quite possible.

I have been busy on other activities for the last six months or so but I will make a start towards the end of next week. I will write again as soon as I have more information.

Very best wishes, Robin.

I thought it kind of him to offer to help, but I did not give the letter much thought, and added it to the ever-growing file of similar correspondence. I wrote again to the Children's Society on the 82nd Anniversary of the day my Father was sent to the foster care home.

Dear _____   October 31, 1995

. . . You will understand my cynicism regarding this search for information about my Father's past, given my Parents' futile efforts over 60 years. I am still waiting for the Society to acknowledge that the existence of my Father's Brother (William Henry Snow - August 29, 1912) was known to them and evidence lay in his case file for 82 years!

This information was withheld from my Father . . . This acknowledgment may never be forthcoming as the existence of my Father's Brother is studiously avoided in all correspondence.

Regrettably, the revelations of the Child Migrants Trust are validated in this case as well. Be that as it may, I would still like to retain some faith in human nature and will persist in my search for information with or without the cooperation of those "keepers" of the information.

. . . Before I decide to accept your offer, I would like some assurance that I will not simply receive information that I already have. . . . While I have no problem with authorizing a Birth Relative Initiated Research, I would like to know in advance what this search entails and what it would be reasonable to expect as results.

. . . Sincerely, Perry Snow

I received a reply from their researcher who confirmed they could obtain Birth, Marriage, and Death Certificates for £6.00 ($13.38). The researcher charges a fee of £7.50 ($16.72) per hour and provides an intermediary service to make an initial approach to any relatives traced.

They did not think they would have any greater success than I would in tracing school records. The researcher explained that the index cards have the names of anyone who was ever in the care of the Children's Society and confirmed that William Henry Snow was not in their care. They did not answer my question if he was ever in Barnardo's care. Is there no family member cross-reference in their system? Do they not share information with other child-care organizations? My Father could not have been the only Snow in all of England over all of these years to be a ward of the Children's Society or other child-care organizations.

The Children's Society.

A VOLUNTARY SOCIETY OF THE CHURCH OF ENGLAND AND THE CHURCH IN WALES

Dear Mr. Snow   2 November 1995

. . . the issue of your father's brother William Henry Snow, b. 1912. As you will see from the copies of your father's case file that accompanied my letter of 2nd June 1995, the Society does not hold any additional information about his brother.

He is noted only once in the case file, this being the admission form completed in 1913.

The evidence from the case file would suggest that the Society had never been aware of the whereabouts of William Henry Snow and Annie and their Son, William Henry, . . . Later correspondence does not contain any reference to the couple's address.

The Society never shied away from this fact as is shown by a letter written to your father . . . Indeed, the Society suggested that he contact his guardian, John George Snow, to see if he could offer any insights into the whereabouts of his parents.

The Society did not attempt to withhold this information from your father . . . In terms of . . . the index cards, the reason that they do not contain any reference to William Henry Snow is simply that he was not taken into the Society's care. The cards note only the names and briefest details of individuals who were actually cared for by the Society,

. . . The cards are not a general index to other family members who may have been noted in the case files as part of the admission process.

. . . While I can appreciate your feelings of frustration about trying to locate details of your father's brothers and sisters, the matter is not helped by the lack of information in the case file. . . . Yours sincerely,

They again ignored my request for release of the entire file. They did not provide written reasons why they did not comply with my request. The letter contained a scribbled family tree and a note that said, "I thought this might clarify the relationships involved here. I thought you might have worked this out already!" And just how might my Father, or I, have

"worked this out?" They never told us Annie Gifford was J. G. Snow's Second Wife; J. G. Snow and William Henry Snow were Father and Son; and Annie Gifford and William Henry Snow were Stepmother and Stepson.

They commented William Henry Snow was single in 1913. This turned out to be incorrect. They did not answer my question why they never informed my Father of his Brother's existence. They did not provide any explanation why they never informed me of this when I first contacted them. They did not explain why they told my Father his Grandfather was his Father. It was obvious from their reply such futile correspondence could continue for years.

I was grateful for what I had discovered, but at the same time saddened, that he died before I could share this with him. I was a somewhat discouraged about the search. Although I had confirmed many facts about his origins, I still had very little with which to continue. I still had nothing to verify his alleged birth date of either September 09, 1909, or September 17, 1909. His Mother had been identified as Annie Gifford. I did not know if she had been married before her marriage to his Grandfather J. G. Snow. "Gifford" could be her maiden or married name.

I had only approximate birth years but no locations of birth for her and his Father William Henry Snow. J. G. Snow's children Amy and Jack were likely deceased. I had no idea how to trace William Henry Snow, Jr. The incompetence I had experienced with the Children's Society did not inspire my confidence in their researcher. I decided not to retain their researcher. I resented their ever-present appeals for money. They made enough money from their exploitation of the British Home Children.

A MEAGER FAMILY TREE 1995

1 John George Snow, Born 1857? Location? Married 1877? Died 1940 Croydon, Surrey, England
+First Wife? Born 1857? Location? Married 1877? Died?
  2 George Snow, Born 1880? Location? Married 1902? Died?
  2 William Henry Snow, Born 1884? Location? Married 1902? Died?
  +Annie Gifford, Born 1875? Location? Married 1904? Died?
    3 Frederick George Snow, Born 1909? Larch Road, Balham, London, England, Married 1935, Port Arthur, Ontario
1 John George Snow, Born 1857? Location? Married 1877? Died 1940 Croydon, Surrey, England
+Second Wife Annie Gifford, Born 1875? Location? Married 1904? Died?
  2 John Allen Snow, Born 1905? Croydon, Surrey, England
  +Margaret? Born? Location? Married 1925? Died?
  2 Amy Alice Snow, Born 1907? Croydon, Surrey, England
  +Stephen J? Born? Location? Married 1927? Died?

These are the scraps of information and misinformation they gave my Father from 1929-1984. They consistently identified his Mother as Annie Gifford/Snow, but they never identified her as anyone's Wife. They told him his Father was John George Snow and on other occasions said he was his Guardian. They once told him his Father was William Henry Snow. They never told him that John George Snow and William Henry Snow were Father and Son and that the former was married to Annie Gifford. They once told him John Allen Snow was his Brother and on another occasion told him, he was his Stepbrother. They told him Amy Alice Snow was his Stepsister. They never once told him that he had a natural Brother named William Henry Snow Jr. They did not volunteer this information to me when I first wrote to them. They had a copy of his

Baptism Certificate in their possession from the day he was apprehended, and did not give him a copy until he was 48 years old.

1929 (Age 20): We could find no entry of your birth. Your full name is Frederick George Snow. You were born at Larch Road, Balham, sometime in September 1909. Your mother's name is Annie Gifford and your father is believed to be William Henry Snow. Your guardian Mr. J. G. Snow may furnish you with further particulars.

1931 (Age 22): There is very little information I can give you respecting your parents and relatives. You were left by your parents with a Mr. J. G. Snow who consented to your emigration. I am afraid there is nothing further we can do for you.

1937 (Age 28): I can add nothing to the letter which was sent to you from this office on the 30th January 1931. You were deserted by your father and mother. We were unable to obtain a copy of your birth certificate, as your birth was not registered.

1942 (Age 33): Frederick George Snow was born at Larch Road, Balham, London, on September 17, 1909. He is the son of John George Snow and Annie Snow, formerly Gifford.

1949 (Age 40): We do not have any details regarding your people. You had a stepsister Amy Alice Snow and a stepbrother John A. Snow.

1957 (Age 48): I have searched your file and can find no other information than that supplied to you previously over the years since you left England. I did obtain a copy of your Baptism Certificate and enclose it herewith. You may already have a copy as one was sent to Thomas Keeley in December 1936. . . . We searched in 1929 with no success. It seems that you were not registered.

1984 (Age 75): I am unsure if we will be able to help you. I am not clear whether in fact you have received information from our records relating to the time in our care. If you would like to avail yourself of this information, I can retrieve the records.

Your identity consists of a collection of beliefs you hold to be true about yourself. My Father's lifelong identity consisted of the lies the Children's Society told him.

> All I know about myself was what the Waifs and Strays Society told me. They said I was born at Larch Road, Balham, London, England on September 17, 1909. They told me I do not have a Birth Certificate, as no one registered my birth, so I am not sure on what day I was born. I never knew I was baptized in the Church of England in 1913, until I was 47 years old in 1957. I don't know why they never gave me a copy before this. I was almost 50 years old before I had proof that my name was really

'Snow.' There was no Father's name on the Baptism Certificate, so I guess I was illegitimate.

I really don't know who my Parents are. They told me William Henry Snow was 'believed to be' my Father, but I do not know who he is. They told me John George Snow was my Guardian, but later told me *he* was my Father. My Mother was Annie Snow (formerly Gifford). I don't know if she was married, or who she was married to, when she had me. They told me my Parents deserted and abandoned me, and left me with my Guardian John George Snow. This never made sense, if he was my Father.

His children -- Jack and Amy Snow -- thought they were my Brother and Sister. I just never believed they were. The Waifs and Strays Society told me once they were my Brother and Sister and years later they told me they were my Stepbrother and Stepsister. I do not know if I have any real Brothers or Sisters. I don't know why I never saw any of my family in England in the 15 years I was there in a foster home and Boys' Home.

Most people have two families, you know. There is the one you came from, and the one you create when you get married, and have your own children. People take it for granted everyone has two families. You don't realize how much people talk about the families they came from. I could never do that. I would have loved to talk about my Parents, Brothers, and Sisters, but I could only talk about the family Gert and I created. Without her, I would not have had any family at all. I'm sorry I can't tell you any more about myself. I don't know who I am.

Had I not undertaken his search, I would not have been able to identify him any more than could he. *All* the information the Children's Society reluctantly gave me in 1995 could have been given to him when he first inquired in 1927, or anytime in the following 55 years. They could have simply given him the facts that would let him know who he was. A few lines of truthful information would have been sufficient. Why did they not? I imagine they would answer with the arrogance of the bureaucrat. "Your father never asked for *these* specifics."

They never told him what he wanted, needed, and begged to know. This was so cruel to him. Their obstinacy in releasing this vital information to me is spurious and contemptible. I had serious doubts about how much time, money, and energy my search had taken after only one year. I wondered if it would ever end, or whether it would become an all-consuming, endless, and circuitous search. The more I learned of his unknown life, the more I was saddened by the unnecessary loneliness of his life.

Chapter 3: A Kind Stranger Joins the Quest

I was often tempted to abandon my search. I wondered what difference it would make to anyone to find out about my Father's past. Each time I began to doubt, some new piece of information turned up that inspired me to continue. I decided if my Parents persisted all their lives, the least I could do was make an effort. If they believed that answers existed to their questions, and did not accept the limited information they were given, then so could I. At times, I felt guided, nudged, pushed, shoved, and finally driven along the path of this search.

You may be familiar with the phrase, "There is a light at the end of the tunnel!" My Mother is most fond of saying, "There is a light inside the tunnel!" A light came on inside this lonely tunnel, just when it became darkest. I received a letter in November 1995 from someone whom I had not expected to hear. A "kind stranger" in England became intrigued with this mystery and took it upon himself to solve it. Robin -- on his own initiative -- found Birth Certificates for my Father's Half Brother Jack, Half Sister Amy, and newly identified Brother William!

These people suddenly became real for me. They were no longer just names. When I held proof of their identities, I could claim them as my own. Jack became my Half Uncle, Amy my Half Aunt, and William Henry Snow Jr., [sic] my Uncle. I quickly learned the importance of these certificates, as each provided more pieces to the puzzle. The Waifs and Strays Society had identified my Father's previously unknown Brother as William Henry Snow Jr. This was incorrect. He was William Alfred Snow.

CERTIFIED COPY OF AN ENTRY OF BIRTH
Registration District: Streatham, Wandsworth County: County of London
When Born: 29 August 1912   Where Born: 77 Pevensey Road
Name: **William Alfred Snow**
Name and Surname of Father: William Henry Snow
Name, Surname and Maiden Surname of Mother: Annie Snow formerly Gifford
Occupation of Father: Journeyman Carpenter
Informant: Annie Snow 77 Pevensey Road

This Birth Certificate became a crucial piece of the family puzzle. My "Man in England" did a remarkable job. When he wrote he would be "pleased to research some of my missing links," I had no idea he would expend so much effort. He spent many hours in libraries, Family History Centres and Record Offices all over London. He mailed me a copy of the London A-Z road map! He is remarkably kind and thoughtful. I photocopied and pasted pages together to make a large map, and highlighted relatives' addresses.

Since the Vicar of St. Peter's Church had my Uncle's name wrong, I wondered how much of the other information was credible. I also wondered how much time and money it would have cost, if I had retained the Children's Society researcher. I was cynical enough to assume they would have persisted for some time, at some cost, and looked all over for William Henry Snow's Birth Certificate. I faxed them and asked them to confirm whether William *Alfred* Snow was ever in their care. They replied the next day.

The Children's Society

A VOLUNTARY SOCIETY OF THE CHURCH OF ENGLAND AND THE CHURCH IN WALES

Dear Mr. Snow   27 November 1995

Thank you for your fax of 26 November 1995. I am writing to confirm that I have again searched the records in the name of <u>William Alfred Snow</u> and have found no card in this name.

There is therefore no evidence that your uncle was ever under the care of The Children's Society.

I am glad that with the help of your agent you are managing to make some progress with your research and I wish you well with it.

I will leave it to you to contact me again if you ever wish any further assistance from the Children's Society.

Yours sincerely

I was relieved to find my Uncle had not been in their care. I wondered just how useful was their Index. To establish whether he was ever under the care of other child-care organizations, would I have to write to each of them separately? If I found other Snow siblings or relatives, would I have to make separate inquiries to every other child-care organization? Why do they not have an index of the Parents of the children who were in their care? Do these organizations not communicate with each other?

Robin found Birth and Marriage Certificates for my Half Uncle Jack and my Half Aunt Amy. In all, he sent me 80 certificates that cost only £480.00 ($1,070.40), as he obtained them for £6.00 ($13.38) each. Had I known what Certificates to request from the General Register Office, it still would have cost £1600.00 ($3,568.00). I was very grateful for these savings.

```
┌─────────────────────────────────────────────────────────────────┐
│              CERTIFIED COPY OF AN ENTRY OF BIRTH                   │
│  Registration District: Croydon  County:  County of Croydon       │
│  When Born:  10 July 1905            Where Born:  141 Sussex Road  │
│                    Name:  John Allen Snow                          │
│  Name and Surname of Father:  John George Snow                    │
│  Name, Surname and Maiden Surname of Mother: Annie Snow formerly Gifford │
│  Occupation of Father:  House Painter                             │
│  Informant  A. Snow 42 Sussex Road                               │
└─────────────────────────────────────────────────────────────────┘
```

```
┌─────────────────────────────────────────────────────────────────┐
│              CERTIFIED COPY OF AN ENTRY OF BIRTH                   │
│  Registration District: Croydon       County:    County of Croydon │
│  When Born:  18 March 1907            Where Born:  144 Selsdon      │
│  Road                                                              │
│                    Name:  Amy Alice Snow                           │
│  Name and Surname of Father:  John George Snow                    │
│  Name, Surname and Maiden Surname of Mother: Annie Snow formerly Gifford │
│  Occupation of Father:  House Painter                             │
│  Informant:  Annie Snow 144 Selsdon Road                         │
└─────────────────────────────────────────────────────────────────┘
```

He looked long and hard for traces of my Grandmother Annie Gifford. He checked the birth records from 1859-1876, but we did not know where she was born, so could not identify her from these records. He searched the Croydon Directories and found a listing for George Frederick Snow at 157 Brighton Road (1911-1912) and 131 Sussex Road (1925). J. G. Snow was listed at 5 Parker Road (1914) and Dean Road (1925). This information confirmed that the people identified were the right ones.

For some time I thought a William Henry Snow listed at 16 Broadway Avenue (1912-1930) might have been my Grandfather, but this later proved not to be the case. These addresses are all a few blocks from each other and close to St. Peter's Church. My Great Grandfather J. G. Snow lived at Dean Road for 26 years until his death in 1940. My Granduncle George lived his life in Croydon for 42 years until his death in 1952. This information allowed me to create a more accurate chronology of the years before my Father's apprehension.

From 1905-1909, the Snow family was intact in Croydon. J. G. Snow (47-51), Annie Gifford/Snow (27-31), Jack (1-5), and Amy (2) lived together. According to the Vicar of St. Peter's Church, Annie (31) "ran off" with her stepson William Henry Snow (26) to have my Father in 1909. J. G. Snow (51) was left to look after Jack (4) and Amy (2). Sometime in 1913, Annie (35) returned to Croydon with my Father (4) and his Brother Bill (6m). She allegedly left my Father with J. G. Snow (55), Jack (8), and Amy (6).

The Vicar arranged his apprehension in May 1913 for reasons unknown. They kept him in the Children's Convalescent Home in Croydon from May-September, 1913. The Vicar applied to the Waifs and Strays Society to have my Father become their ward, because they could no longer pay to have him kept in this hospital.

I updated the sketchy Snow Family Tree and was inspired enough by the discovery of relatives to buy a Genealogy computer program. I thought if my Uncle Bill were still be alive at the age of 83, he would collect a pension, so I wrote the Department of Social Security.

Contributions Agency
Department of Social Security
Newcastle Upon Tyne, England   30 November 1995
Dear Mr. Snow: RE: MISSING RELATIVES
. . . Information held in the Department's records is kept in strict confidence and cannot be disclosed.
The function of this Department is primarily concerned with the maintenance of National Insurance records of the insured population and the payment of National Insurance Benefits. We do not record details of next of kin nor family histories. I am sorry I am unable to assist you.
Yours sincerely

I had hoped they might simply verify if he was alive! If he were not, I could search for a record of his death. I wrote to them again a few months later to inquire about whether British Home Children might be eligible for Social Security Benefits. They replied that he was not, as National Insurance came into effect in 1948, twenty-three years after my Father was sent to Canada. They added that they "do not get involved in cases which involve family histories or where people are unknown to each other."

In December 1995, Robin located the burial plots of J. G. Snow and Amy in Croydon. There was no Snow family plot in Croydon. He speculated that Arthur J., noted on Amy's Death Certificate might be her Son, and after a great deal of search, located him. Arthur gave me his Nephew's address in British Columbia. I wrote him but he did not reply. Arthur said Jack and his Wife had a Daughter named Eileen who had moved to Canada many years ago. She must have been the "Niece" who called my Father while hitchhiking through Fort William in 1955.

Arthur had no recollections of a Grandmother named Annie Gifford/Snow and had never heard of George Snow or William Henry

Snow. He recalled seeing a picture of my Father standing in the snow and holding his Son. This must have been a picture from St. Anthony Gold Mine my Father sent his Grandfather in 1938. Arthur believed Jack and his Wife divorced. She died in 1989. Arthur gave me the last known address at a Home for the Aged in Ireland where Jack (90) lived.

I wrote Jack in late January 1996 but did not receive a reply. He died on April 26, 1996. His Lawyer wrote that he found my letter in Jack's effects, but there was nothing in his belongings that would be of any use in my inquiries. He kindly sent me a copy of Jack's Birth Certificate. I wrote the Lawyer again and asked if he could give me a copy of Jack's obituary, but I did not receive a reply. I had hoped it might identify other Snow family members.

I went to the Calgary Public Library and found telephone and addresses of Snow's in Croydon in a telephone book. In February 1996, I made up sixteen packages and mailed them to every Snow in Croydon. Some were returned as, "Moved -- no longer here," and others did not reply. Some wrote very nice letters and offered helpful suggestions. Others gave me what they knew of their Snow ancestors. It was worth a try!

In April 1996, Robin found listings for Snow's and Gifford's in Kelly's Directories for Balham and Tooting. I highlighted the addresses on the A-Z map. They were all within a few blocks of one another. While this did not establish familial relationships, it implied some possible connections. From 1907-1914, a Herbert Gifford lived at 2 Larch Road, Balham, London -- the alleged address of my Father's place of birth. Was this where my Grandmother went to have my Father in 1909? Could Herbert be her Father, Brother, Uncle, or Cousin? Perhaps my Grandmother stayed with another of her family when she had my Uncle Bill in Tooting in 1912. These two addresses were less than a mile apart.

Robin drove around London and located some of these addresses. He found only new buildings at Larch Close. He took some interesting slides in Croydon. One was of J. G. Snow's house at 3 Dean Road, where they apprehended my Father in 1913. I expected a picture of a run-down slum but instead it was a very ordinary house on a very ordinary street. This was where Amy had her two children and where J. G. Snow died in 1940. Another was of St. Peter's Church located at the end of Dean Road. Others were of 131 Sussex Road where my Granduncle George lived all of his life, 141 Sussex Road where Jack was born, and 144 Selsdon Road where Amy was born. Robin and I both got on the Internet and our communications were enhanced.

179

In May 1996, I wrote to the National Archives of Canada to determine if there were any records of my Father in the Reserve Army Service Corps. They were unable to locate any records of his service, as they destroyed the records of Reserve Forces members when they were 70 years old.

Robin made use of a clue provided in Amy's 1980 letter to obtain important school records from Archbishop Tenison's C. E. School in Croydon. These records listed Jack and Amy as children of J. G. Snow (painter), who lived at 3 Dean Road, Croydon. Jack attended this school from 1913-1919 and left at 14 years old to work with the Croydon Gas Company. Amy attended from 1915-1921. Emily and George were listed as children of George Frederick Snow (painter), who lived at 157 Brighton Road, Croydon in 1911, and 131 Sussex Road in 1912. Emily was born on 23 November 1902 and attended this school from 1911-1917. George was born on 16 June 1904 and attended this school from 1912-1918. He left school at 14 years old to work as a Grocer's Boy.

These bits of information were very useful as they provided birth dates for George's children. Jack and Amy must have attended some other school in Croydon before this one. J. G. Snow (55) tried to look after Jack, Amy, and my Father. He hired a young girl to look after my Father while he looked for work and worked. When he was unable to pay for a sitter, Jack took Amy and my Father to school with him. When they apprehended my Father in April-May, 1913, Jack would have been 7 years 10 months old, Amy 6 years 2 months old, and my Father 3 years 6 months old. Amy wrote in 1980, that my Father was fostered out because he "was not old enough for school" and J. G. Snow could not get anyone to look after him through the day.

What was London like in 1913 when they apprehended my Father? Charles Booth -- of Salvation Army fame -- categorized 909,000 Londoners into eight income classes. The fifth class (337,000) earned 22-30 shillings a week. This barely provided them with enough to eat regularly. The fourth class (129,000) was poor and needed their children's wages to raise the family income above the poverty line. The third class (75,000) was poorer still. The second class (100,000) was very poor and earned 18-21 shillings a week. The first class (11,000) led "savage" lives. He described them as people who degraded whatever they touched, and labelled them as incapable of improvement (Thomas 195). According to this classification, and the Children's Society report of his earnings, J. G. Snow (55) was just above the poverty line in 1913.

Many parents paid neighbours to look after their preschool children in these times. The working poor turned to their relatives for help and lived together to ease their financial pressures. Widows often had to reluctantly turn their youngest children over to the child-care agencies when they became destitute. Children from 6-12 years old were enlisted as caretakers of their younger siblings. In 1905, 20% of all children in the poorer districts of London worked for wages. Only 10% of all these children attended school regularly. Parents sent younger children to school with older school-age children to get them out the way. In 1912, there were more underage children (3-5 years old) in the elementary schools than children of legal age (Parr 15-20). My Father was one of thousands of children whom older siblings took to school with them.

In 1905, a Headmaster of a London school of 400 children reported these conditions to the County Council. The clothing of 280 children (70%) consisted of a ragged coat with scarcely any clothing underneath. They tied rags to their feet. These were their shoes. The clothing of 120 children (30%) was "insufficient to retain animal heat." Two hundred children (50%) had "poor but passable clothing." This consisted of a ragged suit with some underclothing. Forty boys (10%) were very dirty and "verminous," and 120 (30%) were dirty but not verminous. Another group of 120 boys (30%) was "passably clean for boys" and 40 boys (10%) were above average in cleanliness. In 1906, Health Nurses inspected 120,000 London school children, and announced 55% of them clean, 7% partially clean, and 37% verminous. They examined 40,000 infants and found 67% of them "verminous" (Thomas 195).

The Victorian attitudes towards the poor persisted into the early 1900's when my Father was apprehended. They believed poor children were the "raw materials" that would form "the dangerous classes." They believed child deportation would eradicate the children's "memories of pauperism," and would save them from becoming "as corrupted as their parents" (Parr 33).

The British Child Deportation Scheme was in full swing in 1913 and had been operating for almost 30 years. The child-care organizations had already deported tens of thousands of young children. Their solution to the problem of underage children attending school was apprehension and deportation. Once out of sight, they were permanently out of mind. The organizations propagated the myth that children would have a better life in Canada then they ever would have in England. In my Father's case, the clergy acted as procurers of children for the scheme.

The East Surrey Family History Society published an article I wrote about my search (Snow P. 1996). I received a lot of interesting mail as a result. A woman in Australia wrote on behalf of her friend whom the Kingsley Fairbridge organization deported to Australia in 1934. Her friend had four sisters. One stayed in England and another was deported to Australia. Her two other sisters were deported to Canada in the early

1930's. The woman who wrote was instrumental in helping to reunite her friend with her Sister in England after 54 years. I could only pass along her inquiry to David Lorente, whom I am sure was able to help her. How many people all over the world are still searching for their siblings deported to different countries? Why does it take so long?

One man sent me an e-mail offering to search Certificates on his lunch hour as he worked close to the Public Records Office. A woman went to a Family History Centre in London and painstakingly searched their microfiches for every possible Annie Gifford. The list she mailed me was vital in obtaining my Grandmother's Birth Certificate. How kind these people were!

My Daughters Charlotte and Elizabeth gave me a copy of <u>Empty Cradles,</u> a current map of London, and a book of poems for Father's Day. My first thought was that the map was to help me locate relatives' addresses. I realized I was to use it when I went to London to *meet* my relatives. I had occasional thoughts of perhaps someday going to London to do this. It suddenly became a goal. Both announced if they married, that they would retain their Snow surname. I was very touched. I hoped they would not marry men with surnames such as "Job" or "Storm." I went for a long walk and thought of my Father on Father's Day.

Chapter 4: The Unearthing of Relatives in England

Robin found Birth Certificates for J. G. Snow's First Wife (my Great Grandmother), his Sons William Henry Snow (my Grandfather), George Frederick Snow (my Granduncle), and Daughter Alice Emily Snow (my Grandaunt).

CERTIFIED COPY OF AN ENTRY OF BIRTH

Registration District: Wandsworth, Battersea   County: County of Surrey
When Born: 30 October 1857   Where Born: 33 Bolingbroke Road
Name: **Emily Jane Cheer**
Name and Surname of Father: James Cheer
Name, Surname, Maiden Surname of Mother: Jane Cheer formerly Hollingshead
Occupation of Father: Labourer, Colour Factory.
Informant: "X" The mark of Jane Cheer

My Great Great-Grandmother Jane Cheer signed her Daughter's Birth Certificate with an "X." This was typical of the times in which 40% of the British population in 1850 could not sign their names. Half of all children 5-15 years attended school in the 1850's. Mandatory schooling for children only came into effect in the 1870's. When the 1881 Census was taken, 20% of the population could not sign their names.

Robin found J. G. Snow's First Marriage Certificate. He literally married "the girl next door," as they lived at 100 and 112 Brandon Street, Walworth, Surrey. This certificate identified my Great Great-Grandfather as John Allen Snow, and determined J. G. Snow's birth date as 1858.

Robin was unable to find a Birth Certificate for J. G. Snow. The area of the search shifted from Croydon to Wandsworth.

CERTIFIED COPY OF AN ENTRY OF MARRIAGE

Registration District: St. Saviour.
Marriage solemnized at St. John's Church, Walworth, Surrey
When married: 11 June 1878.
  Name and surname: **John George Snow** (21) and **Emily Jane Cheer** (20)
Rank or Profession: Railway Policeman
Residence at the time of the marriage: 112 Brandon Street and 100 Brandon Street.
Father's name and surname: John Allen Snow and James Cheer.
Married in the Parish Church. Witnesses: Thomas Goman, Elizabeth J. Hopgood.

```
CERTIFIED COPY OF AN ENTRY OF BIRTH
Registration District: Wandsworth, Battersea  County: County of Surrey
When Born: 9 December 1879          Where Born: 11 St. Philip's Cottages
                    Name:  George Frederick Snow
Name and Surname of Father:  John George Snow
Name, Surname, Maiden Surname of Mother:  Emily Jane Snow formerly Cheer
Occupation of Father:  Railway Policeman                Informant: E. J.
Snow
```

My Granduncle George's lineage fell into place when Robin found his Marriage Certificate and Birth Certificates of his seven children. His first two children were born in Tooting in 1902 and 1904. Perhaps J. G. Snow and his two sons lived in Tooting in 1902-1904, and when he moved to Croydon in 1905, they followed.

From 1911-1912, his first two children attended Archbishop Tenison's School in Croydon with Amy and Jack. His other five children were born in Croydon but apparently four of them died in infancy. I wrote to the last known addresses of some descendants of my Granduncle George, but these were out of date.

```
CERTIFIED COPY OF AN ENTRY OF BIRTH
Registration District: Wandsworth, Battersea  County: County of Surrey
When Born: 3 August 1881             Where Born: 31 Shirley Grove
                    Name: Alice Emily Snow
Name and Surname of Father:  John George Snow
Name, Surname, Maiden Surname of Mother:  Emily Jane Snow formerly Cheer
Occupation of Father: Railway Ticket Examiner
Informant:  Emily Jane Snow
```

I learned nothing more about my Grandaunt Alice Emily Snow. She likely married, had children, and created another line of descendants, as did my Granduncle George.

```
CERTIFIED COPY OF AN ENTRY OF BIRTH
Registration District: Wandsworth, Battersea  County: County of Surrey
When Born: 29 April 1883             Where Born: 23 Shirley Grove
                    Name:  William Henry Snow
Name and Surname of Father:  John George Snow
Name, Surname, Maiden Surname of Mother:  Emily Jane Snow formerly Cheer
Occupation of Father: Railway Ticket Collector
Informant:  E. J. Snow
```

My Grandfather was finally confirmed as a real person! The paper chase quickly became a people-search. I was thrilled to be able to simply write to anyone to whom I was related, but I was somewhat apprehensive if my letters would be answered.

My first contact with a Snow relative occurred in June 1996 when I wrote to a Second Cousin -- a descendant of my Granduncle George Frederick Snow. She kindly sent me photographs of my Granduncle and Great Grandfather. Another Second Cousin sent laminated family photographs of some of the George Frederick Snow Line.

The initial letters from these people were overwhelmingly kind. People offered to help with my search in any way they could.

Robin found a Death Certificate for my Great Grandmother Emily Jane Cheer/Snow. She and J. G. Snow had only three children before she died in 1904 at the age of 46. She was 22, 24, and 26 years old when her first three children were born in 1879, 1881, and 1883. It is possible she had more children in 1885, 1887, and 1889, when she was 28-32 but none were located.

CERTIFIED COPY OF AN ENTRY OF DEATH
Registration District: Wandsworth, Streatham County Borough of London
When died: 6 February 1904
Name: Emily Jane Snow
Where died: 27 Chetwode Road, Upper Tooting Sex: Female Age: 46 years
Occupation: Wife of John George Snow Decorator (Journeyman)
Informant: John George. Snow Widower

J. G. Snow married my Grandmother Annie Gifford six months after his First Wife died. He made himself younger by one year and she made herself older by four years on their Marriage Certificate. This created an age gap of only 15 years between them. This was apparently acceptable to the Vicar of the Parish Church in Tooting, whereas an actual age gap of 20 years may not have been.

Vicar Reeve was incorrect in stating that my Grandmother was nine years older than my Grandfather was, as the difference was only five years. J. G. Snow was 20 years older than my Grandmother Annie Gifford/Snow was when she was pregnant with my Father by her stepson William Henry Snow.

The Vicar did not mention the disparity in their ages. Instead, she described J. G. Snow as the "rightful husband" who had been so "wronged."

```
╔══════════════════════════════════════════════════════════════╗
║            CERTIFIED COPY OF AN ENTRY OF MARRIAGE              ║
║ Registration District: Tooting.                                ║
║ Marriage Solemnized in The Parish Church in the Parish of Tooting ║
║ When married: 1 August 1904                                    ║
║ Name and surname: John George Snow (45) and Annie Gifford (30) ║
║ Rank or Profession: House Decorator                            ║
║ Residence at the time of the marriage: 17 Gasham St., 2 Rookstone Road ║
║ Father's name and surname: John Allen Snow (Deceased), William Gifford ║
║ (Carpenter)                                                    ║
║ Married in the Parish Church. Witnesses: William Gifford, Catherine Gifford. ║
╚══════════════════════════════════════════════════════════════╝
```

My Grandfather William Henry Snow (21) married Agnes Maud Moore (21) three months after his Mother died. I do not know if they had any children, although there was an Agnes Snow born in Croydon in 1905.

```
╔══════════════════════════════════════════════════════════════╗
║            CERTIFIED COPY OF AN ENTRY OF MARRIAGE              ║
║ Registration District: Tooting.                                ║
║ Marriage solemnized at The Register Office in the Parish of Tooting ║
║ When married: 7 May 1904                                       ║
║ Name and surname: William Henry Snow (21) and Agnes Maud Moore (21) ║
║ Rank or Profession: Journeyman Carpenter                       ║
║ Residence at the time of the marriage: 27 Chetwode Road        ║
║ Father's name and surname: John G. Snow, House Painter. Samuel Handle ║
║ Moore, Cornet Player                                           ║
║ Witnesses: Edward G. Hartland, Eliza Cheer                     ║
╚══════════════════════════════════════════════════════════════╝
```

The most shocking news came when Robin found Birth Certificates for my Father's two Sisters and one Brother. My Grandparents stayed together for at least 11 years after my Father was born and had three other children while he was in the foster home in Rumburgh. Their first Daughter was born just before the beginning of WWI and may have been named after my Grandaunt Lilian Gifford/Keers. Their second Daughter was born just before the end of WWI.

```
╔══════════════════════════════════════════════════════════════╗
║             CERTIFIED COPY OF AN ENTRY OF BIRTH               ║
║ Registration District: Wandsworth, Battersea County: County of London ║
║ When Born: 15 March 1914          Where Born: 33 Meyrick Road  ║
║              Name: Violet Lilian Beatrice Snow                 ║
║ Name and Surname of Father: William Henry Snow                 ║
║ Name, Surname, Maiden Surname of Mother: Annie Snow formerly Gifford ║
║ Occupation of Father: Journeyman Carpenter  Informant: Annie Snow ║
║             CERTIFIED COPY OF AN ENTRY OF BIRTH               ║
║ Registration District: Wandsworth, Battersea County: County of London ║
╚══════════════════════════════════════════════════════════════╝
```

When Born: 22 August 1918   Where Born: 7 Abyssinia Road
                    Name: **Gladys Elsie Snow**
Name and Surname of Father: William Henry Snow
Name, Surname, Maiden Surname of Mother: Annie Snow formerly Gifford
Occupation of Father: Journeyman Carpenter
Informant: Annie Snow

CERTIFIED COPY OF AN ENTRY OF BIRTH
Registration District: Wandsworth, Battersea County: County of London
When Born: 10 December 1920   Where Born: 7 Abyssinia Road
                    Name: **Reginald William Snow**
Name and Surname of Father: William Henry Snow
Name, Surname, Maiden Surname of Mother: Annie Snow formerly Gifford
Occupation of Father: Journeyman Carpenter
Informant: Annie Snow

Robin found Death Certificates for my Grandfather and Grandmother. Peggy Snow was listed as informant and William Henry Snow's Daughter on his Death Certificate. My Uncle Reg was listed as informant on my Grandmother's Death Certificate.

CERTIFIED COPY OF AN ENTRY OF DEATH
Registration District: Hampstead, Metro Borough of Hampstead
When died: 24 January 1959
                    Name: William Henry Snow
Where died: North Western Hospital, Hampstead Sex: Male Age: 75 years
Occupation: Carpenter and Joiner (Retired)
Informant: Peggy Snow, Daughter

CERTIFIED COPY OF AN ENTRY OF DEATH
Registration District: Lambeth, Metro Borough of Lambeth
When died: 10 August 1954
                    Name: Annie Snow
Where died: Lambeth Hospital Sex: Female Age: 76 years
Occupation: Widow of William Henry Snow Carpenter
Informant: R. W. Snow

Thanks to Robin's tremendous sleuthing skills, I was able to contact my Father's family. None of his Siblings or their Families knew of him. I had not determined whether Uncle Bill (84) was alive. Aunt Vi (82) was alive, and although I did not speak with her, I obtained a remarkable account from her children -- my Cousins James and Gladys. Aunt Gladys (76) did not answer my letter. I spoke with one of her children -- my Cousin Ann W. My Uncle Reg died on 13 March 1984. Ironically, my

Father wrote a letter to the Children's Society in early March and received a letter from them dated 13 March 1984 -- the day his Brother died. He wrote his final letter to them on 31 March 1984. I wonder if he had some unusual premonition about his unknown Brother Reg.

I phoned Reg's widow -- my Aunt Freda. When I talked with her about my Uncle Reg, it was like talking to my Mother about my Father. Both spoke of their Husbands in such loving terms. She said he would have been a marvellous Father if they had children. As my Mother described my Father, she described Reg as "lost and alone" when she met him. I am grateful these two women recognized the goodness of these two Brothers and chose them to love all their lives.

The year ended well, with a tremendous conclusion to an intense search for family. I was astounded by one unanticipated aspect of the search. I never would have thought I would be in a position of clarifying relationships and family history for my relatives in England.

I had hoped that if Snow relatives existed in England, I would eventually contact one who would be quite knowledgeable and would ask me, "What do you want to know of the Snow's?" It was quite the opposite. I informed *them* of our common Uncles, Aunts, Cousins, and Grandparents.

Robin suggested it would be a lovely thing for all the Snow descendants to unite in England and to have some sort of memorial for my Father. What a kind thought! What an extraordinary man! My Siblings were somewhat overwhelmed with this family information. We had all lived without having Snow relatives, so it took some time for the information to be processed from names into actual living people. My Mother is extremely happy to have her in-laws identified.

The fall of 1996 marked the second anniversary of my Father's death. I was quite satisfied with the search results to date. At the same time, I was left with the knowledge of the awful legacy of the British Child Deportation Scheme. Why is this aspect of Canadian history so unknown? Must it take a lifetime of searching for the British Home Children to learn who they are? What was to become of their millions of Canadian descendants? Were all of our efforts going to be stymied as well? Just as my Father searched all his life for his Parents, I spent years searching for my Grandparents. Will the next generation spend years searching for their Great-Grandparents? When will this nonsense stop? I wondered what I could do to help others learn who they are, and discover their British roots.

Chapter 5: Assembling the Pieces of the Puzzle

In February 1997, I discovered many Genealogical Websites on the Internet and posted what information I had about the Snow family. I joined the Kent Family History Society once it was established that the Snow family had their origins there. In March 1997, David Lorente searched his indices and confirmed an entry for my Father. It stated he arrived in Halifax on April 13, 1925, and that his birth date was September 17, 1909. Thomas Keeley in 1942 told him he was born on this day and this appeared to be the source of this information.

In July 1997, I tried to find information about the Children's Convalescent Home in Croydon. I hoped to obtain his medical records. It was a Private Charitable Institution supported by voluntary contributions, but not affiliated with child-care organizations. It was converted to a Convalescent Home for Soldiers in 1919. In 1920 it was unoccupied and was taken over by local authorities and transformed into a Relief Station for the unemployed. There are no records. Why was my Father hospitalized here rather than in a free hospital? Why did the Vicar of St. Peter's Church pay to keep him there?

The fall of 1997 marked the third anniversary of my Father's death. In November 1997, I posted a message on a Genealogical Website on the Internet. I asked if anyone had any information about Rumburgh, Halesworth, Suffolk. It was too small to be included in travel literature I ordered from Suffolk. I would have been content to learn of its size.

A woman in Suffolk took it upon herself to seek out his school records in Ipswich. She photocopied school records, transcribed them, and sent them to me as e-mail. This took considerable time and I was very grateful she did this. These records provided me a picture of what it was like for my Father to attend school as a "Waif" in a small village. She drove to Rumburgh and photographed the school he attended and the foster home where he lived from 4-12 years old. She located a class picture of him from 1919! This is the only photograph I have of my Father before he was 20 years old. I examined this picture for hours with a magnifying glass and could not identify him. After I studied the photograph, I had a nap. I had a very unusual dream where my Father clearly said, "I'm standing in front of the teacher!" I woke up and had another look at the picture. I found him.

Christmas 1997 was remarkable because for the first time I exchanged Christmas cards with "my people." The initial telephone contacts were delightful. The Kent Family History Society published my Banished to Canada article (Snow P. 1997). I received a considerable amount of e-mail when I published this article on the Internet. I was encouraged by the supportive messages I received from all over the world, and was somewhat surprised people were so moved. My Mother was quite ill from December 1997 - January 1998. In February, she fell in her apartment and was not discovered until the next morning. She may have suffered a minor stroke, and was unable to reach the 'Panic Button.' She was hospitalized for two weeks. The last time she had been in a hospital was when my youngest Sister was born over 40 years earlier. It was quite an experience for her but she slowly regained her strength and was discharged from hospital. My search for relatives took on a new urgency.

In March 1998, David Lorente sent me the required forms to apply for information from Barnardo's about my Uncle Reg. I forwarded these to Aunt Freda, who authorized the release of his records to me. Barnardo's reply was very disconcerting.

Barnardos   03 March 1998

Dear Mr. Snow

Thank you for your recent enquiry concerning your relative who may have been in Barnardo's care.

Since the BBC documentaries were shown in August 1997 we have received nearly 1,400 enquiries from people seeking information from Barnardo's records. We are also still working with a considerable number of enquiries dating back to the earlier BBC programmes shown in July 1995.

In order to manage this enormous workload we have taken the very difficult decision to respond only to those enquiries which came from people who were themselves in Barnardo's care and who are looking for information to help them make sense of their early life experiences and to help them trace family members. This means that for the forseeable [sic] future we will be unable to research and respond to enquiries such as yours about a deceased relative.

We know that you will be disappointed by this letter and we hope that you will understand that this decision was not made lightly, but rather as a response to the vast number of enquiries from those people who are alive today and are actively seeking their family background information.

Your enquiry will remain on our records and if at any point in the future we find that we are in a position to address enquiries such as yours we will write and let you know.

We would ask therefore that you keep us informed of any change of address.

Yours sincerely

They referred to my inquiry about my Uncle Reg as someone "who may have been in Barnardo's care." They are still processing inquiries since the showing of <u>The Leaving of Liverpool</u> documentary in 1995. When it was shown again in 1997, they had another 1,400 inquiries. They will only process inquiries from people who were themselves in their care -- not relatives. They could not respond to my inquiry about a "deceased relative" for the "foreseeable future." They would keep my inquiry on their records. If, "at any point in the future," they might be able to address it, they would contact me. They asked me to keep them informed of any change of address. They did not even bother to confirm whether or when my Uncle Reg was in their care. How difficult would this have been for them to do?

I imagine they were flooded with inquiries from Australia but I did not feel any sympathy for them. The scandal revealed by the Child Migrants Trust was bound to set off a backlash. I was discouraged to learn they had a three-year backlog of inquiries.

If my Father was alive at the age of 89 today, would Barnardo's ask him for his non-existent Birth Certificate to verify his relationship to his deceased Brother Reg? Would they tell him they could only accommodate enquiries from people who were themselves in their care, and tell him they cannot respond to inquiries about "deceased relatives?" Would the fact he inquired about his Brother make any difference to them?

If my Uncle Reg were alive at the age of 82, would they tell him they were preoccupied with Australian inquiries and he would have to wait a few years for a response? Would they tell him they had an inquiry from his Brother -- my Father?

If my Aunt Freda wrote for her Husband's records, what would they her? Would they tell her they cannot respond to inquiries about "deceased spouses?" Would they tell her they had an inquiry from her Nephew Perry Snow?

By now, I was sceptical enough to believe they would stonewall *any* inquiry regardless of who made the inquiry. I decided these bureaucracies were not going to change. The will, is -- as it has always been -- simply not there. The fall of 1998 marked the fourth anniversary of my Father's death and the fifth anniversary of the beginning of my search. Barnardo's response was the final straw.

In December 1988, the Select Committee on Health reported to the British House of Commons the results of their inquiry into the Welfare of Former Child Migrants (House of Commons 1998). They described child migration as a costly mistake that had caused irreversible and irrevocable damage. One recommendation they made was that the child-care organizations create a central database that inquirers could use as their first point of contact. All former child migrants and their descendants should have immediate access to files that contain relevant information about their backgrounds.

They concluded all the governments and child-care agencies involved are responsible for helping the "surviving casualties." They did not clarify who might compel these organizations to comply. The British government was encouraged to establish a Travel Fund so former child migrants could visit their families in Britain. Child-care organizations were advised to provide free counselling services when family reunions occurred. Canadian, New Zealand, and Australian governments should provide financial support to organizations representing former child migrants.

They recommended the Child Migrants Trust should be adequately funded by the British government. The Child Migrants Trust applied to the British Department of Health for a grant of £110,000 ($245,300) in 1990. They again applied for a grant of £92,000 ($205,160) for the next two years. They received £20,000 ($44,600) in 1990 and nothing for the next two years. From 1993, their funding was limited to £20,000-25,000 ($44,600-$55,750).

In 1992, the Child Migrants Trust asked the British Government to match the £23,000 ($51,290) per year provided by the Australian Government. Their application was refused (Humphreys 224). David Lorente's organization receives no funding from either the British or Canadian government. He made submissions to the Select Committee on Health on behalf of the British Home Children in Canada. He and his Wife Kay paid their own way to attend, but Canadian interests were hopelessly overshadowed by New Zealand and Australian interests -- even though 100,000 of the 150,000 children were deported to Canada.

The British Library gave the Children's Society a grant of £10,000 ($22,300) to catalogue and index the first 6,000 children's files from 1882-1896 (Kohli, 1999). How will this allow descendants of the British Home Children to readily access information? Why would they not catalogue records of the *last* children to be deported to Canada in the 1930's? Some of these people might still be alive. But, perhaps that is the point -- they are still alive.

By beginning with the oldest records, they will ensure that the project will take many years, and the last British Home Child will be dead. This will allow them to tell the descendants they "are awfully busy with cataloguing records from the 1800's," and will not get around to the most recent records for years to come. They can also tell them, "Inquiries from New Zealand and Australia take precedence over inquiries from

Canada." Inquirers will likely receive a reply such as, "Please leave your name and number and we may get back to you at some point in the foreseeable future."

The fall of 1998 marked the fourth anniversary of my Father's death. In December 1998, the British government announced they would provide $2.6 million to former British Child Migrants to reunite them with their families. They did not apologize for the child deportation scheme, but called it "misguided." They offered their 'sincere regrets' and added that further compensation would be "inappropriate" (CBC News 1998). Who "misguided" the scheme? Was it the Royal Family who has been patrons of the child-care organizations for over 100 years?

In April 1999, the British Health Minister announced that £1 million ($2.23 million) was available to Canadian Home Children to reunite with close family in Britain (British High Commission 1999). The Canadian Government did not match this offer. As always, they assume no responsibility for the British Home Children whom they imported to Canada. The younger generation of British Home Children deported to Australia will likely benefit from this Support Fund. The fund will be administered, and applications processed, by International Social Services. A Central Information Index is to be compiled by the National Council for Voluntary Child-care Organizations (NCVCCO) in the fall of 1999. I hope it is comprehensive and all the organizations involved in the British Child Deportation Scheme freely contribute their information.

My experiences with the Children's Society and Barnardo's cause me to believe this index will not have any impact upon the speed with which the organizations reply to inquiries. They do not want the information in the case files to be released. If I were to contact the keepers of this index, all they would tell me is to contact the Children's Society. They would handle my inquiry the same way they did in 1994 -- with obfuscation. Unless the index is cross-referenced, inquirers will have to contact each organization separately for each inquiry.

Many conditions have to be met before someone can benefit from the Travel Fund (British High Commission 1999). British Home Children themselves will be the first -- and perhaps only -- to qualify. They must prove they have traced a close family relative (Mother, Father, Brother, Sister, Aunt or Uncle), and that they intend to meet for the first time. The few surviving elderly British Home Children deported to Canada are in their 80's and 90's. No one knows how many are alive. David Lorente estimated that there may be only 100 and could not say how many were too infirm to travel. They obviously have outlived their Parents, Uncles and Aunts, and many have outlived their Siblings.

Why is the Travel Fund not available for British Relatives to travel to Canada? Surely, it would be easier for this younger group to travel to Canada than it would be for the elderly British Home Children to travel to England. Why is it not available for British Home Children to reunite with their Siblings in Canada?

If my Father were alive today, he would be 90 years old and too infirm to travel. I do not know how he would prove his relationship to his two surviving Sisters without a Birth Certificate. He would have to prove they planned to meet for the first time. His sole surviving Sister Gladys (80) did not reply to my correspondence. He would not have anyone else who would meet the criteria of "close family member."

Spouses, widows, and widowers do not qualify, because the "fund is not unlimited," and is to be used for those children whose parents and siblings are alive. The younger generation of British Home Children deported to Australia have a higher probability of having living parents and siblings. It is sad that spouses of the British Home Children deported to Canada would be so ignored. My Mother (86) would not qualify for the Travel Fund. She will never meet her newly identified Sisters-in-law, Nephews, and Nieces.

First generation descendants, such as me, will not likely qualify for the Support Fund to visit gravesides, birthplaces, and Cousins. If we were to apply, our applications would be considered "sympathetically" and "on their individual merit." I can envision a letter of response to our applications: "The Support Fund has considered your application on its individual merit. It was viewed sympathetically, but regretfully, the Fund is not unlimited, and granting your application may result in insufficient funding for the priority group."

Our Grandparents are deceased. Few of our Aunts and Uncles are alive. Our Cousins do not fit the criterion of "close family relatives." The aged British Home Children and their descendants will have a short time to trace relatives, as money will only be available for three years. The Travel Fund administrators argued that "one or two individuals" might trace relatives after this time, but this is insufficient reason to keep the fund available on an "unlimited basis" (British High Commission 1999).

The International Social Service will determine who will qualify for the Support Fund. No one has a particular right to the fund, and no one has the right to appeal a refusal. Applicants will have to submit to a "means test" and this, along with their partner's financial status, will determine their eligibility. I sincerely hope that this fund will benefit the last generation of children deported to Australia. It does little for the surviving British Home Children in Canada, less for their spouses, and nothing for their descendants.

The literature describing the British Child Deportation Scheme referred to the child-care institutions as "charitable organizations." When it comes to providing vital personal information to the British Home Children and their descendants, these organizations have proven themselves to be most uncharitable. They have been -- and continue to be -- most cruel.

THE GOLDEN LADDER OF CHARITY

The first and lowest level of charity, is to give, but with reluctance or regret. This is the gift of the hand, but not of the heart.

The second is to give cheerfully, but not proportionately to the distress of the sufferer.

The third is to give cheerfully, and proportionately, but not until we are solicited.

The fourth is to give cheerfully, proportionately, and even unsolicited; but to put it in the poor man's hand, thereby exciting in him the painful emotion of shame.

The fifth is to give charity in such a way that the distressed may know the benefactor and receive his bounty without being known to him.

The sixth which rises still higher, is to know the objects of our bounty but remain unknown to them.

The seventh is still more meretorious, namely, to bestow charity in such a way that the benefactor may not know the relieved person, nor he the name of his benefactor.

The eighth and most meretorious of all is to anticipate charity by preventing poverty; namely, to assist a reduced brother . . . so that he may earn an honest livelihood and not be forced to the dreadful alternative of holding up his hand for charity (Maimonides 1135-1204).

Many people asked me how my Father might have felt to learn of his unknown past. Far too many assumed that perhaps "there were things best not known." A better question to have asked was, "Why did he never know who he was?" The answer is now quite obvious. The Children's Society did not want him to know who he was.

My Father had a unique identity as someone's Son, Brother, Grandson, Nephew, and Cousin until he was four years old. They took this identity away from him, gave him a new one, and withheld his own from him. They are thieves. They stole my Father's identity from him.

In <u>Othello</u> (Act 3 Sc. 3), *Shakespeare* wrote:

Good name in man and woman, dear my lord,
Is the immediate jewel of their souls:
Who steals my purse steals trash; 'tis something, nothing;
'T was mine, 't is his, and has been slave to thousands;
But he that filches from me my good name
Robs me of that which not enriches him

195

And makes me poor indeed.[18]

Since he died before I made these discoveries, I can only speculate how he might have felt to learn of them. He simply would have been satisfied to know that he belonged to, and was part of a family. He could have accepted and lived with *any* factual answers to his lifelong questions about who he was. He found it difficult to live with only unanswered questions. The imagination -- if left to its own devices -- tends to follow a negative path. His was fuelled by visions associated with the words, "Abandoned, deserted, and illegitimate." Throughout my search, I heard my Parents softly whisper, "Find the answers." As I discovered the truth, I heard them say, "Tell the story." When I found his family, their voices were louder, and I heard them say, "Write the book!" Was all of the information I discovered simply "too much -- too late" for my Father? Perhaps it is never too late.

PART III: A STOLEN IDENTITY RECLAIMED

I would have dearly loved to have met with my Parents and shared what I had discovered. It was not to be. Not only did the Children's Society rob my Father of his identity, they also robbed me of the opportunity of returning it to him before he died. This book could, and should have ended, with a description of how I returned his stolen identity to him. I can only describe the visit we should have had in the summer of 1994.

A Hypothetical Reunion, Thunder Bay, Ontario, 1994

My Wife and I flew to Thunder Bay with binders full of material to share with my Parents. I could not have made this one trip alone. Mom (81) suggested we go to Chippewa Park for a picnic to review all the material. She packed a lunch of sandwiches and tea. She was ready and waiting at the lobby of her building long before the arranged time. I had become accustomed to saying, "It is my way." Now I say, "It is my way -- and the way of my people." She smiled and we hugged each other. An ever-present twinkle gleamed in her eyes. She left her walker behind and carefully made her way to the car as she leaned on our arms.

Dad (85) waited in his wheelchair outside the entrance of the Home for the Aged. He was dressed in his jacket and tie. He never missed an opportunity to be outside in the fresh air. He used his cane to make his way to the car, and carefully manoeuvred the walk on his artificial leg. I placed his wheelchair in the trunk. They were both frail, but rarely complained. They greeted each other with a kiss and, "Hello, Dearie!" We drove by our former home of so many years -- just for a look. We drove by "The Loop" where we children waited for the bus to take us to Chippewa Park. We admired Mount McKay as we crossed the Swing Bridge over the Kaministiqua River. The loose boards on the bridge rattled and thumped as they always did.

My Wife and I helped Mom from the car at Chippewa Park. Mom took her arm to steady herself for the short walk to the picnic table. Dad insisted on walking with his cane rather than sit in the wheelchair. He raised his chin and proudly walked to the picnic table as he leaned on my arm for support. Neither of them pressed to learn what I had discovered. They were very patient, as they had waited all of their lives to learn anything of his background. We ate and reminisced about the happy times we had as a family at Chippewa Park. We absorbed the view of the Sleeping Giant. The Lake Superior waves pounded up against the rocks of the breakwater and echoed memories of sunny days, warm breezes, picnics, and laughter.

Perry (50), Gert (81), Fred (85), Thunder Bay, Ontario, 1994

Dad finally said, "Now, Perry, what have you found out about your Father? Did you find out who I am?" Mom held his hand in anticipation. I said, "Yes, Dad, I discovered who you are. I found your stolen identity. I'm here to return it to you." He asked, "What do you mean, when you say my identity was stolen?" I replied, "The Children's Society had information about your family they withheld from you. They tried to withhold this information from me." He frowned and said, "I always suspected they knew more than what they ever told me."

"We need to thank a 'kind stranger' in England who made this project his own. Without his tremendous dedication, I could not have done this. Many other people were helpful. They provided me with information I would not have obtained from agencies, organizations, and bureaucracies." We were silent for a few moments, while we expressed our "Thanks" to these unmet friends.

"Dad, I only set out to discover who your Parents were, but I learned almost too much about this thing called the British Child Emigration Scheme. It was a scheme all right." He looked intrigued. I returned his stolen identity to him by relating this story.

Your Great-Grandparents: John Allen Snow and Mary _____

Your Great Grandfather John Allen Snow was baptized at St. John the Baptist Church in Margate, Kent in 1831. He was the eldest of six children. You had three Great Grandaunts and two Great Granduncles. John Allen Snow was a Mechanic when he was 20 years old and a House Painter when he was 49 years old. He married your Great Grandmother Mary Ann _____ in 1858 and had eight children who were born in Canterbury and Margate, Kent. Your Grandfather John George Snow was the eldest born in August 1858 in Margate, Kent. I was not able to find his Birth Certificate. You had four Granduncles and three Grandaunts. Your youngest Granduncle and two Grandaunts may have died at young ages. In the 1870-1880's, one in four children did not survive their first year of life, and adult life expectancy was about 45 years old.

Dad said, "Wait a minute. What do you mean -- John George Snow was my Grandfather? The Church of England told me he was my Father." I replied, "I know what they led you to believe, but it is not true." He said, "If he was not my Father, then Jack and Amy were not my Brother and Sister. Somehow, I just knew they weren't! Who is my Father, then?" I said, "I know it is confusing, but we'll get to that."

Your Grandparents: John George Snow and Emily Jane Cheer

Your Grandfather J. G. Snow ran off to sea and sailing ships when he was 14 years old in 1872. The conditions on these ships were terrible, and he jumped ship when he was 20 years old in 1878. He then worked on the railroad in London and lived at 112 Brandon Street, Walworth, Surrey. Your Grandmother Emily Jane Cheer lived at 100 Brandon Street. When they married, you inherited "Cheer" relatives, who originated in Drayton, Berkshire as early as the 18th Century. There is a Chiers Drive in Drayton that may be named after them. Your Grandmother Emily was the middle child of your Great Grandfather James Cheer who was born in 1831 in Chelsea, Middlesex, and your Great-grandmother Jane Hollingshead who was born in Fulham, Middlesex.

You had three Great-granduncles and two Granduncles. J. G. Snow (21) married his First Wife Emily Cheer (20) on 11 June 1878 in Walworth. Your Uncle George Frederick Snow was born 9 December 1879 in Battersea, Surrey. From 1878-1883, your Grandfather J. G. Snow (20-23) worked for the Railroad as a Ticket Examiner, Ticket Collector, and Policeman. Your Aunt Alice Emily Snow was born on 3 August 1881 at 31 Shirley Grove, Wandsworth, Battersea. I know nothing more of her. She likely married around 1900 and had children -- your Cousins. Your Granduncle George Frederick Snow (19) worked as a letter carrier and lived with your Grandfather J. G. Snow when she was born.

Your Father William Henry Snow was born on 29 April 1883, at 23 Shirley Grove, Wandsworth, Battersea. He was named after your Granduncle (1868) of the same name.

Dad said, "You're telling me that this guy was my Father?"

I replied, "The Waifs and Strays Society led you to believe J. G. Snow was both your Guardian and your Father. In all of your correspondence with them, they never identified him as your Grandfather. Nor did they identify him as the Father of William Henry Snow -- your actual Father. In 1929, they said your Father was *believed* to be William Henry Snow."

He said, "I don't recall that letter. In 1929, I rode boxcars and did not have any address."

I said, "In 1931, they referred to this letter, but never mentioned William Henry Snow's name. They gave you J. G. Snow's address and identified him as your Guardian. In all the correspondence over all the years, William Henry Snow's name never appeared again. Each time you wrote them, and said J. G. Snow was your Father, they never corrected this for you. They could have told you much, much more about yourself. They withheld a lot of vital information from you. They lied to you."

"I'm not surprised -- they lied to me all of my life about my family," he said.

I replied, "In 1942, Thomas Keeley told you that your Mother was Annie Gifford and your Father was John George Snow. He knew the truth."

"I trusted Tom Keeley -- all of us kids did. He was all we had in Canada," he said. Mom reached out and grasped his hand. His face betrayed a mix of joy and pain when he said, "They had the nerve to call *me* a 'Bastard!'"

Your Grandparents appear not to have had any more children. Women usually had children two years apart, so perhaps there were more Uncles and Aunts born between 1885-1891, when your Grandmother Emily was 27-34 years old. Your Uncle George Frederick Snow married Ann Eliza Storer on 25 December 1901 in Battersea when they were both 22 years old. She was literally "the girl next door," as he lived at 47 Alfred Street and she lived at 49 Alfred Street. They had seven children. Your Cousins were: Annie E. Snow (1902), John G. Snow (1904), Arthur R. Snow (1907), Florence A. Snow (1910), Albert E. Snow (1911), Thora K. Snow (1915), and Ernest D. Snow (1920). One of your Cousins sent me these pictures of your Grandfather, Uncle, and Aunt.

George F., & John George Snow   George F., & Ann Snow, 1925.

Your Uncle, Grandfather, and Father were all carpenters, house decorators, and painters. I guess we come by these skills honestly. They likely worked together from 1890-1900, and your Father and Uncle may have apprenticed with your Grandfather. Your Uncle George and Aunt Ann moved to Tooting in 1904 where they had the first two of their seven children. Their other five children were born in Croydon from 1907-1920. They lived a short distance away from your Grandfather. Your Uncle George was at your Grandfather's home at Dean Road when your Mother likely announced she was pregnant and her Stepson William Henry Snow was your Father. This must have caused quite a rift in the family. From then on, there appeared to be no further contact between your Parents and the Snow family. Your Uncle George maintained a close relationship with your Grandfather, but not with his Brother -- your Father. George served in WWI when he was 35-40 years old. He worked most of his life as a Builder's Foreman and lived his life in Croydon.

Your Parents: William Henry Snow and Annie Gifford

Dad, your enigmatic Mother was very difficult to trace, but Robin eventually found her Birth Certificate. She was born on 25 June 1878, at 4 Patmore Street, Wandsworth, Battersea. This was about one block away from where your Grandfather J. G. Snow, Aunt Emily, and Uncle George lived in 1881. Perhaps this is where the Snow and Gifford paths' first crossed. She was born in the same year when Grandfather married his First Wife.

I discovered a few things about your Gifford ancestors. Your Great Grandfather William Gifford was born in 1810 and married Ann _____ in

1830. Your Grandfather William Gifford (1837) was the eldest of seven children. Your Granduncles were: Edward Gifford (1830), William Gifford (1842), Walter Gifford (1844), Robert Gifford (1849), Edward C. Gifford (1851), and Thomas Gifford (1852). Your Grandfather William Gifford was born in Dilton Marsh, Somerset. Your Grandmother Catherine Pearce was born in Norton St. Philips, Somerset. They married about 1862 and had six children. Your two Uncles and three Aunts were: William Gifford (1864), Ada Gifford (1866), Emma Gifford (1867), Frederick Gifford (1872), and Lilian Gifford (1876). Your Mother was the youngest of these six children.

Dad, the Snow family underwent dramatic changes a few years before you were born. Your Grandmother Emily died on 6 February 1904 when she was 46 years old. She and J. G. Snow had been married for 26 years. Three months after she died, your Father William Henry (21) married his First Wife Agnes Maud Moore (21). Four months after your Grandmother Emily died, your Uncle George (25) and Aunt Ann had their second child. Their first was two years old.

Your Grandfather J. G. Snow married his Second Wife -- your Mother Annie Gifford. This happened six months after your Grandmother died. Your Uncle George (30) and his family moved to Croydon in 1908. Your Father William and his First Wife Agnes may have moved to Croydon around this time as well. When your Grandmother died, your Grandfather, your Mother, your Father, his First Wife, your Aunt, Uncle, and two Cousins all lived at the same address.

Your Grandfather J. G. Snow (46) married your Mother Annie Gifford (26) on 1 August 1904 in Tooting. She made herself four years older on the Marriage Certificate to make a difference in their age of 15 years instead of the actual 20 years. I imagine this marriage was unpopular with your Grandmother's family -- the Cheer's. Your Grandfather married a woman 20 years younger than he, and only six months after he became a widower. Who knows what your Uncle George, your Father William, and your Aunt Alice thought of this marriage? It was, after all, their Mother who died, and their Father who remarried. Your Grandparents William Gifford (67) and Catherine Pearce/Gifford (67) witnessed their marriage. William Gifford was a Carpenter, so perhaps the Gifford and Snow families worked together.

Your Grandfather and Mother moved to Croydon in 1905 where they had their two children. Your Half Brother Jack was born in 1905 at 141 Sussex Road, Croydon. He was named after your Great Grandfather John Allen Snow (1831). Your Half Sister Amy was born in 1907 at 144 Selsdon Road, Croydon. She was named after your Grandaunt Amy Snow (1874) and your Aunt Alice Emily Snow (1881). The first few years of this marriage must have been difficult as J. G. Snow was often unemployed. Jack and Amy had to go to St. Peter's Church for food from the soup kitchen. In the meantime, something happened in your Father's marriage. His Wife Agnes (26) may have died, or they may have separated. Interestingly enough, 1905 was the year Mom's Parents decided to leave London with two young children and sail to Canada to settle in Port Arthur, Ontario.

"Coming into Care," Croydon, Surrey, England, 1913

Grandfather: John George Snow (55)	Fred G. Snow (3)
Father: William Henry Snow (30)	Brother: Bill Snow (7 mo.)
Mother: Annie Gifford/Snow (35)	
Half Brother: Jack Snow (8)	
Half Sister: Amy Snow (6)	

You were likely conceived by your Father William (25) and Mother Annie (30) in December 1908. You may have been named after your Uncle George Frederick Snow (1879) or your Granduncle George Frederick Snow (1862). We will never know the exact date of your birth as no Birth Certificate was found for you. The Sevenoaks Council School records listed your date of birth as September 9, 1909. Perhaps they invented this for their convenience, as it is the ninth day of the ninth month of the ninth year. Your birth date of September 17, 1909, appeared once in a letter Thomas Keeley sent you in 1942. He may have taken this date from an Overseas Settlement Grant list.

There were a number of searches for your Birth Certificate. The Waifs and Strays Society searched in 1929 under the surname "Snow" and "Gifford." Although they told you this, you had your reasons not to believe them. The Balham Police apparently also searched in 1957, but no one ever provided you with a copy of the negative result. Had they done so, we might not have continued to request searches. I requested a search this year. After all this, we have to accept that your Mother did not register your birth. The most likely reason was a lack of money.

When your Mother was pregnant with you in 1909, she made the difficult decision -- given her limited choices -- to leave your Grandfather J. G. Snow (52), Jack (4) and Amy (2). Your Father (26) made the difficult decision -- given his limited choices -- to leave his Wife Agnes (26), or she may have been deceased. He impregnated his Father's Wife -- his Stepmother. Your Mother had you at the home of one of her relatives -- Herbert Gifford -- who lived at 2 Larch Road, Balham. I do not know her relationship to him.

I do not know if your Parents were together for your first three years of life, but I would like to believe so. I would like to believe that they loved you and cared for you. You must have inherited your admirable qualities from somewhere. Your Parents were together from 1909-1929 and had four more children together. Dad, you are the eldest of five children. You had two Brothers and have two Sisters.

He said, "Oh, my God! My two Brothers are dead? My two Sisters are alive?"

I replied, "Yes, your two Sisters are alive, as well as your Sister-in-Law."

Your Brother Bill was born on 29 August 1912, at 77 Pevensey Road, Tooting, when you were about to turn three years old. Your Mother may have had him at your Aunt Lillian's home. In May 1913, you were 3¾ years old, your Brother Bill was 9 months old, and your Mother (35) was a month pregnant with your Sister Vi. Your Mother returned you to your Grandfather J. G. Snow (55), Jack (8), and Amy (6) at 5 Parker Road. That must have been very difficult for her to do, as she had left them four years earlier when she was pregnant with you. Since she left them to live with your Father, she had two children by him and was pregnant with her third. Her situation must have been a desperate one. Did she have no other family to whom she could turn? One possible reason she left you there was you may have had German Measles (Rubella) in early 1913. She may have feared exposure during the first trimester of her pregnancy with your Sister Vi.

Dad, you were not simply "abandoned" or "deserted" by your Parents as the Waifs and Strays Society told you. I determined the circumstances from your Case File they reluctantly released to me. Vicar Arthur Reeve of St. Peter's Church in Croydon was instrumental in having you forcibly taken from your family. According to his Wife Inez, your Mother "ran away" and left you with your Grandfather in 1912. Much of the Vicar's account proved to be incorrect, and I suspect this is inaccurate as well. The Vicar intervened because your Grandfather was in financial difficulty. The clergy were also on a Holy Mission to procure children for the British Child Deportation Scheme.

Jack (8) took Amy (6) and you (3½) to school in Croydon because your Grandfather had to work during the day. The three of you sat in the front row and Amy and Jack tried to keep you quiet. Amy thought the "authorities" objected to your being in school, and this was the only reason they apprehended you. I believe her account of events, rather than the Vicar's. In 1912, thousands of older children took their younger siblings to school with them. There were more underage children attending school than older children of legal age. Amy was spared apprehension only because she was barely old enough to be in school. Jack and Amy naturally assumed you were their natural Brother, rather than Half Brother. Your Grandfather did not tell you three any different, but his reasons are more understandable than any reasons the Waifs and Strays Society might have had.

In May 1913, the Vicar arranged for the Police to apprehend you. Your Grandfather likely opposed this. All you remembered was that you might have done something wrong, become lost, or run away. You thought your Mother might have died. They put you in a hospital after they apprehended you. For unknown reasons, the Vicar paid for your stay in the Children's Convalescent Home in Croydon, from May-September 1913. Your Grandfather tried to pay for this as well. It was very unusual for you to have been kept in a private hospital that cost money to have you there. I do not know why you were not placed in a free hospital in Croydon.

Dad said, "I don't remember being in any hospital!"

You were 3½ years old when they admitted you. You must have blocked this from your memory, as you only remembered the Police taking you away and then being placed in the foster home. There are no hospital records of your stay there. When you were apprehended, your family consisted of your Grandfather, one Half Brother, one Half Sister, three Uncles, five Aunts, your Mother, your Father, one Brother, and five Cousins.

Who knew you were in this hospital? Your Grandfather J. G. Snow knew. Your Mother may not have known what became of you. Your Uncle George (32) lived a short distance from the hospital but I do not know if he or anyone ever visited you. He and your Aunt Anne had five children under 11 years old. While you were in this hospital, something significant occurred on the far side of the world. Mom was born on 23 March 1913, in Minnedosa, Manitoba, Canada. You followed your different paths until they crossed 21 years later, when you met, fell in love, and married.

On September 24, 1913, Vicar Inez Reeve applied to the Waifs and Strays Society to have you admitted. The dominant reason for this appeared to be the cost to them of having you in hospital. You had a Medical Examination by Dr. Rose Turner. She estimated your age to be between 3-4 years old. I have often wondered if you were legally old enough to become their ward. She noted you had a squint that might need attention. It apparently was not attended to, and you did not seem to suffer from it in later years. Your tonsils and adenoids were enlarged and they were supposed to be attended to as well but there is nothing in your file to indicate that they were. You were apparently knock-kneed and flat-footed. You were supposed to get a vaccination. A week later, you had another Medical Examination that said you may have had German measles twice before and some other illnesses that were unreadable. The

Vicar knew the identities of your Parents and knew you had a Brother whom they incorrectly identified as William Henry Snow.

You officially became a ward of the Church of England Society for Providing Homes for Waifs and Strays and became Waif Number 18264. The Vicar stated your Parents had abandoned you, and their whereabouts were unknown. I doubt this was true. In your case, the clergy acted as procurers for the British Child Deportation Scheme. Your Grandfather reluctantly signed the admission form in 1913. He knowingly or unknowingly gave them permission to "emigrate" you to Canada. Fortunately, they did not send you to Canada immediately, as they had so many other very young children. What choice did your Grandfather (55) have? He may have feared they would take Amy (6) and Jack (8). In your case, they already had custody of you. He was in no position to oppose them.

The organizations alleged they tried hard to assist families in financial difficulties. From your case file, it does not appear that they attempted to contact or notify any of your relatives when you became their ward. In 1913, they could have been listed in the Telephone Directory. In November, Vicar Inez Reeve arranged for your vaccination by Dr. Rose Turner. She took it on herself to sign a Medical Consent as she stated that there was no one from whom she could obtain consent. Six weeks earlier, however, she managed to have your Grandfather sign his consent for your admission. I do not think she attempted to contact him for this consent. She must also have known that your Uncle George lived two blocks away. I do not know where your Aunt Alice was at this time. Surely, some of your relatives must have been aware of your situation. When you officially "came into care," you ceased to exist for your family.

Vicar Arthur Reeve of St. Peter's Church baptized you on October 08, 1913, Croydon. The Vicar could have written William Henry Snow as your Father on your Baptism Certificate. She knew J. G. Snow was your Grandfather. A copy of this lay in your Children's Society case file for 82 years. They could have give you a copy when you first wrote to them in 1929, and you would have had something with which you could identify yourself. The Waifs and Strays Society sent a copy to Thomas Keeley in 1936. He did not tell you he had this in his possession. He did not tell you who were your Father and Grandfather. He did not tell you that you had a Brother. He wrote and told you that your Grandfather was your Father in 1942. He lied. They kept you in a hospital for five months. On October 23, 1913, they transferred you to their Receiving Home in Clapham. I imagine they put you on the train alone and saved the price of an adult ticket for an escort. You spent 6½ months of your first four years of life in hospitals and institutions.

Foster Care: Rumburgh, Halesworth, Suffolk, England, 1913-1921

Grandfather: John George Snow (55-63)   Fred G. Snow (4-12)
Father: William Henry Snow (30-38)   Brother: Bill Snow (1-9)
Mother: Annie Gifford/Snow (35-43)   Sister: Vi Snow (1-7)
Half Brother: Jack Snow (8-16)   Sister: Gladys Snow (1-3)
Half Sister: Amy Alice Snow (6-14)   Brother: Reg Snow (1)

On December 06, 1913, they discharged you from their Receiving Home and placed you alone on a train for a three-hour ride to Rumburgh. A Social Worker met you and drove you 16 km in a horse-drawn cart to the foster home of Marie & Harry Smith. They agreed to "bring you up" as one of their own, and "hand you over," when called upon. They were old and impoverished, and yet the Waifs and Strays Society sanctimoniously decided that anything was better than having you live with your family or relatives. You were one of almost 1,000 children in foster care in 1914. Your Sister Violet Lilian Beatrice Snow was born on March 15, 1914, to your Father (31) and your Mother (36). She was born five months after you "came into care." Your Father was about to enter the Army. Vi was your Mother's fifth child. When she was born, the others were: Jack (9), Amy (7), you (5), and Bill (1¾). During WWI, your Grandfather J. G. Snow (57-61) worked as a House Decorator and did his best to care for Jack (9-13) and Amy (7-11).

This is the only picture I was able to locate of your Father. It was mounted on cardboard and I soaked it in water to see if there was anything written on the back. There was not.

William Henry Snow (32), WWI, London, England, 1915

Dad asked, "Where on earth did you get this picture?"

I replied, "Your Sister-in-Law Freda mailed it to me." He just grinned.

In WWI, your Father was a Sergeant and a Light Machine Gun Instructor with the Royal Fusiliers. Their Regimental Headquarters was located at the Tower of London. He was badly wounded several times on the Western Front. He had something to do with the design or modification of this gun and was "presented" to King George V.

Dad said, "So, this is my Father -- he looks rather tall." I replied, "Yes, I measured the boards on the building behind him to estimate his height as a little under 2 m. I do not know anything more about his war service. Somehow these records could be obtained."

After two years of foster care, you had a Medical Examination on January 26, 1915. The Waifs and Strays Society did not give me a copy of this report. Dad said, "I don't remember ever seeing a Doctor while I was at the Smiths. If you got sick, you got yourself better."

I managed to obtain some Rumburgh School Records. They had excerpts from a Punishment Book. Your name was not in it. Children were caned for climbing trees, ill-treating smaller children, idleness, inattention, disobedience, laziness, and impudence.

Dad said, "Kids weren't really bad -- you could get severely punished for minor things. I sang in the St. John's Church as a soprano. The Church was a place of comfort for me. It was the only place where I felt I belonged. Some of the hymns helped -- such as Jesus Loves Me."

Your Sister Gladys Elsie Snow was born on 22 August 1918 to your Father (35) and your Mother (40). Gladys was your Mother's sixth child. When she was born, the others were: Jack (13), Amy (11), you (9), Bill (6) and Vi (4). I told him I had a picture of Rumburgh School a kind woman in England mailed to me. He said, "This is a remarkable picture! The roof was thatched and the wind whistled through the window frames. It was always so cold.

On November 12, 1919, you had a Medical Examination by Dr. Turner but they did not give me a copy of her report. This may have occurred during the Spanish flu pandemic of 1918-1919 that killed 20-30 million people worldwide. Your teacher gave each student an orange from the Peace Celebration Fund. He said, "I definitely remember getting an orange. That was quite a treat in those days." I showed him a Rumburgh School class picture. He said, "I remember some of these kids. Some were no better off than I was. At least they lived with their families. There I am in the second row on the left. I'm standing in front of the teacher."

Rumburgh Council School #17, Rumburgh Halesworth, Suffolk, England, 1998.

Rumburgh Council School #17 Class Picture, Halesworth, Suffolk, England, 1920.

On September 27, 1920, you had your second Medical Examination by Dr. Rose Turner in eight years of foster care. She noted your teeth were bad and recommended attention for them. He said, "The first time I ever saw a dentist was when I was an adult in Canada."

On December 10, 1920, your Brother Reginald William Snow was born to your Father (37) and Mother (42). Reg was your Mother's seventh child. When he was born, the others were: Jack (15), Amy (13), you (11), Bill (8), Vi (6) and Gladys (2).

On September 20, 1921, you had another Medical Examination. There was no mention of the condition of your teeth on this report. This examination was in preparation for your transfer to St. Augustine's Home for Boys. Rev W. Linton Wilson completed a report and noted that you were "cheerful and obliging."

During the eight years you were in foster care, your family's life went on without you. Your Father and Uncle George served in WWI and your Mother and Aunt raised their children under difficult wartime circumstances. Your Brothers, Sisters, and Cousins attended school as young children during WWI and did not have any contact with you. None of them knew you existed.

St. Augustine's Home, Sevenoaks, Kent, England, 1921-1925

Grandfather: John George Snow (63-67)	Fred G. Snow (12-15)
Father: William Henry Snow (38-42)	Brother: Bill Snow (9-13)
Mother: Annie Gifford/Snow (43-47)	Sister: Vi Snow (7-11)
Half Brother: Jack Snow (16-20)	Sister: Gladys Snow (3-7)
Half Sister: Amy Snow (14-18)	Brother: Reg Snow (1-5)

On October 12, 1921, they placed you on the train alone for a three-hour ride to Liverpool Station. They pinned a nametag on your shirt, and shipped you like some sort of parcel. What is particularly tragic is that while you were in the Home, your family lived so close to you. Just as they did not know where you were while you were in foster care, they did not know you were in St. Augustine's Home for Boys. My research confirmed everything you said about the harshness of life in the Homes.

You attended Sevenoaks Council School, High Street, Kent, from October 13, 1921-April 17, 1924. Canada made it illegal for children under 15 years old to enter the country, so they may have held you until after you turned 15 in September 1924. In January 1925, Secretary Wescott wrote your Grandfather J. G. Snow and advised him you were "anxious to emigrate to Canada." He reminded him that he signed an agreement to send you to Canada "should the Committee consider it advisable." On February 2, 1925, your Grandfather (67) signed the Consent Form. He signed the form with a shaky hand. Lilian Gifford/Keers (49) witnessed his signature. She may have been your Aunt, who lived at 296 Franciscan Road, Tooting. This address is quite close to where your Brother Bill was born in 1912.

Amy (18) and Jack (20) likely lived with your Grandfather at 3 Dean Road, Croydon. The Waifs and Strays Society did not allow you to see either your Grandfather or your Aunt before they deported you. What a difference this might have made in your life. At least you could have left your homeland knowing at least two people who were your family. The child-care organizations deported 4,000 other children like you to Canada in 1925. Mom was 12 years old when you were deported, and unknowingly waited for you to arrive in Port Arthur, Ontario nine years later. On April 03, 1925, you left on the SS Andania, never to see England again. Your family consisted of your Grandfather, eight Granduncles, one Grandaunt, three Uncles, five Aunts, one Half Sister, one Half Brother, and seven Cousins. Your Father (42) and Mother (47) were likely still together with your Brothers and Sisters -- Bill (13), Vi (11), Gladys (7), and Reg (5).

Early Adulthood as a Waif, Canada, 1925-1935

Grandfather: John George Snow (68-78)	Fred G. Snow (16-26)
Father: William Henry Snow (42-52)	Brother: Bill Snow (13-23)
Mother: Annie Gifford/Snow (47-57)	Sister: Vi Snow (11-21)
Half Brother: Jack Snow (20-30)	Sister: Gladys Snow (7-17)
Half Sister: Amy Alice Snow (18-28)	Brother: Reg Snow (5-15)

After the ship docked at Halifax, Nova Scotia, they pinned a nametag on you, and placed you on a train to Sherbrooke, Quebec. They admitted you to the Gibbs' Home and sent you to a farm. You wrote your first letter to Master Ernest Jago at St. Augustine's from a farm in East Angus, Quebec. There was no copy of a letter of reply in your case file. While you worked on this farm, Amy (18) married Stephen J. (21) in Croydon. Her first child -- your Half Nephew Arthur J. was born in Croydon in 1926. That year, your Brother Bill (14) left home. He maintained loose contact with your Parents after WWII. Your Brother Reg (6) may have been placed with Barnardo's shortly after this. Bill and Reg did not have a close relationship, but maintained some contact after the war.

He asked, "Who put my Brother Reg into Barnardo's?" I replied, "I don't know, and may never know. Barnardo's will not release information about him to me." He snarled, "What's new about that?"

Ironically, of all the places Barnardo's could have placed Reg, they sent him to live in a foster home in Stowmarket, Suffolk. This is a small village very near your foster home in Rumburgh. He may have been in this foster home from 1926-1932 (age 6-12) and in a Boys' Home from 1932-1934 (age 12-14). I hope he was not in the foster home in 1924-1925. It would be cruel to find that you and he were in foster homes only a few kilometres apart from each other. Although child deportation to Canada had dwindled during these years, Reg was fortunate to have not been deported to Australia. He gave good accounts of this home to your Sister-in-Law Freda. I handed him a picture of Reg in the Barnardo foster home. He studied the picture of his unknown Brother.

Back Right: Reg Snow (11), Stowmarket, Suffolk, England, 1931.

In 1928, you were in a hospital in Sherbrooke, Quebec for treatment of your mangled arm. I wrote to Sherbrooke and tried to obtain medical records of your stay, but these apparently do not exist. Amy had her second child -- your Half Niece Elizabeth J. in Croydon. Your Father (45) may have left your Mother (50) that year. They apparently did not marry. His First Wife (Agnes Moore) and her First Husband (your Grandfather J. G. Snow) may have been alive. In these times, divorces were difficult and costly to obtain. While you were in hospital, Bill (16) had been away from the family for two years. Vi (14) had just finished school, and Gladys was 10 years old. Reg (8) had been in the Barnardo foster home for 2-4 years. In 1929, you enlisted in the Reserve Army Service Corps in Sherbrooke, Quebec. I wrote to Canadian Veteran's Affairs, but they said these records no longer exist.

You picked fruit on Hatzic Island, British Columbia during the Depression. You wrote and asked for the whereabouts of your Parents. You described yourself as "one who has been in darkness, and ignorant as to who he is." They told you your Parents "left" or "abandoned" you with a "Mr. J. G. Snow." They could have told you he was your Grandfather and identified your Father to you. They referred to their previous letter of 1929 that you had lost. Half of your first nine years in Canada coincided with the Great Depression. In England, your Grandfather (67-76) likely subsisted on a pension. Your Father (38-42) and Mother (43-47) had been separated for six years. Bill (13-22) had been out of the home for eight years. Vi (11-20) and Gladys (7-16) likely finished school at the age of 14 years old. Reg (5-14) was in a Barnardo's Home.

From 1925-1934, your family consisted of your Grandfather, three Uncles, five Aunts, Mother, Father, two Brothers, two Sisters, one Half Sister, one Half Brother, and seven Cousins.

Your Unknown Family in England, 1913-1934

Name	Relationship	In Care 1913	Foster Care 1913-21	Boys Home 1921-25	Canada 1925-34
John George Snow	Grandfather	55	55- 63	63 - 67	67 - 76
John Allen Snow	Half Brother	7-02 m	8 - 16	16 - 20	20 - 29
Amy Alice Snow	Half Sister	6-02 m	6 - 14	14 - 18	18 - 27
William Gifford	Uncle	55	55- 63	63 - 67	67 - 70
Frederick Gifford	Uncle	49	49- 57	57 - 61	61 - 70
George F. Snow	Uncle	35	35- 43	43 - 47	47 - 56
Ada Gifford	Aunt	46	46- 54	54 - 58	58 - 67
Emma Gifford	Aunt	44	44- 53	53 - 57	57 - 66
Lilian Gifford	Aunt	37	37- 45	45 - 49	49 - 58

Ann Storer/Snow	Aunt	35	35- 43	43 - 47	47 - 56
Alice Emily Snow	Aunt	32	32- 40	40 - 44	44 - 53
Annie Gifford/Snow	Mother	35	35- 43	43 - 47	47 - 56
William H. Snow	Father	30	30- 38	38 - 42	42 - 51
William A. Snow	Brother	9 m	01- 09	09 - 13	13 - 22
Violet L. B. Snow	Sister		01- 07	07 - 11	11 - 20
Gladys Elsie Snow	Sister		01- 03	03 - 07	07 - 16
Reginald W. Snow	Brother		01	01 - 05	05 - 12

Family Life, Thunder Bay, Ontario, Canada, 1935-1994

Grandfather: John George Snow (78-83)   Fred G. Snow (26-85)
Father: William Henry Snow (52-74)   Brother: Bill Snow (23-79)
Mother: Annie Gifford/Snow (57-76)   Sister: Vi Snow (21-80)
Half Brother: Jack Snow (30-89)   Sister: Gladys Snow (17-76)
Half Sister: Amy Alice Snow (28-75)   Brother: Reg Snow (15-64)

You cut lake ice in Jellicoe and prospected for gold around Beardmore. You found work at the Ozone Gravel Pit and built a log shack for your matrimonial home. Your marriage announcement said you were the Son of John George Snow and Annie Gifford/Snow. Had you been able to discover your parent's identities, it would have read differently.

In 1936, your Brother Bill (24) married Eva (28). I do not know where Reg (16) was after he was in the Barnardo Home. Your Half Brother Jack (31) married Margaret (30) in Croydon -- four days after Bill married. Jack and Amy never knew any of your Brothers or Sisters. Your Half Niece Margaret was born to Amy in Croydon in 1936. Your Father (53) married Leah L., so he obtained a divorce from his First Wife Agnes Moore, or she was deceased.

You wrote to Thomas Keeley for information. The Waifs and Strays Society had told him that a search had been made for your Birth Certificate seven years earlier. They gave him a copy of your Admission Form that clearly stated the relationship between your Grandfather and your Father. They left it to his discretion how much information he would pass on to you. He chose not to inform you of the details of your apprehension and identify your family. They gave him a copy of your Baptism Certificate that he withheld from you for another 19 years, as they did not give you a copy until you were 48 years old in 1957.

Your Sister Gladys (20) married William W. (20) in 1938 while you fought forest fires. You wrote to Master Ernest Jago at St. Augustine's

Church Home for Boys and the Old Boys League. They replied that they could add nothing to their previous correspondence. In 1938, you wrote to the Waifs and Strays Society and said you never received their 1929 letter. You expressed doubts whether the surname Snow was really yours. They gave you a copy of their 1931 letter but not the 1929 letter that identified William Henry Snow as your Father.

While you worked at St. Anthony Gold Mine, you received a Christmas card from your Half Brother Jack whom you called "someone claiming to be my brother." The Waifs and Strays Society encouraged you to write to Jack but did not tell you he was your Half Brother. This was your first ever contact with any family member. From the age of 4-28, there was no one in the world with whom you could claim a familial relationship. He must have contacted the Waifs and Strays Society to get your address and there should have been copies of his correspondence in your Case File.

Your Half Sister Margaret (Peggy) Snow was born to your Father William Snow (55) & Leah in 1938. Your Niece Susan W. was born to Gladys (20), and your Nephew Arthur was born to Bill (26). You moved to Peninsula to work at the train station. You quit this job and worked at the wood flume in Heron Bay. It was the worst winter you and Mom experienced.

In 1939, your Sister Vi (24) married James A. (28). Your Father (56) and Mother (61) may not have attended the wedding, as they had been apart for 14 years and your Father had remarried. Bill (27) and Eva (31) were witnesses at the wedding. Gladys (21) had been married for a year, but I do not know where Reg (19) may have been. Your Niece Gladys A. was born to Vi (25).

You received a letter from J. G. Snow (83) in 1939. He signed the letter as "Dad." He was either unable or unwilling to inform you of how you became under their care, or that his Son William Henry Snow was your Father. Your Brothers Bill and Reg were in the British Army in WWII. I have these pictures of them.

Reg Snow (20), England, 1940   Bill Snow (23), England, 1945

Dad said, "These are my Brothers? They have pointy noses like most of you kids. I always thought it was a 'Perry' thing -- but maybe it is a 'Snow' thing." Mom said, "What do you mean, 'pointy?' I call it 'Distinguished!'"

Your Brother Bill (28-35) was with the Royal Artillery and East Surrey Regiment in WWII. He served in North Africa, Italy, Greece, and Palestine. Sometime during the war, your Sister-in-Law Eva, and your Nephews Arthur (5) and Peter (2) were bombed out of their home. Bill returned to England in 1947 and this was the first time Peter saw him, as he had left England shortly after he was born. Your Nephew said Bill was shell-shocked, exhausted, and never the same after the war. Following the war, he worked for the General Post Office until he retired.

Your Grandfather J. G. Snow died in 1940 in Croydon, where he had lived for 25 years. Your Father (59) and Mother (62) did not attend the funeral, nor did any Gifford's. Only your Half Brother Jack (35), Half Sister Amy (33), and Uncle George (61) attended his funeral. You believed he was your Father, because that is what they told you. You wrote to your "Father" and "Brother" for two years and had little to show for it. After J. G. Snow died, you may have felt you lost the only credible link to your family. Ten years of correspondence with the Waifs and Strays Society had produced little information.

In 1941, your Nephew Peter was born to Bill (28) in Wiltshire, England. You worked scaling lumber in Mead in 1941, and then found work at Canada Car and Foundry that lasted for two years. In 1942, Thomas Keeley of the Gibbs' Club gave you with a "To Whom it May Concern" Letter. It incorrectly stated your Parents as John George Snow and Annie Gifford/Snow. He knew William Henry Snow was your

Father, your Brother Bill's identity, and had a copy of your Baptism Certificate.

In 1942, your Nephew James A. was born to Vi (28). She placed him with Barnardo's in September 1942 when he was four months old. Gladys was just a baby when she was placed with Barnardo's as well. When James was five years old, he was placed in a County Council Home in Essex. When he was nine years old, he was placed in a foster home where he lived there until he was 22 years old in 1964. Barnardo's asked him if he could assume responsibility for his Sister Gladys. Until then, he never knew he had a Sister! I was not surprised by now to learn that yet another child in care had a sibling about whom they never knew. He agreed and they lived together for a few years. They found their Mother Vi (56) in the early 1970's when they were in their 30's. They do not know why they were placed with Barnardo's and know nothing of their Father or their Grandparents -- your Parents. Your Half Niece Kathleen J. was born to Amy in 1943. You tried to enlist in the Canadian Army but they rejected you because of your mangled and scarred right arm. You had hoped they would accept you, so you could go to England and possibly find your family. In 1948, your Niece Theresa W. was born to Gladys (30).

I sent a picture of you to your Nephew Arthur. He pinned it to his bulletin board by his desk. Late one evening he recalled a memory "long since buried." He remembered he was 10-11 years old in 1948-1949 when his Mother Eva took him to meet his Grandmother -- your Mother (70). He recalled a gas-lit corridor and a basement apartment. The brown door had the number "1" on it. He described her as an old woman who sat in a wooden chair with a crocheted headrest. She held his hand, kissed his cheek, and plied him with jam sandwiches and a banana -- a rare treat in those days. This was the only time he saw her.

In 1949, you bought the "War Time" house and were off work because of your ulcerated foot. You put in the basement yourself. In 1952, your Uncle George Frederick Snow died in Croydon at the age of 73. In 1952, your Brother Reg (32) married Freda (24). After WWII, he located your Mother (74) and he and Freda lived in the same building as she for two years. They were married for many years before he told her he was raised in a Barnardo foster home. Freda only met your Parents, Brother, and Sisters once. She described your Mother as an accomplished pianist -- even though she was missing a finger -- and "well spoken." She did not have any photographs of her. She described your Father as "nice," and said his home had "exquisite furniture," as he was a Journeyman Carpenter. I have a picture of your Brother Reg's wedding.

Reg Snow (32) and Freda (24), England, 1952

Your Mother died in Lambeth Hospital, London on 10 August 1954 at the age of 76. You were 44 years old, married for 19 years, and Father of five children aged 18, 16, 13, 9, and 7. Mom was two months pregnant. You had just obtained work at Canada Car and Foundry that would last three years until it closed in 1957.

Reg (34) was the informant on the Death Certificate and he made the funeral arrangements. Why was her maiden name of Gifford not on the Birth Certificate? Why was she named as the Widow of William Henry Snow when they were not married? He was alive when she died and apparently paid for her funeral expenses. She did not tell your two Brothers and two Sisters she had been previously married to J. G. Snow and had two children in that marriage. Jack (49) and Amy (47) did not know when she died and had not seen her since they were young children.

Bill (42) had been married for 18 years, and your Nephews Arthur (16) and Peter (13) had only seen her a few times when they were young children. Vi (40) may have been separated from her Husband for 10 years. Vi and Gladys may have attended her funeral. Your Niece Gladys A. (15) and your Nephew James A. (12) lived in different Barnardo Homes and did not know their Parents let alone their Grandparents. Your Nieces Susan W. (16) and Theresa W. (6) never met her.

Your Father William Henry Snow (75) died on 29 January 1959 in Hampstead, London. His Wife Leah predeceased him. He is apparently buried in Highgate Cemetery, London. Your Half Sister Peggy (21) was the informant on the Death Certificate, and lived at the same address when he died. She briefly stayed with your Brother Bill (46) and Eva (43) for a time after his death. You were 49 years old, married for 23 years, and the Father of six children ages 22, 20, 18, 14, 13, and 3. Two years earlier, you received your Baptism Certificate that did not include your Father's name. You had started your correspondence course the year before your Father and worked at the Keefer Seaway Terminal Construction.

Your Nephews Arthur Snow (20) and Peter Snow (18) had only met him once when they were young children. Your Sister Vi (45) may have been separated for 15 years, and may have attended. Your Niece Gladys A. (20) and your Nephew James A. (17) did not know him. Your Sister Gladys (41) may have had some contact with him. Your Nieces Susan W. (21) and Theresa W. (11) had never heard of him. Your Brother Reg (39) did not attend his funeral but your Brother Bill (39) did.

In the 1960's, you bought a new house, completed your correspondence course, and completed your Certified Engineering and Technologist course. You worked in the isolated community of Gull Bay. You obtained your first permanent position with the Ontario Government. Your children married and had your Grandchildren, and your Nephews and Nieces in England married and had your Grandnephews and Grandnieces.

In the 1970's, you continued your search for your Birth Certificate, and obtained your Canadian Citizenship. You retired in 1974 and wrote to the author John Stroud in 1976. The next year you had your left leg amputated. In 1980, you received the only account of how you "came into care" from your Half Sister Amy (73). She died in 1983 at the age of 76 in Croydon, Surrey.

Your Brother Reg (64) died on 13 March 1984 in London, England. Earlier that month, you wrote your final letter to the Children's Society. Your Brother Bill (79) died three years ago in a Home for the Aged in London, England. He had only been there a few months. Your Sister-in-law Eva (80) died last year in a Home for the Aged -- two years after Bill died.

Robin's extraordinary help allowed me to identify many generations of Snow's. Broken branches of the family tree have been spliced together, roots have been revitalized, and family connections re-established.

Like everyone else, Dad, you always belonged to a family. You are not just the product of one man named Snow and one woman named Gifford. You had two parents, who had two parents, who had two parents, etc. There are at least eight separate families in your line that contributed to you being you. With time, effort, and appropriate records, another eight families could be identified. Robin and I identified about a hundred of your relatives. The Waifs and Strays Society forcibly removed you from this intricate family network. It was their deliberate policy to shred this network. Like any fabric, if you pull one strand out of the weave, you weaken it. These are "your people."

As I passed him the Snow Descendant Tree, a gust of wind came through the trees. It was strong enough to make the poplar leaves tremble and the delicate bark of the birches flutter. It blew the sheet away and I ran after it. I retrieved it and looked back at Mom, Dad, and my Wife sitting at the picnic table. I thought I heard something in the breeze that passed by me. It sounded for a moment like soft whispers of English accents. The air was still again. I walked back to the picnic table, and gave him the Descendant Tree.

DESCENDANTS OF JOHN ALLEN SNOW, KENT, ENGLAND, 1812

.1 John Allen SNOW born 1832, Canterbury, Kent, England

 + Ann _____ born 1832, Canterbury, Kent, England

..2 John George SNOW born August 1858, Margate, Kent, England, died 8 March 1940, Croydon, Surrey, England

..+ (First Wife) Emily Jane CHEER born 30 October 1857, Wandsworth, Battersea, married 11 June 1878, Walworth, Surrey, England, died 6 February 1904, Upper Tooting, Surrey, England

...3 George Frederick SNOW born 9 December 1879, Battersea, Surrey, England, died 14 February 1952, Croydon, Surrey, England

...+ Anne Eliza STORER born 1879 England, married 25 December 1901, Battersea, England, died 1960

....4 Annie E. SNOW born 23 November 1902, Tooting Graveney, Surrey, England, married 22 December 1923, Croydon, Surrey, England, died 1990, Tasmania

....+ Wallace T. born 1901, Isle of Wight, England, died 1975, Greenwich, London, England

.....5 Dorcas T. born 1925, Woolwich, Kent, England

.....5 Joan T. born 1926, Woolwich, Kent, England, died 1994, Tasmania

.....5 Wallace T. born 1931, Woolwich, Kent, England

....4 John G. SNOW born 16 June 1904, Upper Tooting, Surrey, England, died 29 July 1974, England

....+ Alice born 1905 Croydon, Surrey, England, married 27 December 1930, died 19 September 1968, Croydon, Surrey, England

.....5 Ronald SNOW born 1931, Croydon, Surrey, England

.....5 William SNOW born 1933 Croydon, Surrey, England

.....5 Eric SNOW born 25 September 1936 Croydon, Surrey, England

....4 Arthur SNOW born March 1907, Wandsworth, Battersea, England, died 1908, Croydon, Surrey, England

....4 Florence SNOW born September 1910, Croydon, Surrey, England, died 1911, Croydon, Surrey, England

....4 Albert SNOW born March 1911, Croydon, Surrey, England, died 1912, Croydon, Surrey, England

....4 Thora SNOW born 29 November 1915, Croydon, Surrey, England, died 1916, Croydon, Surrey, England

....4 Ernest SNOW born 21 September 1920, Croydon, Surrey, England, died 27 December 1997, Australia

        + Joan born 1925 England, married 1946 England

.....5 L. SNOW born 1959, England

.....5 S. SNOW born 1965, Australia

...3 Alice Emily SNOW born 3 August 1881, Wandsworth, Battersea, England

...3 William Henry SNOW born 29 April 1883, Wandsworth, Battersea, England, died 24 January 1959, Hampstead, England

...+ (First Wife) Agnes Maud MOORE born 1883, married 7 May 1904, Wandsworth, Battersea, England

...3 William Henry SNOW born 29 April 1883, Wandsworth, Battersea, England, died 24 January 1959, Hampstead, England

...+ (Second Wife) Annie GIFFORD born 25 June 1878, Battersea, England, died 1 August 1954, England

....4 Frederick George SNOW born 17 September 1909, Balham, died 17 September 1994, Thunder Bay, Ontario

....+ Gertrude M. E. PERRY born 23 March 1913, Minnedosa, Manitoba married 5 September 1935, Port Arthur, Ontario

.....5 Gary Frederic SNOW born 1 June 1936, Port Arthur, Ontario

.....5 Karen Victoria SNOW born 12 August 1938, Peninsula, Ontario

.....5 Sandra Gale SNOW born 5 December 1940, Fort William, Ontario

.....5 Perry Alan Wayne SNOW born 11 October 1944, Fort William, Ontario

.....5 Roger Maurice SNOW born 11 January 1946, Fort William, Ontario

.....5 Wendy Anne Pamela SNOW born 16 February 1955, Fort William, Ontario

....4 William Alfred SNOW born 29 August 1912, Tooting, London, died 1991 London, England, died 1991, England

....+ Eva born 1908, England, married 21 June 1936, St. Pancras, London, England, died 1993, England

.....5 Arthur SNOW born 22 May 1938, Marylebone, London, England

.....5 Peter SNOW born 24 January 1941, Wiltshire, England

....4 Violet Lilian Beatrice SNOW born 15 March 1914, Wandsworth, Battersea, England, died September 1998, London, England

....+ James A. born 15 August 1910, Edrum, Berwick, Scotland, married 25 March 1939, London, England

.....5 Gladys A. born 13 October 1939, Lambeth, London, England

.....5 James A. born 27 March 1942, Newington, Southwark, England

....4 Gladys Elsie SNOW born 22 August 1918, Wandsworth, Battersea
....+ William W. born 1918, England, married 1936, England
.....5 Susan W. born 1938, England
.....5 Theresa W. born 1948 England
....4 Reginald William SNOW born 10 December 1920, Wandsworth, Battersea, England, died 13 March 1984, London, England
....+ Freda born 1928, Ireland, married 26 March 1952, London, England
...3 William Henry SNOW born 29 April 1883, Wandsworth, Battersea, England died 24 January 1959, Hampstead, England, married 1937, England
...+ (Third Wife) Leah born 1908, England
....4 Margaret SNOW born 1938, England
..2 John George SNOW born August 1858, Margate, Kent, England, died 8 March 1940, Croydon, Surrey, England
..+ (Second Wife) Annie GIFFORD born 25 June 1878, Battersea, England, died 10 August 1954, Lambeth, England, married 1 August 1904, Tooting, Surrey, England
...3 John Allen SNOW born 10 July 1905, Croydon, Surrey, England, died 26 April 1996, Cork, Ireland
...+ Margaret born 1906, Croydon, Surrey, England, married 25 July 1936, Croydon, Surrey, England, died 1989, England
....4 Eileen SNOW born 1938 Croydon, Surrey, England
...3 Amy Alice SNOW born 18 March 1907, Croydon, Surrey, England, died 15 February 1983, Croydon, Surrey, England
...+ Stephen J. born 1904 Croydon, Surrey, England, married 31 August 1925, Croydon, Surrey, England
....4 Arthur J. born 17 September 1926, Croydon, Surrey, England, died 17 September, 1999 Thornton Heath, Surrey, England
....4 Elizabeth J. born 1928 Croydon, Surrey, England, died 1985, England
....4 Margaret J. born 1936 Croydon, Surrey, England
....4 Reginald J. born 1938 Croydon, Surrey, England
....4 Kathleen J. born 1943 Croydon, Surrey, England
..2 William SNOW born 1860 Canterbury, Kent, England
..2 George Frederick SNOW born 1862 Canterbury, Kent, England
..2 Mary Ann SNOW born 1865 Canterbury, Kent, England
..2 William Henry SNOW born 1868 Canterbury, Kent, England
..2 Harry SNOW born 1871 Canterbury, Kent, England
..2 Amy SNOW born 1874 1862 Canterbury, Kent, England
..2 Agnes SNOW born 1877 Canterbury, Kent, England

Dad studied the Ancestor Tree very carefully, shook his head, and said, "Well, I guess I am a member of a family, even though I never knew them."

I replied, "Yes, Dad, the moment you were born you were linked by blood to hundreds of other people. It was your birthright to know who you were." He asked, "Did any of these relatives know of me before now?" I said, "No, but many more people will know who you are." He smiled. Mom was overjoyed to see the names of her in-laws. She was extremely happy for him to know he had a family -- just like everyone else. Her eyes filled with tears of love for him.

(NOTE: A comprehensive summary of the genealogical results of this search can be found at http//www.familytreemaker.com/users/s/n/o/Perry-A-Snow)

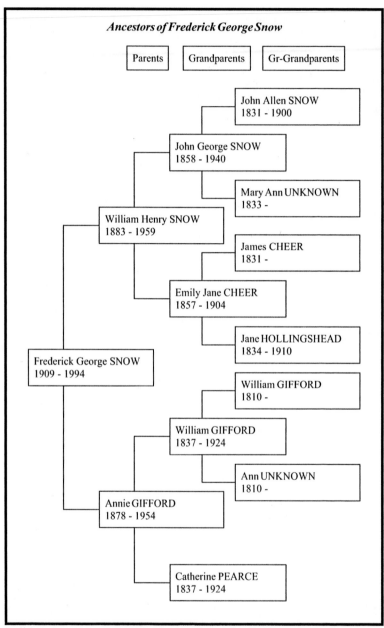

Ancestors of Frederick George Snow

| Parents | Grandparents | Gr-Grandparents |

John Allen SNOW
1831 - 1900

John George SNOW
1858 - 1940

Mary Ann UNKNOWN
1833 -

William Henry SNOW
1883 - 1959

James CHEER
1831 -

Emily Jane CHEER
1857 - 1904

Jane HOLLINGSHEAD
1834 - 1910

Frederick George SNOW
1909 - 1994

William GIFFORD
1810 -

William GIFFORD
1837 - 1924

Ann UNKNOWN
1810 -

Annie GIFFORD
1878 - 1954

Catherine PEARCE
1837 - 1924

I did not set out to research the Perry family but along the way, I discovered a lot of this ancestry. Mom, you are the product of at least eight separate families. When you and Dad conceived me, I inherited the genetic contributions of 16 separate families.

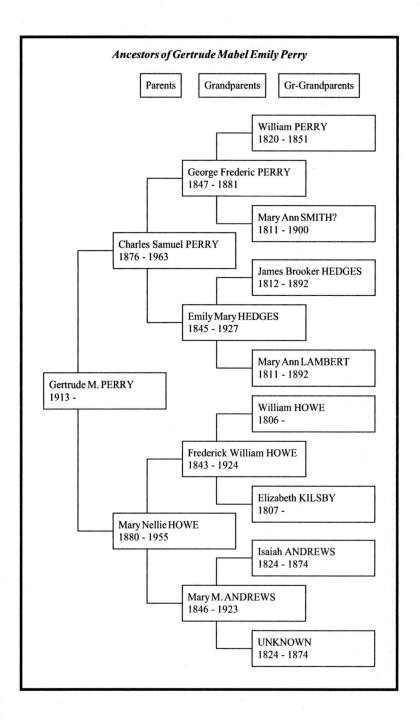

Ancestors of Gertrude Mabel Emily Perry

Parents   Grandparents   Gr-Grandparents

William PERRY
1820 - 1851

George Frederic PERRY
1847 - 1881

Mary Ann SMITH?
1811 - 1900

Charles Samuel PERRY
1876 - 1963

James Brooker HEDGES
1812 - 1892

Emily Mary HEDGES
1845 - 1927

Mary Ann LAMBERT
1811 - 1892

Gertrude M. PERRY
1913 -

William HOWE
1806 -

Frederick William HOWE
1843 - 1924

Elizabeth KILSBY
1807 -

Mary Nellie HOWE
1880 - 1955

Isaiah ANDREWS
1824 - 1874

Mary M. ANDREWS
1846 - 1923

UNKNOWN
1824 - 1874

225

Dad said, "So, what living relatives do I have again?"

I do not know if your Half Sister Peggy (56) is alive. If I could locate her, she may be able to tell us much more about your Father.

Your Brother Bill had two Sons. Your Nephew Arthur (56) has two daughters -- your Grandnieces Coral (33) and Catherine (30). They have four children -- your Great-grandnephew Michael (17), and twin Great-Grandnephew and Great-grandniece Benjamin (4) and Kirstie (4). Your Nephew Peter (53) has one Daughter -- your Grandniece Emma (18). Your Sister Vi (80) has a Daughter and a Son -- your Niece Gladys A. (55) and Nephew James A. (52). They have four children -- your Grandnephews and Grandnieces -- David (26), Shane (20), Jeanette (32), and Heidi (21). Your Sister Gladys (76) has two daughters -- your Nieces Susan (56) and Theresa (46). They have two sons -- your Grandnephews Mark (25) and Steven (19). Your Brother Reg and your Sister-in-Law Freda did not have children.

Fred G. Snow (81), 1994

He said, "I have two Sisters, three Nephews, and three Nieces! I also have 10 Grandnephews and Grandnieces! How nice it would be to talk to these people. Well Dearie, I guess we have a few phone calls to make. First, I'd like to thank your friend Robin, for all he has done. Then I'd like to say 'Hello' to my Family! What do I say to them?"

I said, "Tell your Sisters you are their long-lost Brother. Tell your Nephews and Nieces you are their uncle. I have already spoken to them, and they are waiting to hear from you. They will welcome you back into your Family -- where you always belonged.

This meeting never happened. It should have happened.

When my Father was 21 years old in 1931, he pleaded with the Waifs and Strays Society to "help one who has been in darkness, and ignorant as to who he is." He died on his alleged birthday when he was 85 years old in 1994. He died "in darkness, and ignorant as to who he was."

PART IV: THE PSYCHOLOGY OF THE WAIF
The Development of a Personal Identity

Your Parents conceived you in a moment of love. They were overwhelmed by the wonder of what their love produced when you were born. They knew you were a unique individual, the first time you grasped one of their fingers with your tiny hand. They were overjoyed simply because you were alive, healthy -- and theirs. The unconditional love you felt when you were born was your birthright.

Only one of your Father's millions of sperm survived the frenzied search to find your other complementary half. Only one of your Mother's egg cells was reserved for you. These two infinitesimal cells found each other and united with an unseen spark of life to produce you. All that is you was created the moment you were conceived. An extraordinary and predetermined program unfolded and knitted together an intricate combination of genes to guarantee your uniqueness. The greatest miracle in the world is repeated every time a child is born. From the beginning of time billions of people have been born, but never one exactly like you. Until the end of time, billions more will be born, but there will never be another one exactly like you. No one will ever think your thoughts, feel your feelings, or experience life exactly as you (Mandino 97-98). The Psychiatrist Carl Jung theorized that a powerful spiritual inheritance is transmitted at the moment of our conception. It lives in our subconscious mind, and may contain all the life experiences of all of our progenitors. The collective experience of *all* of humanity may be present in *all* of us.

The first year of your life is a critical period of your development. You and your Mother formed a wondrous unique relationship. The nature of this relationship formed the basis of all other relationships you would have in your life. This included your most important relationship -- the one you have with yourself. Your Mother is the one who taught you to love and trust. The exquisite subconscious program that was designed to ensure your survival began to operate at the moment of your conception. It relentlessly works 24 hours a day on your behalf throughout your life. Before you were born, it automatically regulated your heart rate, blood pressure, body temperature, and breathing. It also recorded the repetitive, relentless, and rhythmic sound and feel of your Mother's heart beat. It indelibly etched this record into your being. Mothers universally rock their children at a rate 70-80 beats per minute. This coincides with the rate of their resting hearts. This frequency and pattern of sound have been used throughout history in healing ceremonies (Perry 7).

The Mother-Child bond reverberates through your being throughout your life. Your heart beats a subliminal sound that echoes your Mother's

227

synchronized heart beat. Perhaps it beats a different sound that echoes your Family's heartbeats. Death and distance do not muffle these unheard sounds. Have you ever "sensed" something from a family member far away? Have you ever been prompted to contact them, to see if all is well? How are these unheard messages communicated?

A loving, stable Mother-Child relationship is a prerequisite for healthy child development. Maternal Deprivation is the term used to describe inadequate mothering, or deficient foster care. It produces a lack of maternal identification and maternal bonding. Young children separated from their Mothers and placed in institutions invariably suffer from *anaclitic depression.* They cry continuously for the first few months and then became indifferent to adults. They lay with their eyes wide open and stare off into space. Their faces are expressionless, frozen, and immobile. If Maternal Deprivation persists for more than five months, normal development is arrested or retarded. The result is that some children cannot walk unassisted and do not develop meaningful speech (Mussen 163). The idea of Maternal Deprivation is not a recent one. As early as 1906, the Committee on Agricultural Settlements in the Colonies noted that there was an "evil psychological effect" upon children separated from their parents (Parr 78).

The adverse effects of institutional care on young children have been studied for many years. The mortality rate for infants in American foundling homes in 1915 was 90-99% during the first year of admission. They died of a disease called "merasmus." They "wasted away" (Juhan, 43-44). In modern times, this is called a Reactive Attachment Disorder of Childhood.

The most severe form of deprivation experienced by children is loss of their Mothers in the first five years of life. This alone contributes to the development of ambivalent feelings about identity, love, and affection. It is known to be associated with feelings of lifelong depersonalization, alienation, and worthlessness. Missildine described the three phases of a grief reaction that children experienced following separation from their Mothers (227-228). They first protested the only way they could. They shook their cribs, cried loudly for their Mothers, and anxiously looked for any sign or sound of her. If they were strongly attached to their Mothers, their protests persisted for some time. Then despair ensued. They continued to whimper for their Mothers, but they gradually gave up hope of ever seeing them again. They grudgingly accepted the food and care offered by their caretakers. They learned to avoid the risk of any form of attachment to transient caretakers. The third reaction was one of detachment. They withdrew into their lonely selves and responded to their caretakers with indifference.

Stroud described how children came into the care of the Waifs and Strays Society as a simple matter. He wrote they grieved, became quiet, found their bearings, and settled into the routine (111). The childhood experience of actual parental abandonment is most harmful. Children, who were led to believe they were abandoned, are equally harmed. The mind does not always differentiate between an actual experience and a strongly held belief. They told my Father his Parents abandoned him. Whether they did or did not is not important. If he believed what he was told, the impact was the same. He was 3½ years old when the Police apprehended him and the Vicar admitted him to the Children's Convalescent Home. He had absolutely no memories of this. He had blocked this traumatic experience from his mind. I was disappointed, but a little relieved when I did not obtain his hospital records. They may have contained some graphic descriptions of his adjustment to the hospital. It is painful enough to imagine his six months there.

For the first year of your life, your physical growth was predominant. Your subconscious mind attended to your needs of nutrition, elimination, and sleep. It finely developed your senses of vision, hearing, touch, taste, and smell. You learned to sit, crawl, stand, and walk. You learned to smile, trust, and love because of parental care taking. In the second year of your life, you became a more socialized person. You continued to grow in height and weight. You walked more confidently and refined your motor skills. You used words in a meaningful way, and could comprehend questions and instructions. In the second year of your life, your subconscious mind continued its important work. It determined the pace and sequence of your physical, emotional and cognitive development. It carefully monitored your progress, guided you, and helped you solve your problems.

Your conscious mind -- the part that actively thinks and decides -- was relegated to a position of secondary importance. People addressed you by your name, and many other names. They bombarded you with positive and negative comments about yourself. These took the form of judgments such as, "You are _____." Your relatively weak conscious mind allowed these judgments to pass unfiltered and uncensored into your subconscious mind. All of these comments were absorbed, recorded, and implanted in your subconscious mind. You believed everything everyone told you -- especially about yourself. If the majority of these messages were positive, you developed a positive self-image. Correspondingly, if the majority of these messages were negative, you developed a negative self-image. Either way, portions of your adult identity are composed of these internalized judgments from this vulnerable period of childhood.

Some of these judgments became powerful determinants of your adult self-image and self esteem. Suppose one of the early implanted beliefs was that, you were unintelligent. It would not matter if you were actually more intelligent than you believed yourself to be. You would act according to your strongly held belief about your intelligence. This one belief could become a self-fulfilling prophecy. "I am not very smart. I can't do anything right. When I try, I fail. I guess it's true. I am not very smart." This one belief could dramatically affect major life choices in education, vocation, and relationships. You are, as a person, who you believe yourself to be. You value yourself according to these beliefs. Implanted beliefs can be blessings or curses.

The British Home Children had many negative beliefs implanted in their minds before they were of an age where they were capable of consciously accepting or rejecting other's judgments of them. They were depersonalized, stripped of their identities as someone's valued child, and bombarded with labels of inferiority. As a young child, your Parents likely allowed you the freedom you needed to develop a degree of autonomy and at the same time set realistic limits for you. They reinforced the critical belief that you were a person of worth and that you belonged to a Family. Your conscious mind developed so that you were able to exercise your judgment. You chose what to believe or disbelieve about yourself. You could reject negative appraisals if they did not fit in with your definition of who you were. You independently developed your unique ideas about who you were. As an adult, you could readily answer the question of "Who Are You?"

How important is your given name and surname to you? Would any another name suffice as a substitute to identify you? How would you feel about yourself and value yourself, if someone forbids you to use your name as the British Home Children were forbidden to use their names in the Homes? We all resent being treated, "Like a number." How would you feel if your identity consisted *solely* of a number, as the British Home Children were identified? Some, like my Father, lived a large part of their lives having doubts their surnames belonged to them.

Two events of major significance occurred in your early childhood. Until you were two years old, you likely referred to yourself in the third person. If your name was Freddy, you said, "Freddy is hungry." Then you underwent a remarkable transformation. You said, "*I* am hungry." This development coincided with the phenomenon of self-assertion. We call this period the "Terrible Two's." It signifies the beginning of the evolution of your adult personal identity. People said, "No" and "Don't," to you for two years and you reiterated the same statements in a defiant way for almost two years.

Both events needed to occur for you to develop your independence and define your existence apart from others. The British Home Children lived in coercive environments. The Rule of Silence enveloped them. They were not allowed to speak, so they had little opportunity to assert themselves.

From the age of four onward, you developed your own unique identity. You learned you were a certain "kind of a person," and belonged to a group called a family. It is to be hoped that, you learned you were important because you were "one of a kind." You learned a consistent set of values that acted as your internal guidance system. Without this, you might have floundered through life plagued with feelings of worthlessness and uselessness. The development of your identity did not evolve by itself. Your Parents provided you with a definition of who you were -- someone's valued child. The British Home Children had these aspects of their identities stolen from them.

We were all sometime, somewhere -- children. There is no demarcation line where we ceased one day to be children and were transformed into adults the next day. Emotionally, the children we once were -- and still are -- live inside our adult shells. The little child in us laughs, cries, dreams, and imagines.

It is difficult to imagine my Father not being traumatized when he was forcibly removed from his family when he was 3½ years old. He was kept in the Children's Convalescent Home for six months. He had no memories of this time. I do not believe any of his family visited him. The Waifs and Strays Society placed him on a train alone and transferred him to their Receiving Home. He may have experienced some separation anxiety when they removed him from his most recent home -- the hospital. He may have sat or lie curled up in a foetal position on a bench and cried the whole time. Perhaps he had learned to suppress his tears, and sat upright and frozen in terror instead.

He may have silently wept again for his Mother for six weeks in the Receiving Home while they transformed him into a Waif. He may have just adjusted to the Receiving Home, when they again placed him on a train alone to yet another unknown destination -- the foster home. To this point, he had been institutionalized for almost one year of the first four years of his life. He again may have struggled with terror during the train ride to the foster home. After eight years there, they again put him on a train alone and sent him to a Boys' Home. Somehow, he learned to survive this brutal environment for 3½ years. When he was 15 years old, they put him on a ship and deported him to Canada. They put him on a train alone and shipped him to the Distribution Centre at Sherbrooke, Quebec. I am surprised he did not develop a phobia for trains!

He was hospitalized for a year after he mangled his arm, and then enlisted in the Reserve Army. He spent a year as a homeless itinerant labourer during the early years of the Great Depression. He lived in a Relief Camp that was virtually a prison for three years. He lived 21 of his first 25 years of life in hospitals, foster care, Boys' Home, indentured farm labour, military, homeless, and controlled environments. If separation from their families was the only trauma experienced by the British Home Children, other positive experiences may have mitigated these effects. Their experiences in Canada exacerbated their early childhood traumas of abandonment, isolation, and rejection in England.

The term Psychology derives from the Greek *psyche* (mind/soul) and *logos* (study). The issue of identity is crucial to Psychology. Your personal identity exists at the centre of your being. It is composed of the collection of beliefs you have about yourself. Your definition of who you are restores any imbalance between what you think, how you feel, and what you do. Your thoughts, feelings, and behaviour must be congruent in order for you to feel a sense of wholeness and integrity. Identity is the feeling you experience every time you say or think, "I." It is what allows you to feel, "Yourself." It is a feeling only you can experience. The British Home Children were not allowed to use their names. They could hardly develop a sense of self.

It is difficult to imagine not knowing who you are. The most important relationship you can have is with yourself. It can be a positive and genuine relationship in which you know who you are and respect yourself. It can be an image relationship in which you may not know who you are, but can respect the image you have of yourself. It can be a rejecting relationship in which you know who you are, but do not respect yourself. Finally, you can be a stranger to yourself. You do not know who you are and cannot respect yourself. You do not have a "self" to which you can be "true."

In Hamlet (Act 1 Scene 3), Shakespeare wrote,

> This above all: to thine ownself be true,
>
> And it must follow, as the night the day,
>
> Thou canst not then be false to any man.[19]

The most important belief you have about yourself is your belief as to your worth. Upon what does your value as a person, depend? Does it depend upon occupation, attractiveness, others' appraisals, skills, money, or material possessions? However you judge your worth, you may judge others the same way. If your personal yardstick for assessing your worth is wealth, you may judge the wealthy as more worthy and the poor as less worthy. It can help to buoy your self-esteem with the balloons of health, relationships, occupation, skills, money, and possessions. How do you value yourself when these balloons break and you hold only the strings? Anyone can feel good about himself or herself when they are healthy, loved, employed, skilled, and have possessions. How do you value yourself when you are ill, alone, unemployed, unskilled, and possession-less?

Your true value as a person rests upon only one thing -- your uniqueness as a human being. Death reminds us of a person's true worth -- that their unique lives are irreplaceable. There has never been, nor will there ever be another exactly like you. No one on earth ever has, or ever will have, your fingerprints, voiceprint, hair, eyes, skin, personality, and DNA structure. You may share many experiences with others, but no one will ever experience the same thing in precisely the same way as you. If you know who you are, you can value yourself as a unique individual. If you do not know who you are, you cannot.

Most of us have an array of conflicting, contradictory, and coexistent appraisals of ourselves. There is a connection between your attitude towards yourself and your attitude towards others. This attitude connection determines the nature of your relationships. While your level of self esteem varies over time, all that is important is the extent to which you occupy one position more than another over a lifetime.

THE ATTITUDE CONNECTION (Snow P. 1988)

	Positive Towards Others	Negative Towards Others
Positive **Towards** **Self**	Trust - Trust Equality Cooperative Mutual Respect Healthy Acceptance - Acceptance Approval - Approval Appreciation – Appreciation Offer - Offer Assertive Move With Love	Trust - Trust Superiority Competitive / Domineering Respect - Contempt Dependent / Vulnerable Acceptance - Rejection Approval - Disapproval Appreciation - Deprecation "Offer" - Seek Aggressive Move Against Anger
	Positive Towards Others	**Negative Towards Others**
Negative **Towards** **Self**	Mistrust - Trust Inferiority Submissive Contempt – Respect Dependent / Vulnerable Rejection – Acceptance Disapproval - Approval Deprecation - Appreciation Seek - "Offer" Passive Move Toward Fear / Guilt	Mistrust - Mistrust Superior / Inferior Enmeshed / Avoidant Contempt - Contempt Mutually / Vulnerable Rejection - Rejection Disapproval - Disapproval Deprecation - Deprecation Seek - Seek Passive / Aggressive Move Toward / Move Away Fear / Guilt / Anger

The Positive / Positive Position:

You trust yourself and others. You believe you and others are equal as human beings. Your relationships are cooperative and healthy. You respect yourself and others. You maintain a positive level of self-esteem independently of others' evaluations of your worth. You accept yourself and others -- in spite of imperfections. You approve of the positive qualities in yourself and others. You appreciate yourself and others for who you and they are -- unique individuals. You and others share what you both need. Positive self-esteem is not a given. You assert yourself to protect yourself from the attempts of others who would elevate their self-esteem at your expense. You "move with" people and are motivated by love. You are most likely to move from a positive/positive position to a negative/positive position when your fear and guilt predominate.

The Positive / Negative Position:

You trust yourself but distrust others. You believe you are superior to others. This belief may be a result of over-compensation for fears of inferiority and becoming submissive. You are competitive and domineering in relationships, as you need to prove your superiority to others. You respect yourself but have contempt for others. You are unable to maintain a positive level of self-esteem independently of others' evaluations of your worth. You are in a vulnerable position because your self-esteem requires you to keep others subservient to you. You accept, appreciate, and approve of yourself but reject, belittle, and disapprove of others. Your self-esteem appears to be high and you apparently offer what others need.

Your style is aggressive as you maintain your inflated self-esteem by intimidating, dominating, and controlling others. You "move against" people, motivated by anger. You are most likely to move from a negative/positive to a negative/negative position when fear and guilt predominate. At an extreme level, this pattern is similar to Paranoid, Narcissistic, Antisocial, or Obsessive Compulsive Personality Disorders. There is room in this description for a yet-undefined pattern I would call Bureaucratic Personality Disorders.

The Negative / Positive Position:

You do not trust yourself but naively place too much trust in others. You believe you are inferior to others. You are submissive in your relationships. You have contempt for yourself and yet treat others with respect. You are unable to maintain a positive level of self-esteem independently of others' evaluations of your worth. You are in a vulnerable position since others' evaluations determine your sense of worth. You reject, belittle, and disapprove of yourself and yet accept, appreciate, and approve of others. You seek love and respect from others. You passively comply and tolerate domination, intimidation, and aggression from others who maintain their self-esteem at your expense. You "move toward" people, motivated by fear and guilt. You are most likely to move from a negative/positive position to a negative/negative position when anger predominates. At an extreme level, this pattern is similar to Dependent and Histrionic Personality Disorders.

The Negative / Negative Position:

You do not trust yourself or others. You vacillate between believing you are superior and inferior to others. Your relationships vary from enmeshed to avoidant, in a confusing pattern of approach and retreat. You have contempt for yourself and others. Your relationships are mutually vulnerable, as you and others are unable to maintain a positive level of self-esteem independently of each other's evaluations. You reject, belittle, and disapprove of yourself and others. You seek love and respect from others, who seek the same from you. Neither is able to offer the same to each other. Your style is a confused one of "move toward" and "move away" from people, motivated by fear, guilt, and anger. You are most likely to move from a negative/negative position to a positive/negative position when anger predominates. At an extreme level, this pattern is similar to Schizoid, Borderline, and Avoidant Personality Disorders

The British Home Children were predisposed to occupy the negative/positive or negative/negative position. Many, out of necessity, developed lifelong coping strategies that deprived them of healthy relationships with themselves and others.

The Childhood Trauma of "Coming Into Care"

When people in financial distress exhausted all of their and their extended families' resources, they reluctantly led their children to the high-walled institutions and placed their children "in care." Half of the children Barnardo admitted from 1882-1908 were for economic reasons. They admitted another third of these cases for "moral reasons." The sanctimonious attitudes towards the families of the poor persisted throughout the history of the British Child Deportation Scheme. The child-care organizations attributed poverty to negligence and unemployment to idleness. They referred to common-law marriages of the poor as "vicious" (Parr 62, 78).

Self-appointed "Child-Savers" benevolently abducted (kidnapped) children. Some were so obsessed with rescuing children from their evil influences (families), that they actively searched for these children of the destitute. The child-care organizations portrayed these families as evil, vicious, tainted, depraved, base, corrupt, immoral, and incorrigible. In modern times, they depicted them as irresponsible, unreliable, untrustworthy, and disreputable. Throughout the history of the scheme, they saw the poor as undeserving of their children. The "Child-Savers" ensured from the outset, that children in care would not know who they were. In their minds, they were convinced they had rescued children, but in doing so, they destroyed their souls. Parents had to sign an Admission Form, that authorized the organization to "bring the child up." This allowed them to "train" children and "send" them to "any situation in the United Kingdom." Few parents anticipated their children would be deported as young as six years old. Once in care, the organizations limited, discouraged, or forbade family contact. Most parents never knew of their children's welfare or whereabouts. Most children never saw their families again.

The organizations usually placed young children in a Receiving Home for assessment and distribution. Once admitted, the first door to their past was slammed shut -- never to be opened again. Admission into care was permanent, and was designed to remove children from their families forever. Children immediately and invariably suffered the traumatic experience of Maternal Deprivation. The younger were the children, the more severe the effects upon normal personality development. From the Receiving Homes, children were placed on trains to foster homes, Boys' or Girls' Homes, or a ship to Canada. Once the train ride ended, another door to their past was irrevocably closed. Each step in the process added to their isolation and alienation from all that was familiar to them.

Those children who suffered the most their losses of identity were those who were deported at very young ages to Canada. Next were those who spent their entire childhood in the Homes and were then deported. Next, were those first placed in foster homes, then a Home, and then deported. This is only because the foster homes offered them some semblance of a family life and exposure to normal daily life. At least in these placements, they were allowed to use their names and to speak. They were still alienated as non-persons, because they belonged to no one.

Children react to trauma differently, depending upon their ages. Infants can only cry. Their emotional expressions range from hyperactivity to apathy. They do not develop attachment nor do they learn to trust. Their eating and sleeping patterns are disrupted. Their language and motor skills are arrested. They fail to thrive physically. Toddlers become hyperactive and do not develop social skills and independence. Preschool children display their distress through repetitive play, avoidance, clinging ness, sadness, dissociation, and regression. School age children react with anxiety, depression, and guilt. Their concentration is impaired and their language development is delayed. Adolescents act out with suicide attempts, substance abuse, delinquency, truancy, and self-mutilation. They suffer identity problems, personality disorders, and eating difficulties (Schwarz & Perry 10-11).

Enuresis was a widespread problem among the British Home Children. Estimates of incidence ranged from 10-66%. Canadians regarded this "low habit" as an indicator of the children's "low beginnings" and proof of their Parents' bad moral lives. Enuretic children were seen as having weak constitutions and lacking in mental vigour and physical development. Some were deported back to England if they could not overcome this problem (Parr 103-104).

Child Training or Brainwashing?

The child-care organizations did not merely "train" children -- they brainwashed them. The term was first used to describe the experiences of Allied prisoners in the Korean War. They were adults who had established identities before their capture. For many, the simple knowledge they had loved ones was enough for them to survive their treatment. British Home Children were prisoners until they were 18 years old and had served their indenture as farm labourers in Canada. Their survival depended upon the speed of their conversion. The brainwashing of helpless, dependent, and vulnerable children was relatively easy for the child-care organizations to accomplish. The children were incapable of resistance and their Families were powerless to protect them.

How do you brainwash someone? You need to have total control over a person to conduct a program of thought reform. You remove him from his familiar environment and assume absolute control of his time. You make him feel powerlessness. You keep him ignorant of what is happening to him and how he is being changed. You strip him of his identity so he will lose confidence in his beliefs. You relentlessly attack his beliefs about his former identity to confuse him. You punish him whenever he displays behaviours consistent with his former identity. You place him into a converted group. They act as models for him to imitate and provide approval once he begins to conform and comply. You provide some rewards when he adapts to his new environment. He acquiesces because he fears the loss of these new relationships if he fails to convert. You work him hard, so he is too tired to resist. If he asks questions, you use this against him. You tell him that his questioning proves there is something inherently wrong with him. You convince him he is evil. He cannot challenge you or the authoritarian structure in a highly controlled and coercive environment. He is always wrong (American Family Foundation 1).

The British child-care organizations began the process of thought reform by transforming the children into objects. The organizations publicly portrayed them as "orphans" who had no Parents and Families. The Child Migrants Trust researched thousands of cases over a seven-year period, and found only one child who had lost both Parents. It suited the pecuniary purposes of the organizations to portray their wards as orphans for 100 years. They called them "Waifs," and implied they were "pieces of abandoned property." They were "things," rather than someone's Son or Daughter. This prevented the public from empathizing with the children as children similar to their own. The organizations depicted the families as undeserving of sympathy and unworthy of consideration. This resulted in the children being treated as an inferior sub-category of the human race by their caretakers. Canadians regarded them in a similar way, and treated them accordingly.

Christian child-care organizations in Canada housed Aboriginal children in Residential Schools. They abused these children to "take the Indian out of the Indian." The British Home Children were dehumanized to "take the taint of their origins out of them." No one challenged, questioned, or opposed the child-care organizations' methods in England or Canada.

Brainwashing is a deliberate process that follows a predictable pattern (Lifton 1989). You place someone in a situation of extreme physical and psychological distress to make him amenable to changing his beliefs about himself. You apply intellectual, emotional, and physical pressure to make sure he converts. You make him confess, expose, and denunciate his former "evil" self. He experiences a death and rebirth of his personality. You deprive him of basic necessities in the early stages of the process, and later encourage him to seek acceptance into a reformed group. His will and power to resist is weakened. He inevitably surrenders his independence and identity. He becomes mentally and emotionally blank. While he is in this vulnerable state, you impose upon him a totally different personality.

There is a predictable sequence to the process of brainwashing (Lifton 1-6).

(1) Assault on identity.
(2) Recognition of guilt.
(3) Self-betrayal.
(4) Breaking point of basic fear.
(5) Breaking point of total conflict.
(6) Desperate gratitude.
(7) Compulsion to confess.
(8) Channelling of guilt.
(9) Logical dishonouring.
(10) Sense of harmony
(11) Final confession.
(12) Ideological rebirth.
(13) Transitional limbo.

Only the first six phases apply to the British Home Children, as adults usually experience the final phases.

1.   Assault on Identity: The individual is physically and emotionally deprived to render him more suggestible. He regresses into a state of helplessness where he surrenders his autonomy. He is coerced into believing he is not the person he once thought he was.

You are a six-year-old child in London, England in 1913. Your Mother tells you she is taking you to see some people who will "take care of you." You wear your best clothes. Your Mother holds back tears as you go through a large gate set into a high stone wall. The huge stone institution frightens you. The people inside look down upon you and your Mother. They lead you away from your Mother and take you into a large hall where strange children stare at you with blank faces. It is eerily still and quiet. Your caretakers take your best clothes from you. You will not see them again. They give you old, worn clothes, and ill-fitting shoes to wear. They cut your hair off in chunks. They bath you in a tub surrounded by the other children. You wonder why the only sound is the splashing of the water in the tub. They roughly dry you with a thin towel and cover you with delousing powder. They say you are, "Verminous." You are in their "care."

You cry for your Mother. Someone slaps your face and says, "You don't have a Mother anymore!" You tell them your name. They slap you again and say, "You don't have a name! You are Boy Number 18264!" The other children just look away or look through you. At night, you wet your bed, and the straw mattress stays wet for weeks. You cannot sleep because you are so afraid. You are never alone or away from the ever-present influence of your caretakers. Peer monitors make note of your every deviation from what they define "acceptable behaviours." They report you to your caretakers for public punishment. They strip you bare and cane you in front of all the other blank-faced children. Every night some child is caned.

You are hungry and cold all the time. Your skin breaks out in sores and your scalp is covered with lice. You constantly work at scrubbing wooden floors in your short pants. You get slivers in your knees and you pull them out yourself. They tell you your Mother is never coming to get you. They say she abandoned you because she did not want you any more. They say you are bad, like all the other children in the Home. You feel confused and completely helpless. You believe what these powerful adults tell you. After a time, you began to believe you do not belong to anyone. They tell you your Mother is dead, you are a deserted Stray, and now you are an Orphan. When they strip you of your name, they strip you of your identity. You have serious doubts about your life before you were "in care." You regard your present life in the institution as reality, and your past life in a family as fantasy. They tell you that you just imagined you were part of a family.

2. Recognition of Guilt. The individual is assailed unmercifully with messages and demands that make him feel guilty. His subconscious mind is impregnated with so many thoughts of his evil-ness that they seep into his conscious mind. The thought of, "You are evil," becomes, "I am evil." His thinking becomes saturated with thoughts of personal evil. He is convinced he alone is the cause of his suffering. He is convinced he deserves to suffer. He expects nothing less than suffering.

As a helpless young child in such a situation, you are desperate for affection and approval from any source. Affection is not forthcoming, so you settle for approval. Powerful adults force you to comply with their expectations and demands. You internalize their negative appraisals. Your survival depends upon this. They can beat you and starve you to death by withholding food. They once placed you on a bread and water diet for three days. You know you cannot do that again. You dare not use your name, for fear of the punishment that would inevitably follow. People have names. You have a number. You are not a person. They do not allow you to speak. They tell you that nothing you could say could be of any importance. You cannot smile or laugh. You learn the best way to not show feeling was to not feel. You "numb" yourself.

They tell you that you are not whom you believe yourself to be -- a member of a family. They ask you hundreds of times, "What did you do, to be in a Home?" You quickly assume that either you must have done something bad, or you were inherently bad. These are the only acceptable answers to their question. You respond by saying, "I was bad." They ask you why you were bad. You answer, "I was evil." They are pleased. If you assert you have a family, they bombard you with questions you cannot answer. "Who are they?" "Where are they?" "Why don't you live with them?" "Why don't they come to see you?" These onslaughts shatter your fragile self-esteem. They make you feel guilty, inferior, worthless, and ashamed -- not so much for what you had done -- but for who you are. You are a Waif. You are a thing. You are tainted by your origins. The word, "Family" fades from your thinking. It becomes synonymous with the words they use. They call your family, "Your Evil Associations."

3. Self-Betrayal: Protestations of innocence are regarded as proof of guilt. The premise is one of, "Only the guilty need to protest their innocence." The individual learns his survival depends upon his confession of secrets already known to his caretakers. He is completely dependent upon them for food, clothing, and shelter. His existence depends upon his compliance. His self-betrayal produces deep feelings of guilt and disloyalty. He confesses to win his caretakers' approval. Once this line is crossed, it is very difficult for him to turn back.

You cannot argue with your caretakers. You are a helpless and anonymous child. They make you eat spoiled food. They force you to wear dirty clothes. They do not change your soiled mattress and you sleep in a urine-soaked bed. They beat you and place you in a dark closet for days. They tell you that your Parents were not married. They call them "vicious" and they deserve to be dead. They call you an "Illegitimate Bastard." You have to agree your Parents neglected you and did not provide for you. You agree you are "Tainted by Evil." You renounce your parents, identity, and origins.

4. Breaking Point of Basic Fear: The captive suffers unbearable emotional conflicts when he is estranged from all that is familiar and his own inner self. He fears total annihilation. His physical and mental integration breaks down. He becomes more anxious and depressed. He has delusions and hallucinations as his psyche tries to protect itself from a fear of total disintegration. He thinks of suicide.

You fear annihilation. You are completely estranged from your family, yourself, and the other children. You cannot speak with the other children because of The Rule of Silence. You do not trust some of them. You learn to dissociate yourself when they punish you or force you to watch others being punished. It is just as painful to watch other children being caned as to be caned yourself. You have few other options other than learning to mentally absent yourself. You are a prisoner. No one knows where you are. You cannot defend yourself. You cannot run away. You are alone and on your own. You live in a state of constant fear. Wild animals "play dead," or collapse into a posture of appeasement to minimize a threat. Children in threatening situations from which they cannot escape, "absent" themselves. Haworth-Attard described the dissociative look as one in which colour drained from children's eyes. This allowed them to wash away their distress, or hide it from others who might take delight in their distress (25).

5. Breaking Point of Total Conflict: The individual becomes confused as to the real truth of his past. His defences weaken because he is totally estranged from his familiar surroundings. His feelings of alienation are exacerbated when he seeks to escape the intolerable stress with self-betrayal. He becomes more estranged from his self.

Your childhood defences are quite inadequate to withstand the brainwashing process. Your "choices" are limited. You either maintain your beliefs about yourself and your past -- and pay tremendous penalties for doing so -- or abandon them. Your newly imposed identity as a worthless thing smothers your previous identity as someone's child. You are driven by self-preservation. You abandon your former beliefs and sacrifice the last remnants of your unique self. You become what your caretaker's want you to become -- a compliant "Waif." It will be difficult to leave this identity behind you. When you are no longer in care, and are 60 years old, they call you an "Old Boy." Since this is the only identity you have, you refer to yourself as an "Old Boy," too.

6. Desperate Gratitude: This part of the brainwashing process could be called, "Grasping at straws." Just as the individual reaches the breaking point, he may be shown unexpected kindness and leniency. This coincides with encouragement to confess. He cooperates with his reform, as this as his only escape from total self-annihilation.

Unexpected kindness is a rare occurrence in the Home. Your caretakers instead show some leniency in punishments as a reward for your compliance. To secure relief from daily torment, you grasp at the only available straw. You become passive, subservient, ingratiating, guilt-ridden, and ashamed. You appear to be a, "Good Waif." When you "came into care," your caretakers stripped you of your legitimate identity. They set it aside as something unclean. They never returned it to you. They kept you naked for a time until you renounced who you "used to be." They did not allow you clothe yourself in your new identity until you agreed you *never* were who you thought you were. They made you admit you were mistaken about this. Then they allowed you to wear your new identity. You learned to express your gratitude to them.

Some of your peers readily accepted their new identities and wore them proudly. Their gratitude was desperate and they professed that becoming a Waif was the best thing that ever happened to them. They thanked their caretakers for rescuing them from their "evil associations," and loudly proclaimed they had "given them a better life than they ever would have had with their families." Such convictions were held even though these children had nothing with which to compare their lives "in care." You secretly wondered just how "evil" were your previous "Associations" -- your Family. You wore the "Waif" identity loosely and vowed you would find the truth about your origins. This new identity constrained you like ill-fitting clothes. The longer you wore them, the more you felt as if you were inside a straightjacket. Very deep inside yourself, you wanted to believe you were not what they said you were. You sustained a tiny belief you had a Family somewhere. This hope kept you going.

The organizations led you to believe Canada was the Promised Land and you would be warmly welcomed. You endured life in the Homes in the hope that eventually you would have "a better life in Canada." Some other children naively believed Canadian families would adopt them. You were sadly disappointed, when you met with a cruel prejudice. Canadians treated you as farm stock rather than as someone's child. They made you live in the barns with the other animals. They segregated you from their families because they feared you would infect them with your "tainted blood." You were imprisoned by your indenture, as you were imprisoned in the Home. There was nowhere for you to run, and no one to whom you could turn for help. All you had for company was the guilt and shame imposed upon you in England and reinforced in Canada. All you had was an imposed identity that would haunt you all your life.

Long after you were in care, you continued to endure an assault on your identity. It was unremitting, merciless, and lifelong. Others asked you all your life who you were. You could only respond by saying your name -- even though you were not certain it was yours. They asked you about your Parents and Family. You replied the only way you could. You repeated these statements, thousands of times. "I am an orphan." "My Parents are dead." "I have no Brothers or Sisters." "I don't know why I was raised in an institution." "I don't have a Birth Certificate." Each time you said these words, you unintentionally reinforced the identity they had imposed upon you. Still, you tried to sustain the flickering belief you had a Family somewhere.

The Legacy: Depersonalization and Dissociation

A Depersonalization Disorder (DSM-IV 1994) is a condition in which you feel like an observer of your life rather than an active participant. Loss of identity is synonymous with depersonalization. You feel your thoughts are not yours, and your body and mind are disconnected. Estrangement from your self can be a frightening experience, as it is your self that anchors you to reality. For most, it is usually a transitory adult phenomenon, similar to an "identity crisis." Occasionally, you may feel "out of touch" with yourself. You might describe the condition of depersonalization as, "I do not feel like myself," or "I do not know who I am anymore." If the condition persisted, your ability to function could be impaired by your distorted perceptions of reality.

British Home Children did not have much opportunity to acquire an identity before they came into care. The organizations took their fledgling identities from them. The only time the children ever felt "themselves," was before they came into care. They did not have the luxury of saying, "I used to know who I was, but now I don't." All they could ever say was, "I don't know who I am." They lived their lives in a constant state of depersonalization. They had nothing with which to identify themselves as individuals. They could not claim to belong to anyone.

The organizations sent their siblings in care to separate foster homes and Homes. They deported their siblings to different countries. They separated siblings they sent to the same country. The children were abandoned in Canada by the organizations that deported them, and rejected by Canadians. Only those who experienced a modicum of human kindness were able to assuage the painful, repetitive experiences of their childhood. Most would suffer lifelong estrangement from themselves and others, in both England and Canada.

British Home Children who were faced with overwhelming emotional or physical pain, from which they could not escape, "ran away" in their minds. The process of Dissociation allowed them to psychologically isolate the ideas, feelings, and memories of their experiences. They could escape temporarily and were later able to act as if they never experienced the trauma. When they dissociated, information was not connected with other information, as it normally would have been. They suffered amnesia as a result. This allowed them to protect themselves from not only remembering the pain, but also re-experiencing the traumatic situations. Amnesia spread from the traumatic incident and further contaminated their imposed identities.

Children subjected to repetitive, overwhelming, and unrelenting trauma, may learn to cope with crises by relying upon the extremely effective psychological technique of dissociation. If used overused, dissociation can become an automatic, habitual response to perceived threat -- even in non-threatening situations. Research has shown that living in a constant state of fear and crises can produce biochemical changes in the brain. Over time, the dissociating coping can become a dominant aspect of children's personalities. When dissociation is so frequent that it disrupts a person's ability to function, it can develop into a chronic condition known as a Dissociative Disorder (DSM-IV 1994). It is usually the result of childhood trauma before the age of nine years old. Symptoms can include any or all of the following: anxiety attacks, depression, mood swings, suicidal tendencies, sleep disorders, phobias, alcohol/drug abuse, compulsions, rituals, hallucinations, eating disorders, headaches, amnesia, time loss, trances, out-of-body experiences, self-injury, self-persecution, self-sabotage, and aggressiveness (Sidran Foundation 1999).

As adults, most British Home Children hid their pasts from their spouses and families. For some there simply was nothing to tell, as their memories were impaired by repression-induced amnesia. Many were ashamed of themselves. An individual develops genuine and close interpersonal relationships because of mutual disclosure of ideas, beliefs, opinions, experiences, and feelings. British Home Children had a difficult time disclosing who they were, as they did not know who they were. What opportunity did they have to disclose themselves in the Home environments where reigned the Rule of Silence? Emotional closeness and feelings of belonging were foreign to them. These experiences made it difficult for others to know them. All yearned to know the families from whom they were taken. This is where they last belonged, and where they felt like people rather than things.

An Acute Stress Disorder (DSM-IV 1994) can develop within a month of traumatic experiences. These contain the potential for loss of life or serious injury, and create intense fear, helplessness, or horror. Children are more susceptible to stress reactions than adults are. Dissociative symptoms can occur during or after the event along with other symptoms such as: emotional numbness, detachment, reduced awareness, feelings of unreality, depersonalization, and amnesia. The traumatic event may be re-experienced as intrusive recollections, images, thoughts, dreams, flashbacks, and distress when reminded of the event. People, places, and activities related to the event may be avoided. Hyper arousal may develop and take the form of sleep difficulties, irritability, poor concentration, hyper-vigilance, startle response, and restlessness. Symptoms usually last a few days and dissipate a month after the traumatic event. Recurrent traumatic experiences perpetuate the reaction and a chronic condition develops.

A Post Traumatic Stress Disorder (DSM-IV, 1994) is characterized by recurrent and intrusive recollections of the event. These can include thoughts, images, perceptions, and dreams about the trauma. People may feel or act as if the traumatic event were happening again. They experience intense distress and severe physical when exposed to aspects of the event. They persistently avoid stimuli associated with the trauma and their general responsiveness is numbed. They may avoid thinking and talking about the trauma, and may avoid anyone and anything associated with the trauma. People are usually unable to recall important aspects of the trauma. They may lose interest and reduce participation in their usual activities. They may feel detached and estranged from others and their usual range of emotional response may become restricted. They may develop a sense of a foreshortened future and may not expect to have a normal life and life span. The condition is called chronic if these symptoms last longer than three months.

If an individual experiences a series of traumatic events, he may have little opportunity to recover from one before having to contend with another. Children are not as resilient as we might think. They do not become inoculated nor are they "toughened up" by their traumatic experiences. Rather, these events can have a profound immediate as well as long-term negative impact upon their adult functioning. The idea of stress and stress reactions is not new. Before WWI, Walter Cannon described how the body responded to stress with either a "fight" or "flight" reaction. The British Home Children were hardly in a position of "fight" in their captive environments. Nor could they "flee" by withdrawing, avoiding, or escaping the stress. They learned instead to "freeze," and dissociate themselves.

Whether the threat is imaginary or actual, the fearful response is immediate. It is an adaptive, inescapable, and uncontrollable reaction in which resources are instantly mobilized to deal with threat. A sophisticated neurophysiological reaction occurs in the brain, autonomic, and immune system. The alarm reaction includes hyper arousal, pounding heart, chest pain, sweating, trembling, shortness of breath, "lump in the throat," abdominal distress, light-headedness, feelings of unreality, fear of losing control, emotional numbness, blurred vision, and hypersensitivity. If the threat is less than first perceived the system reverts to a more relaxed mode. Living a life of constant fear can cause the circuitry of the brain to create over-developed pathways of either 'fight, flight, or freeze' responses (Perry 5).

Severe, prolonged, or recurrent stresses cause tremendous increases in neurotransmitter activity that can significantly alter brain development. Post Traumatic Stress Disorders in childhood can produce irreversible physical alterations of the Central Nervous System. These can cause altered heart regulation, emotional lability, impulsive behaviours, increased anxiety, and sleep abnormalities. The neurological systems can become hypersensitive to future stressful events. Children raised in stressful environments are more susceptible to developing more severe symptoms with each exposure to stress (Schwarz & Perry 4).

The most traumatic event for a child is loss of a parent. Cardiovascular disease, immunological, neuroendocrine, and adult emotional disorders have been associated with parental loss in childhood. These are more likely to occur if parental loss is compounded by the absence of supportive adult relationships following to the loss. Children who suffer a severe trauma such as parental loss before four years old are more at risk to develop severe pre-psychotic and psychotic symptomatology in adult life. Children, who experience trauma later in childhood, are more at risk to develop symptoms that are similar to adult Post Traumatic Stress Disorders. The most consistent physical finding with traumatized children is Autonomic Nervous System hyper arousal (Schwartz & Perry 7).

If a child is hyper-aroused, chronically anxious, and "on guard," any innocuous stimulus can trigger an alarm response. This reaction creates increased anxiety and a chronic hyper-aroused state. A vicious circle is maintained. The "fight or flight" options are not usually available to young, helpless children. Some learn by default, to "freeze." With repetitive stress, these children acquire a sensitized hyper arousal or dissociative syndrome. They automatically "freeze" when overwhelmed by anxiety.

"Freezing" is the first step towards complete dissociation. The entire Central Nervous System is involved whether a child reacts with either hyper-arousal or dissociation. Even though the reactions are different, the system always reacts as it was designed to react. Each exposure to stress strengthens the "freeze" response. It can develop into an automatic response to anticipated or actual threats, or it can become the "normal" state for a traumatized child (Perry et al. 10)

Malignant Memories of a Traumatic Childhood

A memory consists of information about experiences that is conveyed over time. Every system in the body is designed to collect and convey memories across time to ensure the survival of the complete organism. Every living cell has its life cycle that ends in its death. Every cell replicates itself before it dies. Through complex physiological processes, every cell of the body passes on critical information to its replacement and to *every* other living cell. Every skin cell needs to know what its predecessor knew -- that it is a skin cell. If a skin cell was scarred before it died, it passed this information along to its successor. Every cell is intricately connected -- and in some unknown fashion -- in communication with every other cell of the body.

What experiences are collected and transmitted to every other cell in your body? It is entirely possible that every thought, feeling, movement, sight, smell, taste, sound, and experience you have ever had are recorded intact in the billions of brain cells in your mind. Since brain cells do not function in isolation, all of this information may be recorded in, and transmitted to, every other cell of your body. These experiences may exist as memories and may be passed on to every generation since the beginning of time. One could hardly make a case that children of Holocaust survivors are identical in their development compared to children of those who had not experienced this horror.

You inherited your genetically determined physical characteristics when you were conceived. Memories of experiences may be carried from cell to cell *and* across generations. Your brain is changed by your experiences -- all of your experiences -- both good and bad. It is attuned to your internal and external environments. It processes information, stores sensations, and acts to promote survival, by creating internal representations of the external world. The associations between audio, visual, olfactory, tactile, and emotional components of events are stored as memories in the mind (Perry et al. 10). These memories of experiences are recorded completely intact with precise sights, sounds, smells, tastes, sensations, and movements. The mind is designed to process, record, and transmit all of your experiences as memories. Not all of these memories are benign. Some of them are malignant. Most exist at a subconscious level in a dormant state.

Malignant memories can be awakened by external sensory cues or internal cognitive, affective, somatic, or behavioural cues. Once activated, they flood consciousness and trigger either hyper-reactivity or hypo-reactivity. Either set of responses can create depression, and disorganization. High levels of arousal create: cognitive distortions, dissociative and somatic states, emotional and behavioural reactivity, numbness, amnesia, or avoidance. Each time the malignant memory is activated, it takes less and less to awaken it. It lies out of awareness, waiting to be triggered again. Traumatized children who experience repetitive stress are at risk to develop "traumatized brains" that are characterized by deregulated neurological systems. They develop a neurological template that is different from non-traumatized children. It consists of excessive fear, threats, unpredictability, insecurity, frustration, anger, helplessness, powerlessness, hunger, and pain. Young or chronically traumatized children react to a wide variety of triggers that may not be directly connected with the original trauma (Schwartz & Perry 8-15).

The past is not always past. The indelible marks of childhood trauma extend well beyond childhood. Time does not always heal these wounds and traumatized children are more at risk to develop psychopathological symptoms rather than be inoculated against it. Children who lived their lives in fear experience ongoing, repetitious alarm reactions of varying intensities. They adapted to living in an emotional state that varied from High-Medium-Low Stress -- but always in an internal and external environment of stress.

The brain processes information by association and generalization. It connects separate pieces of information, associates them together, and stores the collage as a response to a threat. It also loosely connects bits of information and generalizes from the specific to the broad. Should a threat occur, the brain produces the appropriate response. Often remote cues can set off an inappropriate response because of false associations and false generalizations. The alarm response can be triggered by cues that are only remotely similar to the original cues associated with the threat. The Viet Nam veteran may have initially reacted to the sound of a helicopter but may now inappropriately respond to any sound that is remotely similar. An increase in heart rate may have been part of the initial response to a threat. Long after the threat is gone, an innocent rise in heart rate can trigger an inappropriate alarm response. The brain stored this original memory, associated it with a threat, and now is unable to distinguish between the two cues (Perry 6).

While an adult is capable of cognitively making distinctions between an appropriate and inappropriate response, the child is not. The child simply reacts without knowing why. Malignant memories supplanted whatever initial, safe, secure, and contented memories the British Home Children may have had. The emotional state associated with the former memories did not just fade with time. Their caretakers erased these memories when they stole their identities. The children could not keep these memories alive because they were not allowed to think or speak of their former lives and identities. They could not even find a safe haven in their pasts before they "came into care." They were trapped in the present, cut off from the past, and always fearful about the future.

Even though significant traumatic experiences of early childhood may not recur, their effects leave their mark. Malignant memories are etched in the minds of children by neurochemical changes. They are as much a part of an individual's personality as are any other benign memories. All can intrude upon and transform the individual's present perceptions. No one can help but carry all of these relics of their past into their present. Malignant memories are not entirely passive. They can insidiously intrude into the present transform the present to conform to the template of the past. Even when all is going well, a past memory can sabotage the present.

You know who you are. You have a name you are certain is yours. You have Parents and a known Family from which you came. You know when and where you were born. You know you are someone's Son, Brother, Grandson, and Nephew. You think your thoughts, feel your feelings, and know they are your own. You feel an affinity with others. You conduct your life according to your certain beliefs about yourself, others, and the world in which you live. You feel you belong no matter where you are, or whom you are with. You feel like a legitimate resident on the planet. You are an active participant in your life. A complex collection of beliefs about yourself lies at the centre of your being. This is your unique identity -- this is who you are. It is what makes you a human being -- whose life has value. No one else can be, or claim to be you. Your identity serves you well as your constant companion -- someone with whom you will have a relationship all of your life. It allows you to relate to others and their unique selves. You filter all of your experiences through this core of your self that is composed of predominantly positive early childhood experiences.

You learned to love and trust at an early age. You had a relationship with your Mother that provided the basis for all of your relationships throughout your life. You were raised in a Family from whom you learned who you were. You can relate to others based on the common ground that everyone is someone's Son and Daughter. You experienced your share of pain and disappointments in childhood but these were drowned by more positive experiences of love and acceptance. Your identity is your gyroscope that maintains your stability and keeps you "on track" and "true to yourself." You know where you belong in the "grand scheme of things." You feel complete and whole, because you know who you are.

If you are a British Home Child, you do not know who you are. You have a name but you are not sure it is yours. You do not know your Parents and cannot identify the family from which you came. You do not know when and where you were born. You are no one's Son, Brother, Grandson, and Nephew. You think your thoughts and feel your feelings, but do not feel they are even yours. You do not feel an affinity with others, but feel very much distant from them. You conduct your life according to your uncertain beliefs about yourself, others, and the world in which you live. You do not feel you belong, no matter where you are, or whom you are with. You feel like a foreigner always in a foreign land. You feel like a perpetual traveler rather than a resident. You are a passive observer of your life.

Vague, disparate ideas about yourself lie at the centre of your being. Your identity is composed of labels such as "Waif, Orphan, Boy Number 18264, Home Child, and Old Boy." This is your identity -- this is who you are. You do not have a unique identity. Anyone could be you, or claim to be you. You feel like a thing posing as a person. Your identity does not serve you well because your constant companion is a lonely stranger within, whom you can never know. You feel you have little in common with others, and can only relate to them as a friendly, but reserved stranger. You cannot develop close relationships with others because you never developed a close relationship with yourself. You filter all of your experiences through this shrivelled core of your self that is composed of predominantly traumatic early childhood experiences.

You were deprived of a relationship with your Mother and as a result did not learn love and trust at an early age. You were left with a wound that never completely healed. You had no conscious memories of your Mother but you feel the absence of her love that once was at the centre of your being. You were not raised with your family, so you could not know how to relate to others who were raised within their families. Every person you meet is someone's child. You are not. Your few positive experiences were drowned by more than your share of traumatic experiences of abandonment and rejection. You have no gyroscope to maintain your stability and keep you "on track" and "true to yourself." You do not know where you belong in the "grand scheme of things." You feel incomplete and feel there is something missing inside you. It is your Self.

PART V: THE UNIVERSAL RIGHTS OF A CHILD

The United Nations Convention on the Rights of the Child (UN Convention 1989) declared that a child was a human being. Many of their articles could be used to evaluate the British Child Deportation Scheme. To what extent did they conduct themselves according to the "best interests of the child," and ensure their protection, care, and well-being? What legal grounds did they have to separate children from their families? How was it in the children's best interests to *not* maintain direct and regular contact with their Families? Could the child-care organizations' "emigration" of children be considered as the illicit transfer and non-return of children abroad? How did the Rule of Silence conform to children's right to free speech? Could censorship of children's correspondence be considered unlawful interference?

If it was illegal for these school-age children to work 16-hour-days in England, how was it permissible for them to do so in Canada? What British or Canadian Child Labour Laws did they violate? To what extent were the children protected from physical violence, injury, abuse, neglect, and maltreatment? How did the child-care organizations protect children in their care from economic exploitation and sexual abuse? To what extent did they ensure children in their care enjoyed a full and decent life? How did they safeguard children's dignity, promote their self-reliance, and facilitate their active integration into society? How did they make sure children received adequate medical care and an education? Estimates of physical, sexual, and emotional abuse or neglect vary from 33-50%. This means that 30,000 - 50,000 children did *not* benefit from being "in care" and being deported to Canada.

A few articles of the Rights of the Child Declaration defined a child's right to an identity.

Article 7:1. Children should be registered immediately after they are born. They have the right from birth to a name, a nationality, and, as much as possible, to know and be cared for by their parents.

Article 8:1. Countries should respect the right of children to preserve their identities -- their names, nationalities, and family relationships -- without unlawful interference.

Article 8:2. Countries should help children re-establish their identities, where they have been illegally deprived of some or all of the elements of their identities -- their names, nationalities, and family relationships.

Article 9:3. Unless it is contrary to children's best interests, countries should respect children's rights to maintain relationships and regular, direct contact with both parents.

Article 9:4. Separation of children from families can occur because of detention, deportation, imprisonment, exile, or death of one or both parents or the child.

Countries should provide family members with essential information about the whereabouts of the absent family members, unless it is not in children's best interests.

Article 10:1. Countries should deal with applications of children or their parents to enter or leave a country for family reunification in a positive, humane, and expeditious manner.

Article 10:2. Children who live in different countries than their parents have the right to maintain regular, direct contacts with their parents.

Article 11:1. Countries should fight the illicit transfer and non-return of children abroad.

Article 16:1. Children should not be subjected to unlawful interference with their privacy, family, home, or correspondence.

Article 16:2. Children are entitled to legal protection against such unlawful interference with their privacy, family, home, or correspondence.

While the child-care organizations perhaps were not responsible for registering children's births while they were in care, they made sure they were baptized. Parents were impoverished and could not afford the cost of registering their children's births. Why did the organizations not register the children's births after they were baptized? Was it simply a matter of money?

I have seen Birth Certificates from the 1920's-1930's with only a Mother's name. Is the name of only one Parent sufficient to register a birth? What is the minimal amount of information needed to register a child's birth? I doubt any parent had to produce their child as proof at a Registry Office when they registered a birth. What would it take child-care organizations to register the children's births retroactively? Would it take an Act of British Parliament to register their 100,000 names? Could I register my Father's birth now? He did not have a Birth Certificate or anything to prove he was British. Could I apply to have him declared a British Citizen?

The child-care organizations continue to violate the rights of former children in their care (and their descendants) to their identities, by withholding vital information. It is naive to assume they will voluntarily and speedily help former wards (and their descendants) establish their identities. They themselves are responsible for having illegally deprived children of their identities.

FUTILE LIFELONG SEARCHES

My Father wrote to the Children's Society for 55 years. It took me a year and four requests to obtain relevant information from his case file. I felt that I was simply 'Canadian Enquirer #_____,' who persisted in asking about 'Case File Number 18264.' It may take many years to get information from Barnardo's about my Uncle Reg who was in their care.

My Father would have answered the question of why the child-care organizations went to such great lengths to ensure they erased children's identities. He would have said, "There is strength in numbers -- so divide and conquer." They first isolated children in care from their families. Then they isolated siblings in care from each other. Children in foster care in small villages had no contact with other children in foster care. Children in the Homes had no contact with children in other Homes. They segregated children from society-at-large in England. They deported siblings to different countries. They separated siblings deported to Canada from each other. They separated those who knew each other from the Homes. Communication with friends or relatives in England was censored. Frequent movement from one farm posting to another ensured that any ties between the British Home Children would be severed.

Part of the grand Victorian scheme was to ensure that children would never establish ties between themselves. Their only links with Britain were through the sending agencies. As long as the organizations made sure that a Brother would not find his Sister in Canada, there was little risk that unrelated children would ever unite. As long as the organizations withheld the secrets to their identities, the helpless children became powerless adults.

My Father would also an answer why the organizations did not want the children to know who they were. He would have said, "The bonds of Family are strong." Throughout history, wars have been waged because a family member was wronged. Family members defend, protect, and look after its members "own best interests." The organizations identified the captive children as "no one's children," so they were easily exploited. They had no Family from whom could they could solicit support. Their Families did not know where they were, or what kinds of lives they led.

Imagine this search scenario. Your Grandparents were John (30) and Annie Straye (30) who lived in London, England in 1908. They had three children: your Father Henry (10), your Aunt Jane (8), and your Uncle William (6). Your Grandfather John Straye died in an accident in 1908. Your widowed Grandmother was Irish and had no relatives in England. Your Grandfather's impoverished family was unable to help. Annie could not work and care for the children. It was a hard winter and she had little money for food and fuel. The children became ill shortly after your Grandfather's death. She went to the Parish Church for food for the children. One day, some people came from Barnardo's and performed a "Benevolent Abduction." They took your Aunt Jane and your Uncle William away. Your Father Henry was at a neighbour's at the time. The next day, some people from the Waifs and Strays Society came and took him away. These three children -- your Father, Uncle, and Aunt -- never saw each other again. All they remembered was their Siblings' names and approximate ages.

They Waifs and Strays Society placed your Father Henry in a Home in Kent for two years. They shipped him to Canada on the SS Sardonia on March 15, 1908, when he was 12 years old. He went to the Gibbs' Home in Sherbrooke and was sent to work on the farms in Southern Ontario. Your Aunt Jane was placed in a Barnardo foster home in Somerset until she was 12 years old, and sent to a Girls Home until she was 14 years old in 1914. She stayed in England. Your Uncle William was placed in a Barnardo foster home in Sussex for four years and shipped to Australia when he was 10 years old in 1912.

As an adult in Canada, your Father Henry tried to locate his Sister and Brother. He wrote to the Waifs and Stays Society, as he was their ward. They denied any knowledge of his Siblings. They had been in Barnardo's, but the Waifs and Strays Society either did not know, or did not tell him that. Your Aunt Jane in England contacted Barnardo's but they only told her your Uncle William had been sent to Australia and they did not know his whereabouts after 1912. They told her they had no information about your Father Henry. Your Uncle William contacted Barnardo's and tried to find information about your Father and your Aunt. They told him they had no contact with Jane since 1911. The three of them tried for 50 years to find each other, and eventually gave up. Neither organization shared information or consulted with each other about your inquiries.

Suppose you wrote to the Children's Society and Barnardo's today, asking for information about your Father, Aunt, and Uncle? What do you think they would tell you? The typical procedure for processing an inquiry from Canada such as yours follows an unvarying course. You write to the Children's Society asking about your Father. You know he was in their care. Your letter takes a week to be delivered to England. You wait a few weeks for a reply. In the past, you would have waited years for a reply. Someone writes a letter to you saying they have received your letter! They pass it on to someone else. You wait weeks for a reply. Someone manually searches for your Father's name in an index card system. The information on these cards is scant, and usually consists of dates of coming into care, placement in Homes, and shipping dates. This is information you already know. The cards are not cross-referenced as to Parents, Siblings. This allows them to tell you that they do not know if any of your other relatives were in their care. Someone writes to you to confirm that your Father was in their care. You already knew this.

You write to them asking for information. After a few weeks, they write that your letter has been passed on to someone else. You wait for weeks again. Someone reads the information you have provided. They compare this with the information they have in your Father's case file. They write to you and confirm the information you have, but do not volunteer any other information. You ask them for specific information. Their reply is evasive and they tell you that the information is either confidential or not available. They state that your Aunt and Uncle were not in their care. You take them at their word and either give up, or persist in asking questions. The more you write to them, the longer it takes them to reply. You ask for a copy of your Father's entire file and they reply that the file is the property of the organization and they have no legal obligation to release information to you.

If you write to Barnardo's they might acknowledge that your Aunt and Uncle were in their care. They would tell you they have no other information and that they are busy processing inquiries from the British Child Deportation Scheme to Australia of 1947-1967. Just as your Father would not have found his Sister and Brother, you would likely not find your Aunt and Uncle. Your Aunt would not know her Brothers. They would not know their Sister. Your Uncles would never know each other. You would never know your Aunt and Uncle.

I do not believe the proposed Central Information Index to be compiled by the National Council for Voluntary Child-care Organizations (NCVCCO) will significantly alter the search process. It may take years for the organizations to contribute their information -- and some may not even participate. In the hypothetical case above, if you did not know to which organization your Father belonged, all this index would do is confirm he was a ward of the Children's Society. The index might identify your Uncle and Aunt as wards of Barnardo's. When you contacted them, the predictable process of responding to inquiries would ensue as described. The ponderousness of the past and present will likely persist with the predictable end result.

I do not believe the Canadian descendants of the Home Children nor their unknown British relatives can or should rely upon their respective governments for assistance in their searches. Neither government in the past has shown a significant interest. The Select Committee on Health recommended "further study" and a "conference" of governments, sending agencies, child migrant representatives, information technology experts, and genealogists, etc. They intend to "discuss the problems" faced by former child migrants in obtaining information. The problems are already quite obvious -- the organizations do not want to release the information. They fear repercussions if proof of their perfidy is made public.

In the past, an association of British Home Children in Canada would have possessed a degree of strength higher than any individual member. It is too late for that. It is not too late for Canadian descendants of the British Home Children to seek each other out. We do not need to remain as invisible as our Parents and Grandparents. We can help each other reclaim our families' stolen identities. It is not too late for our British relatives to seek each other out and help each other locate their "Lost Children."

The Internet may provide an outstanding instrument for us. It may allow us to rely less upon the child-care organizations for information. If knowledge is power, then ignorance is powerlessness. By withholding vital information, these organizations have ensured that familial ties will remain severed. Throughout the history of the scheme to Canada, the organizations strategically placed themselves between the children and their "evil associations" -- a.k.a. family. They made sure they would not re-establish their natural bonds. To date, they have succeeded because both groups relied upon them for vital information that was rarely forthcoming. Our British relatives and we Canadian descendants can accomplish our goal without relying upon the cooperation of our respective governments and the organizations responsible for this absurd situation.

The Surviving British Home Children in Canada

An attempt must be made to locate and identify the surviving British Home Children in Canada. The few hundred of them in Canada are in their 80's and 90's. Some may live independently but most may be hospitalized or living in Homes for the Aged. Since so many siblings were separated and isolated from each other when they were deported to Canada, the current situation is preposterous. Your Mother could have been a British Home Child. She and her unknown Sister in Canada could have spent their lifetimes writing to England, searching for each other. Her Sister -- your Aunt -- could be currently living in a Home for the Aged in the same or another Canadian city. They would never find each other, as each would not have retained their maiden names when they married. Can you imagine the joy of helping to reunite them? Can you imagine how wonderful it would be for them to reunite with their families in Britain? It is *not* too late for them.

Each year I am moved on Remembrance Day. As the numbers of war veterans diminish with each successive year, the day will come when the last veterans of the last war die. There will be a national service to mourn their passing. They will continue to be honoured in perpetuity. Their history will be remembered for all time, because it has been sufficiently documented. The day will come when the last British Home Child dies in Canada. His immediate Family will not even know that he was the last. There will be no British Home Children history to remember in Canada. Why is this?

Just as every Canadian veteran of every war has been identified, it is time to identify every one of the British Home Children who were deported to Canada. I want to know their demographics. How many were boys and how many were girls? How many came from Scotland, Ireland, Wales, and England? How many returned to Britain? What were their ages upon entry to Canada? Who were their Parents and Siblings? Which of their Siblings were sent to different countries? How many of them married, separated, divorced? How old were they when they died? How many of them served in WWI and WWII? How did their lives compare with the Canadian population?

They could be readily identified. All someone would need to do is simply ask them how they came to Canada, and if they came *without* their families. Some would not want anyone to know. All would be surprised that someone would bother to ask. Most would willingly volunteer information about themselves, if they knew the purpose for which the information would be used. Someone could ask residents of Homes for the Aged, members of Pensioners Organizations, Union Pensioners, Royal Canadian Legion, Canadian Association of Retired Persons, etc., how they came to Canada. All someone would need to do is place an advertisement in newspapers and magazines read by the aged. The most efficient method is one of someone asking the aged, obtaining an informed consent, and submitting their information to an Internet web site. This site could be designed to help them search for and find their families in Canada, Australia, and Britain. Anyone connected to the Internet could act as an agent on their behalf. The same could be done in Australia.

Their Canadian Descendants

If you are a Canadian reader, you may be a descendant of one of the 100,000 British Home Children. One of them could have been your Parent, Grandparent, Uncle, or Aunt. Why do you not know if you are or are not a descendant? I am a first generation descendant, and yet have met few others. There are four million of us in Canada. If you are a descendant, 10% of the town or city in which you live may be composed of other descendants. In Calgary, where I live, there may be 80,000 others. Why do we not know of each other? Unless we act, we will never know of each other, and will remain as isolated and helpless as were our Parents, Grandparents, Uncles, and Aunts in their searches.

The British Home Children are Canada's Invisible Immigrants. Every other group that immigrated to Canada has been clearly identified. Their cultural and historical associations have preserved their experiences and contributions to the national mosaic. Our government has not adequately recognized the British Home Children. People like my Father, for most of their lives could not claim to be British, Canadian, or British-Canadian. We need to identify our ancestors and make them visible. We need to replace their shame with our pride and ensure their role in Canadian history is acknowledged.

In 1995, the Canadian government granted $4.5 million to build a permanent monument to Canada's Immigrants at Pier 21 in Halifax, Nova Scotia. It celebrates the profound contributions of a million immigrants from 1928-1971. These included British evacuee children, war brides and their children, and 100,000 other refugees. There is no mention of the contribution made by 100,000 British Home Children (Pier 21 1999). The Pier 21 Society did not answer my letter when I inquired why the British Home Children were not included.

Those of us who are first or second-generation descendants need to decide if we are as ashamed of our heritage as were our ancestors. If so, we will not readily identify ourselves. If not, we will volunteer whatever information we have about our families, so that our Parents, Grandparents, Uncles, and Aunts can find their siblings in Canada and their families in Britain.

Unless you know for certain that your Parents, Grandparents, Uncles and Aunts came to Canada accompanied by their families, then you yourself might be a descendant of a British Home Child. If you asked ten people, you knew how their Parents, Grandparents, Uncles, and Aunts came to Canada, at least one might turn out to be a descendant of a British Home Child. If you informed them how their information might be used to help identify and reunite British Home Children with their

Siblings in Canada and their Families in Britain, most would be willing to cooperate. You could obtain an informed consent, and submit their information to an Internet web site designed to help them search for and find their families in Canada, Australia, and Britain. Someone could place an advertisement in a local paper inquiring who might be a descendant. The same could be done in Australia.

Their British Relatives

We Canadian descendants do not know who you are. You do not know who we are. You need to identify yourselves, and each other in England, as relatives of British Home Children. I do not believe Barnardo's statement they *never* had an inquiry regarding children deported to Canada. These 100,000 British Home Children could have 400,000 British Siblings. They have 3-4 million Canadian descendants. Their British Siblings could now have 12-16 million British descendants. Combined, there could be 15-20 million Canadian and British Cousins who do not know each other.

All you would need to do is ask your families and friends if any of them had a relative that was part of the British Child Deportation Scheme to Canada. They are likely elderly and living in Homes for the Ages. They could be asked if they had siblings who were sent to Canada. Pensioner Associations and other organizations for the elderly could be surveyed. All someone would have to do is place an advertisement in newspapers and magazines read by the aged. You could ask them for information, obtain an informed consent, and submit their information to an Internet web site designed to help them search for and find their relatives in Canada and Australia. Can you imagine the joy of helping an elderly person find their Brother and Sister? I know how my Father would have felt to be able to meet his two Brothers and two Sisters.

I believe that millions of Canadian descendants and British relatives could combine their tremendous resources to ensure the restoration of severed family ties. We both know something of our common families. Each group has information or access to information that the other group does not have. I believe that the people we seek, are seeking us. The British Home Children and their descendants wanted -- and continue to want -- to know who they are. Our British relatives wanted -- and continue to want -- to know who we are. Only the child-care organizations prevented -- and continue to prevent -- us from doing this.

British Home Children Websites

Someone could create Internet websites: The British Home Children Society (Canada), The British Home Children Society (Britain), and The British Home Children Society (Australia.) Perhaps one site would be best. I do not have the expertise to do this, and I have my Practice to maintain. I do not know the most appropriate legal method of creating such societies, but someone does. These Societies could exist solely on the Internet. Membership in each could be in the millions. The primary purpose of such websites could be devoted to identifying the British Home Children, their Canadian/Australian descendants, and their British relatives. Voluntary registries could be established for each country. Newsgroups could share information. Links could be established with relevant genealogical websites. Each site could provide addresses of resources in each country. The Home Children Societies could collectively advocate for the release of information from the child-care organizations.

Fruitful Electronic Searches

This is the Electronic Age! Why do the organizations persist with processing paper? If they were genuinely concerned with the efficient processing of inquiries from British Home Children and their descendants, they would use computer resources. They are content to process inquiries as they have for the past 100 years. They have many self-serving reasons for not releasing information to inquirers.

The potential of the Internet is unlimited when it comes to the free exchange of information. My experience with the Children's Society and Barnardo's has left me quite cynical regarding their willingness to help restore severed family relationships. I found the Internet to be of immeasurable help. When I posted an inquiry to find out general information about Rumburgh, Suffolk, someone sent me a picture of his school and a class picture. Others found Census information, Birth, Marriage, and Death Certificates that were vital to validating family relationships.

Once I established the identity of my Uncle Bill, Robin found my Father's family for me. Many other strangers expended time and energy to help me with my search. If they -- with no other motive than goodwill -- could be so helpful, what would a potential relative be willing to do? We could be of tremendous help to each other. We could ask each other to search on each other's behalf in our respective countries.

Records of the lives of the British Home Children exist in each country. As they went about the business of their lives, they left a paper trail of Birth, Marriage, and Death certificates. The were employed, paid taxes, served in the military, lived in homes, voted, etc. Kind Canadians descendants could help British relatives as British strangers had so generously helped me with my search.

Each British Home Children Society website could have an on-line form for submitting information. Someone could construct an appropriate database. Millions of Canadian/Australian descendants and British relatives could voluntarily submit whatever information they had to this database. We could search these for information, exchange information, and rapidly establish familial links.

In the example above, your hypothetical Father Henry Straye was deported to Canada. You knew he had a Sister named Jane, and a Brother named William. You could submit your information to the British Home Children Society (Canada) database.

(SAMPLE)
BRITISH HOME CHILDREN SOCIETY DATABASE:
Name: Henry Straye
Date of Birth: September 1898   Location: London, England.
Father: John Straye
Date of Birth: 1878   Location: England.
Mother: Anne Straye
Date of Birth: 1878   Location: Cork, Ireland.
Marriage Date: About 1898   Location:
Sister: Jane Straye
Date of Birth: 1900   Location: England.
Brother: William Straye
Date of Birth: 1902   Location: England.
Foster Home: Tunbridge Wells, Kent, England.
Foster Parents:
Ship to Canada: SS Sardonia.   Arrival Date: March 15, 1908.
Receiving Home in Canada: Gibbs' Home, Sherbrooke, Quebec.

Suppose your Aunt Jane in England was looking for her Brothers -- your Father and your Uncle. She knew her Brother William was deported to Australia, but nothing more. She did not know that her other Brother (your Father) was sent to Canada. She would submit what she knew to the British Home Children Society (Britain) database.

Suppose your Uncle William had died in Australia, but his Son (your Cousin) was looking for his Aunt Jane in England and his Uncle William. He would submit whatever information he had about his Father. All it would take is for *one* of you to search the databases for the surname "Straye." You could instantly contact your Aunt in England and your cousin in Australia.

A Brother in Canada, a Sister in England, and a Cousin in Australia could be instantly reunited electronically. Each of you could piece together the fragments of your information. Your Aunt Jane would have the information she needed to obtain Birth, Marriage, and Death Certificates of her Siblings. The mystery would begin to unravel. You would no longer be alone. Jointly you could insist the child-care organizations release their records.

Suppose, for example, that a British searcher was looking for an Uncle named Cornelius Van Loon. All he knew was that his Uncle was deported to Canada in the 1920's. He did not know which organization sent him. His Father was deceased. If he were to search the website, he would score a "hit" on information I submitted.

If he e-mailed a message to me, I could instantly send him this reply.

> "Cornelius Van Loon was born on 09 February 1908.
> His Brother Frederick was born on 20 April 1909.
> They entered Sevenoaks Council School on October
> 10, 1921.   They previously attended Ebury Bridge
> Local Council School, St. George's Road, London,
> England.   They were wards of the Waifs and Strays
> Society and lived at St. Augustine's Church Home for
> Boys, St. John's Road, Sevenoaks, Kent.   The Master
> of the Home was Ernest Jago.   Their last day of
> attendance was 17 January 1922.   They were shipped to
> Canada in 1922.   Cornelius was 14 and Frederick was
> 13 at the time."

Can you imagine how crucial this information might be to someone? This British searcher could now obtain Birth Certificates for both of his Uncles.   They would identify his Grandparents and narrow down a location.   These little bits of information could be enough to accelerate his search to a successful conclusion.   A free exchange of information could be this simple.   The alternative for him would be to write the Children's Society for further information.   They would tell him they are busy with the inquiries of the living.   He would have to wait years.

An unknown number of British Home Children found their way into the United States.   No one knows what became of them.   The Americans had their version of a child placement scheme called the Orphan Train Riders.   The Children's Aid Society and the New York Foundling Hospital transported 150,000 - 200,000   "orphan" children to the American Midwest from 1854-1930.   They placed them on farms.   The child-care organizations placed advertisements in newspapers entitled "Homes Wanted for Orphans."   The process was very much like a mail-order catalogue. Farmers submitted their specifications for a "blond, blue-eyed, two-year-old girl." The organization shipped the child and obtained a receipt from the farmer. Unlike Canada, agents accompanied the children on the train. They took the children to churches and town halls in groups to be inspected and selected. Siblings were often separated, never to see each other again (DiPasquale 2).

I suspect that these children fared better than the British Home Children who were deported to Canada did. Perhaps the Americans regarded these children as similar to their own because they were native-born. Canadians did not regard the British Home Children as similar to their own -- they were regarded as unwanted foreigners. There may be 500 original Orphan Train riders alive today, and two million American descendants. The Americans have a national organization dedicated to preserving the records and researching these children and their descendants. An excellent web site appears to be successful in helping people with their searches. Because of the American Access to Information Act, searchers do not appear to have met with the same difficulties as descendants of the British Home Children. Why can we not establish similar websites for Canada, Australia, and Britain?

The Power of Persistence

The child-care organizations must be puzzled by the persistence of the original British Home Children in their efforts to restore family ties. They now must contend with a first and second generations who want to know who they are. I had thought my Father's case was isolated and unique, but have learned that it was typical. We need not conduct solitary searches. Millions of us in Canada and Australia along with millions of our British relatives can help each other with our searches. The Internet will allow us to do so. There is strength in our numbers, and a power to our persistence. Together we need not tolerate the arrogance and indifference of the British child-care organizations. In Canada, Australia, and Britain, we are 20 million voters.

Millions of Canadians, Australians, and Britons can communicate with each other on the Internet. We can share our information and sew together the torn fabrics of our identities. We can jointly decide upon the best method of obtaining vital information from the British child-care organizations. We have asked them and we have pleaded with them. We have sought out the support of our governments. Perhaps now is the time to demand our Families' files. They can keep the paper that is precious to them. All we want is the information -- now! I want my Uncle Reg's entire case File -- now! I am not prepared to wait years for Barnardo's to "get around to me."

We may need to consider legal alternatives to compel the child-care organizations to release our Families' files to us -- intact, uncensored, and unedited. The Government of Canada has an Access to Information and Privacy Act that allows public access to historical records and National Archives (Public Works 1999). Does Britain have a corresponding law? What is the British Access to Personal Files Act, 1987? The British Report to Parliament recommended that the Right to Privacy Laws be waived. Is this an alternative that can be pursued by legal action? Barnardo's is of the opinion that they are "not required by law" to release information to appropriate family members. The Children's Society has an "Interim Policy and Guidance Re: The Ownership of User Records" that allows them to limit the release of information. They regard the case files as confidential and their property. They regarded the children as their property as well and treated them as such.

Who did the spontaneous and massive outpouring of grief following Princess Diana's death not move? No one anticipated the magnitude of such a universal response. The flowers in London were metres deep. Suppose millions of us decided to pick a particular day to write a letter to Queen Elizabeth, the Prime Ministers, and Members of Parliament in Canada, Australia, and England? I wonder how many Canadian, Australian, and British Members of Parliament have family members who were British Home Children? We could always ask them. Suppose we again sent a follow-up letter a week later, and another a week after that? I wonder how deep the mail would pile up at our respective Houses of Parliament.

What do you suppose would happen if, on the same day, we sent a copy of our letters to every newspaper editor and television producer in our hometowns and cities? I wonder at the response. Financial supporters of the child-care organizations might reconsider their contributions. Barnardo's revenues for 1998 were £105 million ($234 million). Revenues for the Children's Society in 1998 were £28.7 million ($64 million) (Charities Direct 1999). Will it take Acts of Parliament or Supreme Court actions in our three countries to compel these organizations to release information on demand to those entitled to receive it? Will it take a class action suit initiated by millions of Canadian, Australian, and British families?

At the very least, we Canadian and Australian descendants can locate and identify the surviving British Home Children in our countries. We can help them find their Brothers and sisters in our countries. We can tell their stories and make them visible. We can help them take their place in a chapter of our history books become proud immigrants. We can ensure that while their lives were lived unnoticed, their deaths will not. We can seek each other out and help each other with our searches in our respective countries. I know our British relatives have tried to find their deported Brothers, Sisters, Nephews, Nieces, and Cousins. I know the British organizations thwarted their efforts, just as they did their best to stymie our efforts. They can help us because they are on-site and close to the information sources. We can help them.

If the British child-care organizations will not willingly cooperate with us, then we can combine our efforts and can compel them to release the information that is vital to our searches. We have asked, sought, and meekly knocked on their doors. Perhaps we jointly need to knock a little louder.

> Ask, and it shall be given you; seek and ye shall find;
>
> Knock, and it shall be opened unto you.
>
> For everyone that asketh, receiveth;
>
> and he that seeketh, findeth;
>
> And to him that knocketh, it shall be opened (Matthew 7:7,8)

For over a hundred years, thousands of British Home Children pressed their pens and pencils to scraps of paper and wrote to the child-care organizations that deported them to foreign countries. They worked many hours to save the pennies to buy stamps and paper. They wrote to the only people they knew in England -- their caretakers. They desperately asked, "Can you help me find my Mother?" They anxiously awaited all their lives for information that was rarely forthcoming.

Whales do not have vocal cords, and yet they send messages through thousands of kilometres of ocean. They wait for their messages to reach their specific targets and bounce back to them. They follow this sound trail to its source. They pursue this pathway and ignore the clutter of others' cries along their way. They know which course is theirs alone. The British Home Children were 100,000 lost souls. Their hearts continued to beat, but their cries were absorbed by the vast Canadian solitude that surrounded them. Their sad cries were, "Where is my Mother?" Their sadder cries were, "Who is my Mother?" Their saddest cries were, "I am lost. Who do I belong to?"

My Father, like thousands of other British Home Children, wrote and asked, "Can you help me find my Mother and Father?" First generation descendants write and ask, "Can you help me find my Grandmother and Grandfather?" Unless there is a significant change, the second generation will write and ask, "Can you help me find my Great Grandmother and Great Grandfather?"

There is still some unfinished business. I need to go to England and trace my Father's footsteps of long ago. I need to visit my Grandparents' gravesides. I need to know who they were. I need to talk to them, and tell them about their Son. I need to return a part of my Father to them. I want to meet his sole surviving Sister (my Aunt), his Brother's Wife (my other Aunt), and his Nephews and Nieces (my cousins). I want to talk to them, and tell them about their Brother, Brother-in-law, and Uncle.

All my Dad ever wanted was to know his Family. All I want is for his Family to know him.

[1] Kenneth Bagnell, "Britain's Children Who Came to Stay," The Review: Canada's Child Immigrants, Volume 64, Number 5, Issue Number 355, (1980a), p. 5.

[2] Kenneth Bagnell, "Britain's Children Who Came to Stay," The Review: Canada's Child Immigrants, Volume 64, Number 5, Issue Number 355, (1980a), p. 9.

[3] "Town of Marathon-History." Noront International Trade Services, Inc., Thunder Bay, Ontario. June 18, 1997. <http://www.marathon.noront.ca/history.html>

[4] Correspondence: Assistant Superintendent, Metropolitan Police, Balham Police Station, Balham, London, England, to Fred G. Snow, October 24, 1957.

[5] Correspondence: Secretary Col. E. St. J. Birnie, The Church of England Children's Society, London, England, to Fred G. Snow, November 11, 1957.

[6] Karen Matthews, "Young child's torment in a long voyage." Article courtesy of Geelong Advertiser, Saturday, November 19, 1994.

[7] Karen Matthews, "A childhood rediscovered and a 'family' reunited." Article courtesy of Geelong Advertiser, Saturday, December 10, 1994.

[8] Correspondence: The Church of England Society for Providing Homes for Waifs and Strays, London, England to Fred G. Snow, February 07, 1929.

[9] Correspondence: The Church of England Society for Providing Homes for Waifs and Strays, London, England to Fred G. Snow, January 30, 1931.

[10] Correspondence: Thomas Keeley, Gibb's Home, Sherbrooke, Quebec to Secretary W. R. Vaughan, The Church of England Society for Providing Homes for Waifs and Strays, London, England, December 08, 1936.

[11] Correspondence: Secretary W. R. Vaughan, The Church of England Society for Providing Homes for Waifs and Strays, London, England, to Thomas Keeley, Gibb's Home, Sherbrooke, Quebec, December 23, 1936.

[12] Correspondence: J. Frost, Assistant Warden, St. Augustine's Home for Boys, Sevenoaks, Kent, England, to Secretary W. R. Vaughan, The Church of England Society for Providing Homes for Waifs and Strays, London, England, September 29, 1937.

[13] Correspondence: J. C. Mason, Secretary, Old Boys League, London, England, to Fred G. Snow, February 8, 1938.

[14] Correspondence: Secretary Col. E. St. J. Birnie, The Church of England Children's Society, London, England, to St. Peter's Vicarage, South Croydon, Surrey, England, October 29, 1957.

[15] Correspondence: Secretary Col. E. St. J. Birnie, The Church of England Children's Society, London, England, to St. Peter's Vicarage, South Croydon, Surrey, England, October 29, 1957.

[16] Correspondence: Superintendent, Wandsworth Registration District, Wandsworth, England, to The Church of England Children's Society, London, England, November 08, 1957.

[17] Correspondence: The Children's Society, London, England, to Gertrude Snow, August 17, 1976.

[18] William Shakespeare. From Othello. "The Complete Works of William Shakespeare," May 23, 1999.
<http://www-tech.mit.edu/Shakespeare/Tragedy/othello/othello.3.3.html>

[19] William Shakespeare. From Hamlet. "The Complete Works of William Shakespeare," June 1999.
<http://www-tech.mit.edu/Shakespeare/Tragedy/hamlet/hamlet.all.html>

Appendix:
Addresses of British Child Care Organizations

BARNARDOS: Head of After Care, Barnardo's, Tanners Lane, Barkingside, Ilford, Essex, England, 1G6 1QG. Phone: 020 8550 8822 Fax: 202 8551 6870. Email: AfterCare_Barnardos@compuserve.com. Website: http://www.Barnardos.org.uk.
Records of: Children's Aid Society, Liverpool Sheltering Homes, Marchmont Homes, McPherson Homes, Sharman's Home.
BOYS AND GIRLS WELFARE SOCIETY: Central Offices, Schools Hill, Cheadle, Chesire, England, SK8 1JE. Phone: 061 428 5256
CATHOLIC CHILDREN'S SOCIETY (WESTMINSTER) a.k.a. CRUSADE OF RESCUE: 73 St. Charles Square, London, England, W10 6EJ. Phone: 081 969 5305
CATHOLIC CHILD WELFARE COUNCIL: St. Joseph's, Watford Way, Hendon, London, England, NW4 4TY. Phone: 020 8203 6323. Fax: 020 8203 6323. Email: ccws@compuserve.com. Website: http://www.vois.org.uk/cathchild.
CHURCH ARMY HEADQUARTERS: Independents Road, Blackheath, London, England, SE3. Phone: 081 318 1226 Fax: 081 318 5258
CHILDREN'S SOCIETY: 1881 Formerly Waifs and Strays: Edward Rudolf House, Margery Street, London, England, WC1X OJ1. Phone: 0171 837 4229 Fax: 0171 837 0211.
The Post Adoption and Care Counselling Research Project, Queens Road, Peckham, London, England, SE15 2EZ. Phone: 020 7732 9089. Fax: 020 7277 5760. Email: julia.feast@the-childrens-society.org.uk. Website: http://the-childrens-society.org.uk.
FAIRBRIDGE: Waterloo Road, London, England. Phone: 020 7928 1704. Fax: 020 7928 6016. Email: info@fairbridge.org.uk.
FAMILY CARE SOCIETY: 511 Ormeau Road, Belfast, Ireland. Phone: 01231 691133. Fax: 01232 649849.
FEGAN'S CHILD AND FAMILY CARE: FORMERLY MR. FEGAN'S HOMES INC. (1870): Mr. A. G. Wincent, Secretary, 160 St. James Road, Tunbridge Wells, Kent, England, TN1 2HE. Phone: 0892 38288.
INVALID CHILDREN'S AID SOCIETY (1881): 126 Buckingham Palace Road, London, England, SW1W 9SB. Phone: 071 730 9891
JEWISH WELFARE BOARD OF GUARDIANS: 315 Ballards Lane, London, England, N12 8LP.
JOHN GROOMS (1866): 10 Gloucester Drive, Finsbury Park, London, England, N4 2LP. Phone: 081 959 3292

LIVERPOOL CATHOLIC ORGANIZATION: (Renamed Nugent Care Society 1998): 150 Brownlow Hill, Liverpool, England, L3 5RF. Phone: 0151 708 0566

MIDDLEMORE HOMES: 31 and 33 Merrits Brook Lane, Northfield, Birmingham B31 1PP. Phone: 021 476 3519

MILL GROVE (CHILDREN'S HOME AND MISSION 1899): 10 Crescent Road, South Woodford, London, England, E18. Phone: 081 504 2702

MISS SMYLIE'S HOMES: The Secretary, 15 Rock Hill, Black Rock, Dublin, Eire.

NATIONAL CHILDREN'S HOME (NCH) ACTION FOR CHILDREN: (Founded 1869 by Dr. Stephenson Bowman). 85 Highbury Park, London, England, N5 IUD. Phone: 020 8203 6323. Fax: 020 8203 6323. Website: http://nchafc.org.uk.

PACT: 15 Belgrave Road, Rathmines, Dublin 6, Eire. Records of: Bethany Homes, Church of Ireland Social Services, Nursery Rescue Society, Protestant Adoption Society, and Protestant Community.

PRESBYTERIAN ORPHAN SOCIETY: 45 Howard Street, Belfast, Northern Ireland, BT1 6NE. Phone: 0232 23737

QUARRIER'S HOMES: Bridge of Weir, Renfrewshire, Scotland, PA11 3SA.

SALVATION ARMY: 101 Newington Causeway, London, England, SE1 6BN. Phone: 020 7367 4840. Fax: 020 7367 4712.

SHAFTESBURY HOMES AND 'ARETHUSA' 1843 (AND RAGGED SCHOOLS): 3 Rectory Grove, London, England, SW4. Phone: 071 720 8709

SPURGEONS' HOMES 1867 STOCKWELL ORPHANAGE: Birchington, Kent, England. Phone: 0843 41381

THOMAS CORAN FOUNDATION: 40 Brunswick Square, London, England, WC1N 1AZ. Phone: 071 278 2424

Bibliography

Allen, Garland E. Science Misapplied: The Eugenics Age Revisited. April 28, 1999. <http://www.techreview.com/articles/as96/allen.html>

American Family Foundation, Inc. Dr. Margaret T. Singer's 6 Conditions for Thought Reform. April 28, 1999. <http://www.csj.org/studyindex/studymindctr/study_mindctr_singer.htm>

Bagnell, Kenneth. "Britain's Children Who Came to Stay." The Review: Canada's Child Immigrants, Volume 64, Number 5, Issue Number 355, 1980a.

- - - . The Little Immigrants: The Orphans Who Came to Canada. Toronto, Ontario, Canada: Macmillan of Canada, 1980b.

Barr, Eleanor. "Mucking Out at Sturgeon Lake." Ignace Visitor's Guide, Ignace Driftwood Magazine, Ignace, Ontario, 1987.

Bean, Phillip and Joy Melville. Lost Children of the Empire. London, England: Unwin Hyman, 1989.

Berton, Pierre. The Great Depression 1929-1939. Toronto, Ontario, Canada: McClelland & Stewart, 1990

Brennan, Brian. "Man's quest took a lifetime." Article courtesy of Calgary Herald, March 16, 1995.

British High Commission, Canada. "Cash fund for child migrants." April 16, 1999. <http://www.bis-canada.org/Releases/NR320399.htm>

British Isles Genealogical Register Index: Surrey and London. Federation of Family History Societies, Birmingham and Midland Institute, Birmingham, England, 1994.

"Charities Direct." 1999. July 13, 1999. <www.caritasdata.co.uk/indexchr.htm>

CBC News. "British Child Migrants to Receive Payment." 16 December, CBC News, 1998. Toronto, Ontario, Canada. April 28, 1999. <http://www.newsworld.cbc.ca/cgi-bin/templates/view.cgi?/news/1998/12/15/children981215>

Corbett, Gail H. Barnardo Children in Canada. Toronto, Ontario, Canada: Woodland Publishing, 1981.

DiPasquale, Connie. "A History of the Orphan Trains." 1999. April 21, 1999. <http://www.ukans.edu/carrie/kancoll/articles/orphans/or_hist.htm>

DSM-IV Diagnostic and Statistical Manual of Mental Disorders, 4th ed. Washington: American Psychiatric Association Press, 1994.

Harrison, Phyllis. The Home Children. Winnipeg, Manitoba, Canada: Watson & Dwyer, 1979.

Haworth-Attard, Barbara. Home Child. Montreal, Quebec, Canada: Roussan Publishers, 1996.

"House of Commons: Select Committee on Health - Third Report." Welfare of Former British Child Migrants. 1998. May 10, 1999. <http://www.parliament.the-stationery office.co.uk/pa/cm199798/cmselect/cmhealth/755/75502.htm>

Humphreys, Margaret. Empty Cradles. London, England: Transworld, 1994.

Juhan, Deane. Job's Body. Barrytown, New York, New York: Station Hills Press, 1987.

Keeley, Thomas. "Canadian News." Gibbs' Club, Autumn Number, September, Sherbrooke Quebec, September 1939.

Kevles, Danial J. In the Name of Eugenics. New York: Knopf, 1985.

Kohli, Marjorie P. Young Immigrants to Canada. 1999. May 16, 1999. <http://dcs1.uwaterloo.ca/~marj/genealogy/news.html>

Lifton, Robert J. Thought Reform and the Psychology of Totalism: A Study of "Brainwashing" in China. University of North Carolina Press: Chapel Hill, North Carolina, 1989. At Encyclopaedia of World Problems and Human Potential. 1999. April 21, 1999. <http://www.uia.org/uiademo/hum/h0865.htm.>

Mandino, Og. The Greatest Miracle in the World. New York, New York: Bantam Books, 1975.

Matthews, Karen. "Young child's torment in a long voyage." Article courtesy of Geelong Advertiser, November 19, 1994.

- - - . "A childhood rediscovered and a 'family' reunited." Article courtesy of Geelong Advertiser, December 10, 1994.

McLaren, Angus. Our Own Master Race. Toronto, Ontario, Canada: McLellan & Stewart, 1990.

Mennill, Paul. The Great Depression Years: Canada in the 1930's. Scarborough, Ontario, Canada: Prentice-Hall of Canada, Ltd., 1978

Missildine, W. Hugh. Your Inner Child of the Past. New York, New York: Simon and Schuster, 1963.

Mussen, Paul H. et al. Child Development and Personality. New York: Harper and Row, 1963.

"North-Western Ontario - Geography." 1999. Noront International Trade Services, Inc., Thunder Bay, Ontario. 1998. June 18, 1997.

<http://www.northwestinfo.com>

Parr, Joy. Labouring Children: British Immigrant Apprentices to Canada, 1869-1924. Montreal, Quebec, Canada: McGill-Queen's University Press, 1980.

Perry, Bruce D. How the Brain Stores and Retrieves Physiologic States, Feelings, and Behaviors and Thoughts from Traumatic Events. In Splintered Reflections: Images of the Body in Trauma. (Edited by J. Goodwin and R. Attias). New York: Basic Books, 1999. At Civitas Academy. April 28, 1999. <http://www.bcm.tmc.edu/civitas/home.htm.>

- - - , et al. Childhood Trauma, the Neurobiology of Adaptation and "Use-dependent" Development of the Brain: How 'States' become 'Traits.' At Civitas Academy. April 28, 1999. <http://www.bcm.tmc.edu/civitas/home.htm.>

"Pier 21 Society." July 13, 1999. <http://pier21.ns.ca/execsumm.html>

"Public Works & Government Services, Canada." Accessing the Historical Records of the Government of Canada. Access to Information Act and the Privacy Act. 1999. May 10, 1999. <http://www.archives.ca/www/svcs/english/atip.htm>

Schwarz, E. and Bruce D. Perry. The Post-Traumatic Response in Children and Adolescents. Psychiatric Clinics of North America, 17 (2): 311-326, 1994. At Civatas Academy. March 12, 1999. <http://www.bcm.tmc.edu/civitas/ptsdChildAdoles.htm>

Shakespeare, William. Othello. "The Complete Works of William Shakespeare," May 23, 1999. <http://www-tech.mit.edu/Shakespeare/Tragedy/othello/othello.3.3.html>

- - - . Hamlet. "The Complete Works of William Shakespeare," June 11, 1999 <http://www-tech.mit.edu/Shakespeare/Tragedy/hamlet/hamlet.all.html>

Sidran Foundation. Dissociative Identity Disorder. June 14, 1999. <http://www.sidran.org/didbr.html>

Snow, Gertrude. One Set of Footprints. Thunder Bay, Ontario, Canada: Unpublished Manuscript, 1986.

Snow, Perry. "Banished to Canada." Kent Family History Society Journal, December 1997, Volume 8, Number 9.

- - - . "Banished to Canada." East Surrey Family History Society Journal, June 1996, Volume 19, Number 2.

- - - . "The Attitude Connection." Self-Management Seminars, Calgary, Alberta, 1988.

Stroud, John. Thirteen Penny Stamps: The Story of the Church of England Children's Society (Waifs and Strays) from 1881 to the 1970s. London, England: Hodder & Stoughton, 1971.

Thomas, W. I. Eugenics: The Science of Breeding Men." Thomas, W. I. American Magazine, Volume 68, 1909. At Ward, Lloyd & Robert Throop. The Mead Project, 1997. October 19, 1997. <http://paradigm.soci.brocku.ca/~lward/SUP/Thomas/Thomas_22html>

Town of Marathon-History." Noront International Trade Services, Inc., Thunder Bay, Ontario. June 18, 1997. <http://www.marathon.noront.ca/history.html>

UN Convention On The Rights Of The Child. G.A. res. 44/25, annex, 44 U.N. GAOR Supp. (No. 49) at 167, U.N. Doc. A/44/49 (1989). June 07, 1999. <http://wwwl.umn.edu/humanrts/instree/k2crc.htm>

Wagner, Gillian. Barnardo. London, England: Weidenfeld & Nicholson, 1979.

- - - . Children of the Empire. London, England: Weidenfeld & Nicholson, 1982.

Index

Waldron, Edwin, 64
Wandsworth, Battersea,
    England, 220
Wayves and Streyves, 14
Wescott, Reverend A. J., 151,
    211
Williams, Charles J., 64
Wilson, Reverend W. Linton,
    147, 152, 210

Winnipeg, Manitoba, 37, 39,
    41, 156
Woolwich, Kent, England, 220
Worby, Reginald M., 166
World War I, 72, 114, 135, 186,
    201, 207, 210, 247, 259
World War II, 41, 68, 72, 76,
    113, 212, 215, 216, 259

Young, Ronald B., 145, 149

Printed in the United States
3429